2

Confronting the New Conservatism

Confronting the
New Conservatism

The Rise of the Right in America

EDITED BY

Michael J. Thompson

New York University Press

NEW YORK AND LONDON

NEW YORK UNIVERSITY PRESS
New York and London
www.nyupress.org

Library of Congress Cataloging-in-Publication Data
Confronting the new conservatism : the rise of the right in
America / edited by Michael J. Thompson.
p.   cm.
Includes bibliographical references and index.
ISBN-13: 978-0-8147-8298-9 (cloth : alk. paper)
ISBN-10: 0-8147-8298-1 (cloth : alk. paper)
ISBN-13: 978-0-8147-8299-6 (pbk. : alk. paper)
ISBN-10: 0-8147-8299-X (pbk. : alk. paper)
1. Conservatism—United States. 2. Political culture—United
States. 3. Political parties—United States. 4. United States—
Politics and government.   I. Thompson, Michael, 1973–
JC573.2.U6C653 2007
320.520973—dc22
2006025996

New York University Press books are printed on acid-free paper,
and their binding materials are chosen for strength and durability.

Manufactured in the United States of America
c 10 9 8 7 6 5 4 3 2 1
p 10 9 8 7 6 5 4 3 2 1

Contents

Acknowledgments

I would like to thank Sam Aboelela, Stephen Eric Bronner, John Ehrenberg, Elena Mancini, Frances Fox Piven, Brett Stoudt, Debbie Wolf, and Greg Zucker for discussions and comments that helped me flesh out the general idea of this book, as well as all the contributors for their enthusiasm for the project. I would also like to thank my editor at NYU Press, Ilene Kalish, for her interest in this project from its inception and for her excellent editorial work. Finally, I would like to thank Mark Major for compiling the index.

Introduction

Confronting the New Conservatism

Michael J. Thompson

Conservative politics has been on the rise in America throughout the postwar era. Although conservatism has generally been the politics of the minority, the past several decades have seen a new assertion of conservatism in many domains of politics and culture, which has reshaped American political and public life in the process. America's supposed conservative turn has taken many different forms, from the election of Ronald Reagan to the presidency in 1980 to the Contract with America in 1994 to the recent aggression in the Middle East. But in the end, conservatism in America has consistently defined itself against the liberal establishment and has sought a redirection of American political and cultural life.

This book is an attempt to come to terms with various aspects of conservative political, social, economic, and cultural ideas, movements, and predispositions in contemporary American life. The essays collected here are each in their own way an attempt to reveal the deeper mechanisms that have come to define different aspects of conservative movements and politics: neoconservative foreign policy, the problem of populism, "cultural rage," family values, gay marriage, far right-wing movements, the conservative turn in the courts, and the renewed attack on the welfare state, among other and related topics. As a whole, this book sees both a continuity and a distinction between "old" and "new" conservatism. On the one hand, there is a continuity with certain older forms of racial backlash, with provincialism, and with nationalism. But at the same time, there is something quite new about contemporary American conservatism: that it latches on to liberal notions of private property and the rule of law; that it embraces markets, celebrates the autonomy of the individual, and most importantly sees itself as a "progressive" movement promising renewal, growth, and the expansion of freedom and moving away from the despotism that social democratic liberalism has created.

This book is also a response to an earlier study of conservatism in America. In 1962 the sociologist Daniel Bell published an edited volume titled *The Radical Right* that examined the right-wing movements of the 1950s and 1960s and their origins. For Bell and his contributors, the overall explanation for these movements was a response to modernity, expressed as a liberal democratic consensus, and a "status anxiety" felt by small numbers of people and their reaction to a changing, modernizing America. "What the right as a whole fears is the erosion of its own social position, the collapse of its power, the increasing incomprehensibility of a world—now overwhelmingly technical and complex—that has changed so drastically within a lifetime."[1] The conservatism analyzed by the contributors to *The Radical Right* did not fit into the understanding of a postwar democratic consensus that had emerged with the New Deal and the expansion of American capitalism in the immediate postwar years. The right-wing impulse they examined was considered a minority, a sociological and political oddity that needed to be explained.

But this situation has radically changed. What this book calls the "new conservatism" is not the purview of a minority; it has become hegemonic in the public discourse, has displaced a waning postwar liberalism as a public philosophy, and has succeeded in attaining political and ideological power in many branches of government and within many of the organs of the public sphere. A new culture has been constructed with new predispositions, and it is at the level of culture *as well as* at the level of political and economic institutions that any fruitful analysis of the present situation must proceed. It may not be that most Americans self-identify as "conservative," but this hardly matters since only a small minority of Americans identify themselves as "liberal," about 20 percent, whereas 40 percent consider themselves "mainstream" and the remaining 40 percent, "conservative."[2] These are general figures to be sure, but they indicate the skewness of political ideology that has dominated political culture over the past decade.

But even if the data do not show a radical turn toward the right among Americans' political attitudes, the nature of the right turn in American politics is real. The new conservatism speaks the language that many different sectors of the American public want to hear: it wants to erode the centralization of political power; restore authority to traditional institutions and to civil society; rely on the free market in economic life; and base social life on voluntary associations and community.[3] On the surface, it advocates what Michael Oakshott termed "rational prudence" in assessing the policies and legacy of postwar liberalism. Multiculturalism has led to division rather than integration; government attempts at reducing or eliminating poverty have only worsened the problem; the bloatedness of the welfare state hampers economic performance, competition, and innovation; the power of the national state has become a new leviathan squashing individual liberty and choice; and so on. It is this mask of pragmatism that has allowed conservative ideas and policies to become "mainstream" themselves. In this sense, the very distinction between "mainstream" and "conservative" needs to be called into question.

The causes of the rise in conservative politics are many and multilayered in themselves. Indeed, the phenomenon of "backlash" is central. The reaction to the 1960s and the cultural and institutional shifts that were then occurring alienated many middle-class and working-class whites from the broader political project of liberalism. As Douglas Massey has recently argued, "liberals increasingly turned to the courts and executive branch to force working-class whites and local political bosses to accept whatever changes they mandated from above."[4] There are also structural accounts that see the crisis of the welfare state as effecting a shift in support from liberal to conservative parties.[5] But whatever the case may be, the actual interests that mobilize the new conservative politics in America are multiple and complex, and they require a more nuanced analytic approach. It is for this reason that this volume is a series of essays, each pursuing a different approach to the phenomenon.

Conservatism has always been associated with reaction, with tradition, with stability. But the new conservatism is something different in this regard: it has been able to assert itself as the locater of crisis, as an ideology that points to the cultural and political situation of the present and claims that it has broken down and that it, alone, has the power and the insight to fix it, to make the crooked straight.[6] What the new conservatism has done is not look simply to the past but look toward postwar liberalism and social democracy as serious distortions of social policy and public morality. It argues that liberalism as a public philosophy has led to cultural and moral decay due to its emphasis on the liberty of the individual and the separation between public and private, which has starved the public sphere of morality and the guidance of tradition and authority.

Outside the realm of culture, the new conservatism has argued for the primacy of capitalism and markets as the core tool for the organization of economic life. Classical liberalism was defined by its liberal theory of property and labor: one has a right to the fruits of one's labor. New Deal liberalism was able to harness the optimistic modernism of Progressivism and merge these with a political rationalism and a populist egalitarianism.[7] The new conservatism has been able to merge the concerns of cultural conservatives—who traditionally had also been anticapitalist in many respects—with the antiprogressivism of the business community, which had always sought to privilege its interests against those of working people or the broader community. New conservatism has become an unabashed apologist for economic inequality just as it has harkened back to the traditional values of family life.

It should also be said from the outset that this book is also conceived as an intervention itself—an intervention into what the authors collected here agree are the corrosive effects of conservatism on American democracy itself. The essays here provide different arguments for why the new conservatism is itself anathema to the most robust traditions in American politics and history. And they argue that, in each case, what is at stake is the viability of a more tolerant, more open, more egalitarian social order that privileges a substantive notion of human freedom over the more narrow, anachronistic concepts of liberty advocated by conservative critics and political actors. Confronting the new conservatism therefore requires a rethinking of democratic politics for the present on behalf of those who seek to uphold the liberal legacy in American political life. Without this, the democratic institutions and culture that have been forged throughout the twentieth century will be in peril.

NOTES

1. Daniel Bell, ed., *The Radical Right* (New York: Doubleday, 1963), 2.

2. See Jacob Hacker and Paul Pierson, *Off Center: The Republican Revolution and the Erosion of American Democracy* (New Haven, CT: Yale University Press, 2005), 25–44. Also see the work of James Stimson, *Public Opinion in America: Moods, Cycles, Swings* (Boulder, CO: Westview, 1998), and Morris Fiorina et al., *Culture War?* (New York: Pearson Longman, 2005).

3. See Robert Nisbet, *The New Absolutism* (New York: Harper and Row, 1988), 62.

4. Douglas Massey, *The Return of the "L" Word* (Princeton, NJ: Princeton University Press, 2005), 27. Also see Robert Wiebe, *Self Rule: A Cultural History of American Democracy* (Chicago: University of Chicago Press, 1995), 229–231. This

theme is also dealt with in a more popular manner by Thomas Frank, *What's the Matter with Kansas?* (New York: Metropolitan Books, 2004).

5. For this account, see Joel Smith, Allan Kornberg, and Neil Nevitte, "Structural Factors in the Conservative Resurgence," in *The Resurgence of Conservatism in Anglo-American Democracies,* ed. Barry Cooper, Allan Kornberg, and William Mishler (Durham, NC: Duke University Press, 1988), 25–53.

6. For a discussion of this aspect of the new conservatism, see Claus Offe, "Ungovernability: On the Renaissance of Conservative Theories of Crisis," in *Observations on "The Spiritual Situation of the Age,"* ed. Jürgen Habermas (Cambridge, MA: MIT Press, 1987), 67–88.

7. See Theodore Lowy, *The End of the Republican Era* (Norman: University of Oklahoma Press, 1995), 23.

Part I

What Is the New Conservatism?

Chapter 1

America's Conservative Landscape
The New Conservatism and the Reorientation of American Democracy

Michael J. Thompson

The history of America's political culture has been one of flux, of convulsion. It has seen seismic changes in its understanding of democracy, its concept of citizenship, and its view of the nature of politics, the state, and the economy; it has recast its ideas about race, gender, and the concepts of political participation and human liberty. It is against these aspects of newness in American democratic political life and culture that American conservatism has always fought. Older versions of conservatism were unabashedly racist and elitist. Adherents to this credo argued for the privilege of the few over the many. Whether it was the ideas about slavery by thinkers such as John C. Calhoun or George Fitzhugh or the "scientific" defense of class inequality by William Graham Sumner or the antimodernist pessimism of Henry Adams, all were critical of the progressive impulses of liberalism, universalism, and equality, the doctrines that were in fact the driving forces behind American democratic culture.

This conservative disposition in American politics and culture differs in some important respects from the brand of conservatism that has emerged over the past three decades and with more intense force over the past decade in particular. Hostility to the welfare state, a renewed sense of localism and provincialism, a growing apathy to economic inequality and its political consequences, and a new acceptance of economic and social hierarchies all point to what I call a "new conservative" landscape: a political and cultural moment where American politics has taken a turn toward embracing some of the more antidemocratic elements in culture, politics, and economics. The "new conservatism" espouses a hatred for economic equality, a renewed respect for institutional authority in politics as well as for the authority of tradition (i.e., religion) in culture and personal life, and a crude brand of nationalism. But it is more than ideology that informs social movements and elites. It is also a disposition created by certain shifts in economic and political life that have made many Americans more prone to accept many conservative ideas. Indeed, what seems to puzzle many liberal social and political thinkers is the extent to which conservative ideas and policies are embraced by the same people that tend to be most harmed by their effects.

But what, specifically, is "new" about the new conservatism? Writers like Thomas Frank have argued that it should be seen as a "Great Backlash," or a political and cultural response to the new leftism of the 1960s. "While earlier forms of conservatism emphasized fiscal sobriety, the backlash mobilizes voters with explosive social issues—summoning public outrage over everything from busing to un-Christian art—which it then marries to pro-business economic policies."[1] Frank's contention is not unique; in fact, it is how we generally conceive of the conservative reaction in contemporary politics.[2] But I think it is much more than this. There is a real sense in which the rise of conservative thought is actually a much deeper, more profound shift in American politics and culture. It is a reaction against a deeper transformation that occurred in American society beginning in the late nineteenth century and that carried over into the early twentieth century, a reaction that effected a reordering of political and economic institutions but also, more fundamentally, reshaped the prevailing ideas about democracy and equality in America. What is broadly known as the Progressive movement sought to redefine American democracy in thought and in practice. It was a reaction against the laissez-faire liberalism of the eighteenth and nineteenth centuries and its narrow understanding of liberalism and individualism. The Progressive movement sought a reconstruction of democracy through a reinterpretation of the state, economy, the individual, society, and the relation of all these spheres to one another. What Progressives were able to conjure was a vision of democratic life that emphasized association, cooperation, the centrality of the state for achieving broader public ends, and the need to fuse the economy to standards of the public good, while still maintaining individual liberty in thought and speech. They fostered a move from communal and local ideas about political life toward a national concept of the public good and national goals. But most important, people associated with this movement sought to deepen American democracy by limiting economic power and eroding elite authority. They sought to forge a "new democracy" that would be appropriate for a modern world. The new conservatism should be seen as a countermovement to this reordering of American life; and the result, I argue, has become nothing less than the wholesale reorientation of the American democratic project.[3]

Part of my argument is that the contours of what can be called the "new conservatism" are not simply rooted in antiliberal ideas but in fact are grounded in many of the broader notions and assumptions of American liberalism itself: the sanctity of private property, individualism and autonomy, economic entrepreneurialism, a privileging of the private sphere over the public sphere, and a hostility to the state. American liberalism is something that can be, and has been, used for progressive ends. It has been able to challenge the pre-liberal political formations and social relations that plagued American political development especially in economic relations and, over time, in race and gender relations as well.[4] But as Louis Hartz has pointed out, American liberalism could also lead to its dialectical opposite, the very thing that it opposed.[5] I want to argue something similar here: that the peculiar brand of American liberalism has given rise to and also maintains certain aspects of the new conservative impulse in American politics, that the new conservatism is "new" precisely because it has been able to attach itself—even if only rhetorically—to so many of the core notions of political liberalism that define American political culture.

The new conservative disposition in American politics is primarily the result of the increasing social atomization and individualism of modern American life, which has eroded secular forms of association such as unions and social and political organizations and created an environment where both economic elites and old-style conservatives—such as members of the religious right—can push their respective agendas. Both groups are, to be sure, minorities of the population as a whole, but through the erosion of secular associational life, they have been able to gain significant traction in pushing their issues onto the public scene and the policy arena. The very source of conservative ideas is a curious mixture of liberal and traditionalist ideologies, and this makes conservatism a fairly pliable political and cultural doctrine. The popular—or perhaps populist—support for different dimensions of new conservative ideas come from different sectors: Some segments of the American electorate support fiscal conservatism, an emphasis on free markets, the dismantling of the welfare state, and so on. Others are drawn to the emphasis on traditional values, to religion, to the ideas of strong leadership and authority, and the like. But these different emphases are symptoms of a larger phenomenon. The rise of conservatism in American politics and the acceptance, or at least the broad toleration, of many conservative ideas—although by no means all conservative ideas—need to be linked to a more general erosion of democratic culture in the United States. Whereas the liberalism of the 1950s and 1960s was a dominant intellectual paradigm or, borrowing a phrase from Eldon Eisenach, "regime in thought" for much of the postwar era, it has waned as a political ideology capable of confronting the changing trends in modern economic and social life.[6]

The new conservative landscape I am describing can be defined through three different but interlocking dimensions of modern American social life and political culture: first, a redefinition and reappropriation of liberalism with a more radical emphasis on individualism; second, a resurgent capitalism that has brought back a new and resilient form of economic hierarchy and that has rearranged previous forms of economic life; and third, the narrowing and "provincialization" of everyday life—structured partially by the suburbanization of American culture—which feeds the other two dimensions and narrows the sphere of social interaction largely to the realm of work and family at the expense of broader forms of civil society. These three dimensions of the new conservative landscape are part and parcel of the reworking of America's democratic institutions and the relation between state, society, the individual, and the economy that were the product of what Robert Wiebe has called the "revolution in values" that occurred during the late nineteenth and early twentieth centuries. It is this combination of factors that largely defines and drives contemporary American conservatism.[7]

From New to Old Liberalism

Central to the thinking of the new conservatism in America is the emphasis on individualism as a means toward enhanced personal and political liberty. In economic life, emphasis on the interests of the individual in the marketplace, on competition, commerce, and so on, all point to a renewal of what was once known as the "old liberalism": a brand of liberalism that emphasized the notion of the individual as fundamentally asocial and ahistorical. Even outside the sphere of economics, the prevailing notion in American political culture has been the primacy of the negative liberty of the individual. The laissez-faire liberalism of the nineteenth century saw society as a collection of atomized individuals freely pursuing their self-interest. In John Dewey's words, "the individual of earlier liberalism was a Newtonian atom having only external time and space relations to other individuals, save that each social atom was equipped with inherent freedom."[8] This led, in the view of many Progressive and reform thinkers of the time, to an atomized society of self-interested individuals where the very idea of public purpose was lost and the rootlessness of modern life would erode any meaningful notions of democratic life. These thinkers did not want to eradicate the ideas of individualism or even the liberal notion of private property, but they did see that the effects of liberal capitalism were leading American democracy toward crisis. Their solution was to create a new concept of democracy that emphasized the role of the state and sought to protect the public from wanton private interests.

Nineteenth-century American social thought was characterized by a laissez-faire liberalism and an individualism without any kind of institutional restraints on economic activity. This led not to the ethical and moral ends that the formulators of classical liberalism—namely, thinkers such as Locke—had envisioned but to a highly unequal society that was fragmenting at the very core. The laissez-faire doctrine had pervasive influence on economic policy, ideas about economic life, and the making and interpretation of law. Central to this thinking was the notion that there existed "laws" of economic activity, derived from thinkers such as Adam Smith and David Ricardo. Profit seeking, speculating, competition —all were considered "natural" in that they were products of truly free people maximizing their respective self-interests. The Social Darwinists of the late nineteenth and early twentieth centuries sought to ground this concept of individualism in ethical terms, constructing a rationalization of industrial society and economic inequality and social atomization.[9]

But the central premise of the ideas of writers such as Herbert Croly, Walter Weyl, John Dewey, and others who sought a reformulation of modern American democracy was the culmination of a broader trend in American social thought that began in the 1870s and the realization— influenced to a large extent by the effect of German social and moral thought on young American social theorists—that laissez-faire liberalism was in fact corrupting American political life.[10] Influential thinkers, such as George Herbert Mead in his *Mind, Self, and Society,* put forth a conception of individuality that is essentially constituted by one's relations to society and to others.[11] The insight of these efforts in social theory was that individuals were to be seen as embedded in more complex social systems and were not to be seen as isolated, atomized selves. This meant that the older epistemological ideas that grounded classical liberalism could no longer hold: individuals were individuals, to be sure, but they were constituted by their social environment just as much as they helped to constitute that environment; they were not radical subjects but were intersubjectively related to the public around them. Mead, who also marched with striking laborers in Chicago, was conscious of the political implications of his work within the context of laissez-faire individualism: the very ideas of the individual and of society were being fundamentally reshaped and rethought, and this meant a wholesale reconstruction of what American liberalism and democracy actually meant, both formally and substantively.[12]

This constituted a reconstruction of liberalism and of the very idea of democracy itself. The "new liberalism" saw individuals as embedded in a broader social, cultural, and economic context. It refused to see the individual as absolute and instead saw the individual as dependent on the complex networks and social systems that modern economic and social life had constructed. It argued that the role of the state had to move beyond one that was largely decentralized with respect to its control over economic life and become a centralized administrative state that would seek to intervene in hampering the negative effects that accompanied the creation of a modern industrial society.[13] The conditions that individuals inhabited therefore became a causal variable as to the type of liberty and personal development they would be able to achieve. As Dewey remarked about this new liberalism in his essay "The Future of Liberalism," published in 1935, "such liberalism knows that an individual is nothing fixed, given ready-made. It is something achieved, and achieved not in isolation, but with the aid and support of conditions, cultural and physical, including in 'cultural' economic, legal, and political institutions as well as science and art. Liberalism knows that social conditions may restrict, distort, and almost prevent the development of individuality."[14]

Walter Weyl's notion of a "socialized democracy," put forth in his book *The New Democracy,* was similar to the thrust of Dewey's ideas. For Weyl, the older problems of laissez-faire individualism were being supplanted by the newer ideas that placed emphasis on the inherent social embeddedness of individuals and the political consequences of that embeddedness:

> In the socialized democracy towards which we are moving, all these conceptions will fall to the ground. It will be sought to make taxes conform more or less to the ability of each to pay; but the engine of taxation, like all other

social engines, will be used to accomplish great social ends, among which will be the more equal distribution of wealth and income. The state will tax to improve education, health, recreation, communication, "to provide for the common defense, and promote the general welfare," and from these taxes no social group will be immune because it fails to benefit in proportion to cost. . . . The political liberties of the people will be supplemented by other provisions which will safeguard their industrial liberties.[15]

Weyl, like Dewey and other thinkers of the time, was aware of the atomizing effect of modern capitalism. But for all of them, capitalism itself was never the real problem. They were all pointing to the ideas and values that made up classical liberalism: the notion of hedonic individualism and utilitarian notions of human action. Their enemies were therefore not big industry per se but, rather, the roots of English and Scottish political economy and ethical theory. The fragmentation of American social and political life was the result of the ethical notions of individualism in economics and ethics that could protect the institutions of unequal wealth and shatter any cohesive sense of a true democratic commonwealth.

The older version of liberalism and its emphasis on laissez faire had led to plutocracy, the erosion of any meaningful sense of individual autonomy, and the desiccation of democratic political life. The thinkers who transformed liberalism philosophically were matched by the social scientists and public policy technocrats who reconstructed the American state into the modern welfare state during the New Deal. The transformation of liberal thought in late-nineteenth and early-twentieth-century American thought was a significant shift in the practice and self-consciousness of democracy. The aims of government were now to be seen as activist rather than minimalist in nature. The essential liberties such as freedom of speech, religion, and the like were all to be maintained, but the new concept of liberty depended equally on the type of social conditions that were existent. Since individuals were no longer to be seen as atomized utility maximizers but as individual members of a broader public, the goal of democracy was to enhance the capacity for liberty through protecting public aims and, wherever possible, to enhance those aims as well.

This "new liberalism" came under severe attack ideologically in the middle and late twentieth century, and this has been the defining strand of conservative thought in America over the past three decades. The transformation of liberalism in the hands of conservative thinkers can be seen, in some ways, as one of the most important shifts in modern American political life and thought. The return to the basic doctrines of the "old liberalism"—to the emphasis on individual autonomy, a hostility to the state, and the reordering of social life enshrining the market mechanism as the institutional and ethical manifestation of human liberty—all began to emerge midcentury with influential thinkers such as Ludwig von Mises, Friedrich Hayek, and Milton Friedman, among many others. Although for some time they were isolated voices of dissent from the academic and public policy mainstream, their ideas would gain currency, most especially among a business elite that sought to reclaim its capacity to operate free from the constraints of the state.

The problem was how to do this while at the same time forging a popular consent among the broader public. This was achieved by purging liberalism of its political implications. Now, the true end of liberalism was to be seen in market rather than political terms. Freedom and liberty were redefined from the ideas of "new liberalism," which saw individual life as embedded in a web of social and economic relations and argued for the need to regulate those relations, to the ideas of the "old liberalism," which placed greater emphasis on civil society than the state when it came to determining democratic life. But the restoration of the ideology of laissez-faire liberalism legitimated other forms of political and social life. It renewed a populist hatred toward the state, it fanned a cynical attitude toward intellectuals and toward expertise, and it brought democracy away from the realm of the state and brought the political, at least at an ideological level, back to the local sphere. This renewed understanding of liberalism, individualism, freedom, the state, and society lay the ground for a justification of a new kind of American life: one that has become dominated by the renewal of an older capitalist ethos and legitimated return of hierarchy.

Resurgent Capitalism and the Transformation of Economic Life

The breakdown of the ideas associated with "social liberalism" made it possible for a return of the power of capital in late-twentieth-century America and for a restructuring of American economic life as well. The shift of social and political power away from capital and toward a new social contract with labor that had been achieved with the New Deal made it clear to economic elites that their interests were now constrained. Not only was the market itself to be extolled as a guarantor of liberty—as

Friedrich Hayek and Milton Friedman had argued in their writings—but the new consolidation of power by the business community would also begin to make real the fears of the thinkers that had constructed the idea of a new republic based on a "socialized democracy." A new economic culture centered around the entrepreneur, around capital and competition, would give flesh to the new ideology of liberalism that was emerging. A new legitimation of American capitalism could now take root.

Through neoliberal reforms that began to shed state regulation of the business community, a new form of economic life began to emerge. The older social compact between capital and labor began to break down as unionization decreased and its political power waned. Inequality began to surge, and the consequent inequities of political power began to be seen as a new legitimation of this form of economic life, and its social consequences were growing in acceptance.[16] In place of once pervasive populist angst against the rapaciousness of capital, accumulation, and conspicuous consumption, the new ideas that began to permeate popular consciousness actually saw these as legitimate ends of economic life. No longer was economic life tied to moral ends; now, thanks in part to the restoration of the "old" laissez-faire liberal ideology, work and consumption were individualized. Now, one labored for oneself, and the corporation became the necessary institution within which one could realize those ends. And in the process, it did not matter that one was legitimating hierarchies and forms of daily life that were anathema to any kind of democratic consciousness; what mattered was that one accept the *bellum omnium contra omnes* of modern working life for the fruits that it would supposedly bear. The focus on competition—both within as well as between industries and corporations—fostered an intensified emphasis on the atomized individualism that was created by the "old liberal" ethos. And with the waning of unions from structural economic causes also came a new skepticism of all forms of collectivism, specifically unionization.[17] The individual was left to face economic life alone. With this has come a new acceptance and internalization of hierarchy and order at the level of personality, a new toleration of economic royalism, and a predisposition toward forms of social authority based on wealth.[18]

In the ideology of new conservatism the interests of economic elites have been elided with more traditional conservative ideas about hierarchy and order. More classical American conservatives were essentially in opposition to capitalism, seeing it as rootless and modern, and they stood against establishing orders and hierarchies based on a system of "bourgeois social relations that undermined all tradition."[19] But new conservatism, contrary to seeing capitalism as undermining traditional constellations of family and communal life, sees capitalism as a central part of the fabric of American life, even as reinforcing it, a change attributable to the liberal theory of property that underlies American economic life.

This resurgent capitalism has taken advantage of the decline of support for the regulative state and the expansion of global markets that began to intensify with the fall of the Soviet Union in the early 1990s. As an ideology, "neoliberalism," which was embraced not only by conservative thinkers but also by the "new Democrats," has as its goal the placement of the market at the core of every facet of social life.[20] It seeks the hegemony of the market over other forms of association and other institutions—such as the government and unions—and it places political emphasis on the "interests of private property owners, businesses, multinational corporations, and financial capital";[21] it has placed market exchange at the very crux of social and political life and has succeeded in making capitalism a new public philosophy that has redefined public aims as well as the cultural life of the majority of Americans.[22] By reordering society around the imperatives of the market, the ideology of individual labor and property (another crucial aspect of classical liberal thought) has become writ large and has been used—oftentimes erroneously—to repeal everything from industrial regulations to taxation on the wealthy.[23]

But there is more than the mere macroeconomic patterns of wealth distribution and the political power that it carries with it that should be of concern when considering how the transformation of American economic life has fed into a new conservative landscape. One aspect of the transformation relates to the theme that I developed in the first part of this essay, the wholesale return to an atomistic individualism with economic as well as ideological connotations. One of the key elements of much conservative thought is the reconceptualization of economic life from seeing economic relations as political in nature—i.e., as relationships that engender relations of dependence and control—toward relations that are of free contract between uncoerced individuals. The interests of workers become akin to the interests of the corporation itself and its leaders, and all concerns about economic inequality become weakened.[24] Furthermore, with the globalization of work and capital has come a quickening change in economic life and, in turn, a new resignation of individuals in the face of the economic institutions within which they live and work.[25]

America's new economic life is therefore characterized by a renewed emphasis on hierarchy as well as a new passive acceptance of the inequalities that it creates. As capitalism and modern work life have become increasingly naturalized in the minds of most Americans, they cease to be objects of critical reflection. The result is the emergence of a new form of despotism, one that is not tied to the ideas of status that characterized the ancien régime but, rather, a new one based on the idea of "merit" and the myth of the liberal theory of property and ownership. This has led to an acceptance of power relations within economic relations that has allowed elites to reassert their interests and their power, reshaping many domains of social life in their own interests (from environmental policy to labor laws to efforts aimed at deregulation and so on). And they have succeeded to a large extent because of a dwindling critical discourse about American capitalism, a discourse that had been quite strong throughout much of American history. The consequence has been, at the social level, the primacy of elite economic interests at the expense of public interests and, at the personal level, a new passive acceptance of the kinds of authority that economic life exhibits as well as a proliferation of consumption, which lends itself to a new passivity in critical political terms and to a new narrowing of social life.

The New Provincialism

The emergence of a newly entrenched economic hierarchy is only part of a broader story that tells of the emergence of the new conservatism. The reestablishment of economic inequality and hierarchy, as well as the new passive acceptance of these inequalities, spring from a broader context in American social life. Indeed, the intellectual program of transforming liberalism into a renewed emphasis on the individual and, in turn, on the consumptive individual as the apex of social achievement and status finds its ultimate expression in the new suburban landscape and antiurban bias that has slowly emerged in America over the postwar period and that is only intensifying. The move away from urban centers, the decline of public space, the detachment of families from one another, and the subsequent narrowing of political and cultural horizons that result I call the "new provincialism," a mindset that has its grounding in the homogenized enclaves of most American suburban towns and that—along with more rural areas in the country—constitute an antiurban bias in American politics and culture.

As early as 1922, Walter Lippmann saw the need to provide a treatment of public opinion in modern democratic life, one that stressed the need to move beyond the older, now outmoded understanding of democratic citizenship, which emphasized the local and the forms of knowledge that were required to maneuver through smaller, more localized political and social life. The new, complex, modern world made it necessary to dispense with the older notions of democracy. "It is no longer possible," Lippmann wrote, "to believe in the original dogma of democracy; that the knowledge needed for the management of human affairs comes up spontaneously from the human heart. Where we act on that theory we expose ourselves to self-deception, and to forms of persuasion that we cannot verify. It has been demonstrated that we cannot rely upon intuition, conscience, or the accidents of casual opinion if we are to deal with the world beyond our reach."[26] But Lippmann's fear is precisely what has, in many sectors of American life, come to pass.

American culture has always demonstrated an explicit tension between its cosmopolitan, urban spheres and its more traditional, provincial ones. And traditionally, it was always the former that was able to hold much of the political power and influence. What the new conservatism has shown is that the reaction from the nonurban—indeed, one could call it anti-urban in its very form—has been able to rise and influence and shape aspects of American politics and culture. The new conservatism therefore not only possesses an economic agenda to expand the power and influence of capital, but it has also given room to the provincial and antiliberal traditions and sectors of American society that are firmly based in homogenized suburban enclaves that emphasize "family values" and domesticity and that thrive on the notion of isolation, especially from urban areas.[27] Furthermore, America's "suburban civilization" has eclipsed even the older ideas about political community idealized by thinkers like Jefferson and Tocqueville and has seen the shrinking of public space and the emphasis placed on the individual not as a member of political community but, rather, as a property-owner/taxpayer whose interests, more often than not, reside in the most immediate concerns of property.[28] As a consequence, older forms and institutional expressions of public space and the public sphere have broken down, leaving in their stead the sphere of consumption, with the shopping mall displacing the public square.[29]

The ideas of new conservatism require a fundamental tie to locality as the primary place of political life. The proliferation of suburban life and the rise of living standards led to a pursuit of comfort and disconnect from the strange and, therefore, to a new emphasis on localism. Although it is true that the new conservative disposition is a broad coalition of interests and ideas, fed not simply by radical right-wing movements, Christian fundamentalism, and the prerogatives of economic elites, it is also and perhaps most essentially based on the quietism and localism that the new provincialism provides. With the expansion of suburban life comes a renewed tie to locality, but in the most narrow economic sense; with it also comes the spatial crystallization of economic and racial inequality, which fosters robust forms of segregation not only between racial, economic, and ethnic groups but also between the suburb and the city.[30] This segregation ineluctably leads to the insulation of ideas about political and cultural life, the emergence of suburban life and culture, and the cultural and political effects of atomistic individualism and consumption. Suburban life cultivates and indeed is in many ways dependent on the notion of "detachment."[31] What is prized in suburban life is the idea that one can live in a form of separateness from others, protected from "difference" and from what may be uncomfortable to deal with.[32] This detachment shapes ways of thinking and the things to which individuals are exposed, having an important impact on notions of publicity and alienating most Americans from difference as well as from the space for dialogue, which cultivates a sense of isolation and apathy. Social atomization, a subsequent decline in secular associational life, and the erosion of political consciousness all have their place in the new provincialism. The new individual that inhabits these spaces eschews public life and has little outside the sphere of work and the family, constituting what Richard Sennett has famously termed the "fall of public man."

Moreover, the new provincialism is a mindset fused in many ways to the interpenetration of contemporary economic life and residential space. The erosion of public space and the detached separateness of suburban life undermines the possibility of alternative activities outside the family and work. Sennett's idea of a "new puritanism" where private life, the family, privacy, and intimacy become the focus of modern life is insufficient as an explanation of what actually happens in suburban life. It is true that these issues form the basis of what is desired by suburbanites, but it is tied to an insatiable consumption that undermines any idea of puritanism.[33]

But how does all of this merge with conservative ideas and ideology? First and foremost, there is the problem of the liberal legacy and its implications for suburban life. Since the suburbs were created along the lines of economic and racial homogeneity, the white flight from cities that occurred throughout the 1950s and 1960s was therefore strongly opposed to liberal programs of the 1960s through the 1970s that sought to desegregate schools and housing. The hostility toward top-down programs that sought to shape American life along more racially egalitarian lines—the problem of housing segregation between black and white municipalities was the prime target of liberal programs such as New Jersey's Mt. Laurel— helped move many suburban citizens toward political positions that alienated liberal democrats. Second, new conservative ideas meshed with more populist political ideas and have made many Americans—even those that do not self-consciously identify themselves as conservative—more susceptible to rhetorically manipulative conservative arguments through what Larry Bartels has called "unenlightened self-interest."[34]

The essence of the new provincialism is therefore not bound up simply with space itself; it is more accurate to say that the detachment and spatial relations that constitute the majority of American living environments shape political and cultural attitudes and ways of understanding because of the return to the emphasis on localism. Historically there is some evidence that correlates the expansion of local forms of political power with the expression of racist and antiliberal ideas. The plebiscitary democratic reforms of the early twentieth century are one example of this. Although on its surface it may seem ironic to argue that the reforms pushed forward by Progressive thinkers and politicians have had antidemocratic effects, the political reality is somewhat different. As Philip Ethington has insightfully argued,

> No sooner were the direct democracy reforms in place than we witness the rise of intolerance politics. The "tribal twenties" were typified by a victorious anti-immigrant movement (culminating in the Restriction Act of 1920 and 1924, and the Anti-Japanese Alien Land Laws of California); race riots; the rise of the Ku Klux Klan in the urban North; big-city mayors who waged openly ethno-racial campaigns (James Michael Curley in Boston and William Hale Thompson in Chicago); the intensification of race segregation in the urban North.[35]

Ethington points out that the emergence of local power corresponded historically to the venting of populist ideas about race and ethnicity. In the new provincialism we can see once again the way that isolated forms of community—isolated economically as well as racially and ethnically—can lead to certain populist ideas about both domestic and foreign policy, shape attitudes about "the other," and re-create certain antiliberal tendencies when it comes to the expansion of social rights.

It is not that all forms of nonurban life *make* people conservative; it is more that the emphasis on localism that was always at the heart of the flight from the cities has produced a narrowness of political interests, of cultural exposure, and, as a result of the elimination of a political public space, an erosion of political life more broadly. The enclavization at the residential level therefore leads to certain forms of thought, life, attitudes, interests, and desires that were not necessarily at the heart of earlier forms of urban life. In the end, what I have called the "new provincialism" has served as a broad spatial and cultural context for the new conservative disposition. It raises serious issues with respect to the ways in which economics, culture, political ideology, and interests mesh to form the conservative landscape, and it is a crucial variable in understanding the distinct change that has been occurring in American democratic life during the past several decades.

The Reorientation of American Democracy

What I have broadly called the "new conservatism" is therefore not a monolithic force in American politics and culture. Rather, as I have tried to show, it is a fundamental reorientation of the American democratic project away from what was initiated with the Progressive and New Deal eras: an emphasis on the sociality of the individual, the importance and primacy of the public interest over the interests of the few, and the constraint of arbitrariness of economic power. If the new conservatism can be seen as a reaction to modernity, than the two-fold nature of modernity needs to be pointed out in order to understand the different groups and interests that have coalesced around it. On the one hand, political modernity is the separation of public and private, the creation of the secular state and its separation from religious authority and tradition. This form of political modernity—which has its roots in Hobbes and Locke—has been the object of reaction and resentment of contemporary populists, Christian fundamentalists, and other detractors of the cultural and political implications of liberalism and political modernity. The other side of political modernity is the facet that emphasizes the attainment of modern political life through the expansion of the democratic franchise, the elimination of what Locke in his *Second Treatise of Government* called the natural liberty of man, which he defined as being "free from any superior power on earth."[36] This was a political insight that drove the efforts to prevent the emergence of hierarchical social relations characteristic of feudalism and to overturn the inequalities that they engendered. It gave individuals a critical standard to assess the political nature of the world around them and motivated them away from tyranny and toward a more liberatory politics. And it is this that conservatives hate: the erosion of authority, the expansion of equality, and the expansion of freedom all seem to them to be the breakdown of society itself. Conservatism becomes the beacon of the maintenance of society in the face of nihilism and equality destroying the traditional forms of authority and "hierarchy that is native to the social bond."[37]

Both of these aspects of modernity are the enemies of the new conservatism, albeit not always simultaneously: economic conservatives may not have a problem with the separation of church and state, and, on the other hand, religious conservatives may be critical of the effects of economic inequality and the preponderance of the market. But where they have come together is their mutual interest in the reduction or complete annihilation of the power of the state and its ability to intervene in the affairs of civil society, whether this is in terms of the market or school prayer. And it is here that the new conservatism has its ideological base. But the reorientation of American democracy has not occurred simply through this amalgam of interests, ideas, and groups. Rather, it has occurred through the ability to translate these concerns as interests of mainstream American society. Simply put, the proponents of the new conservatism have been able to construct a public philosophy that has, over time, slowly displaced the liberal public philosophy that had dominated much of the twentieth century.

This reaction to modernity is nothing new in the history of conservatism in Western politics, but it constitutes a serious threat to the legacy of democratic politics in America. Moreover, the three interlocking dimensions of the new conservatism that I outlined serve not only as a means to understand the historical moment but, more importantly, as a means to understand and comprehend the politics of the present. Each of the three facets of the new conservatism distinguish the older forms of radical right-wing politics from the subtler forms of conservative predispositions and policies that have emerged over the past several decades in America. Furthermore, they explain the particular way that new conservative intellectuals, popularizers, and political figures have been able to weave a new public philosophy that has in many ways displaced the older liberalism that dominated the postwar American scene. It explains how elite economic interests have been able to merge with more populist grassroots movements by seeking the end of state intrusion into civil society— in the interests of economic deregulation for the former and a return to local control of schools and other local institutions for the latter. This new conservative landscape is one that has seen the rise of political apathy, the emergence of a new provincialism, and the construction of a new economic hierarchy that distributes all forms of social power unequally and against the interests of democratic political life, all under the intellectual rubric of a "true" liberty and democracy. This has been achieved through the return to the "old liberalism" that dominated the era before the Progressive movement and New Deal liberalism. The new conservatism is therefore not simply a disposition; it is a concrete set of policy objectives that seek out affinities with different groups and with the broader public, much of the time unwittingly against other interests they might possess, and it is one that will continue to shape American political life unless and until another public philosophy is forged.

NOTES

1. Thomas Frank, *What's the Matter with Kansas?* (New York: Metropolitan Books, 2004), 5.

2. Also see Robert Wiebe, *Self Rule: A Cultural History of American Democracy* (Chicago: University of Chicago Press, 1995), 223–246, and Douglas Massey, *Return of the "L" Word* (Princeton, NJ: Princeton University Press, 2005), 11–36. More recent studies have emphasized the emerging conservatism as a result of the South's class transformation. See Byron Shafer and Richard Johnson, *The End of Southern Exceptionalism: Class, Race, and Partisan Change in the Postwar South* (Cambridge, MA: Harvard University Press, 2006).

3. This argument is made explicitly by conservative thinker Robert Nisbet, who argues that the expansion of the American state under the Wilson administration—itself influenced by the current of Progressive thought at the time— marks the beginning of the slow process of social decay that affects contemporary American society. For a discussion, see Nisbet, *The Present Age* (New York: Harper and Row, 1988), 40–83.

4. For a discussion of the way that liberal ideas shaped modern economic and labor relations, see Karen Orren, *Belated Feudalism: Labor, the Law, and Liberal Development in the United States* (Cambridge: Cambridge University Press, 1991), 68–117. For more on race and gender relations, see J. R. Pole, *The Pursuit of Equal-*

ity in American History (Berkeley: University of California Press, 1993), 174–213 (race), 351–407 (gender).

5. "Ironically, 'liberalism' is a stranger in the land of its greatest realization and fulfillment. But this is not all. Here is a doctrine which everywhere in the West has been a glorious symbol of individual liberty, yet in America its compulsive power has been so great that it has posed a threat to liberty itself. Actually, Locke has a hidden conformitarian germ to begin with, since natural law tells equal people equal things, but when this germ is fed by the explosive power of modern nationalism, it mushrooms into something pretty remarkable. One can reasonably wonder about the liberty one finds in Burke." *The Liberal Tradition in America* (New York: Harcourt Brace Jovanovich, 1955), 32.

6. Eldon Eisenach, *The Lost Promise of Progressivism* (Lawrence: University of Kansas Press, 1994), 1–7. On the waning of liberal ideology in the postwar period, see Theodore Lowi's classic argument in his book *The End of Liberalism* (New York: Norton, 1969).

7. Robert Wiebe, *The Search for Order, 1877–1920* (New York: Hill and Wang, 1967), 133–163.

8. John Dewey, "The Future of Liberalism," in *New Deal Thought,* ed. Howard Zinn, pp. 28–35 (Cambridge, MA: Hackett, 2003), 30. For a more in-depth discussion of Dewey's transformation of liberalism, see David Fott, *John Dewey: America's Philosopher of Democracy* (Lanham, MD: Rowman and Littlefield, 1998), 29–62; John Lugton Stafford, *Pragmatism and the Progressive Movement in the United States: The Origin of the New Social Sciences* (Lanham, MD: University Press of America, 1987), 175–196; William Caspary, *Dewey on Democracy* (Ithaca, NY: Cornell University Press, 2000), 140–173; James Gouinlock, *Excellence in Public Discourse: John Stuart Mill, John Dewey, and Social Intelligence* (New York: Teachers College Press, 1986), 25–42; Robert Westbrook, *John Dewey and American Democracy* (Ithaca, NY: Cornell University Press, 1991), 275–376.

9. William Graham Sumner was one of the most influential of these thinkers. See his *What Do Social Classes Owe One Another?* (Caldwell, ID: Caxton, 2003 [1883]). Also see Richard Hofstadter's classic discussion of this strain in American politics, *Social Darwinism in American Thought* (New York: George Braziller, 1965), 51–66. For a critical view of the extent to which conservatives during the Gilded Age actually relied on Darwinian ideas and principles, see Irving Wyllie, *The Self-Made Man* (New Brunswick, NJ: Rutgers University Press, 1954), as well as Robert C. Bannister, "The Survival of the Fittest Is Our Doctrine: History or Histrionics?" *Journal of the History of Ideas* 31, no. 3 (1970): 377–398, and John G. West, "Darwin's Public Policy: Nineteenth-Century Science and the Rise of the American Welfare State," in *The Progressive Revolution in Politics and Political Science: Transforming the American Regime,* ed. John Marini and Ken Masugi, pp. 221–251 (Lanham, MD: Rowman and Littlefield, 2005).

10. For a discussion of this period, see John Garraty, *The New Commonwealth,*

1877–1890 (New York: Harper and Row, 1968), 309–336; Wiebe, *Search for Order*; Morton White, *Social Thought in America: The Revolt against Formalism* (Boston: Beacon, 1963), 3–58; and James T. Kloppenberg, *Uncertain Victory: Social Democracy and Progressivism in European and American Thought* (New York: Oxford University Press, 1986).

11. "[T]he human individual belongs to an organized social community, and derives his human nature from his social interactions and relations with that community as a whole and with the other individual members of it." George Herbert Mead, *Mind, Self, and Society* (Chicago: University of Chicago Press, 1967), 229. Philosophically, this insight has been developed further by contemporary social theorists. Specifically, see Hans Joas, *G. H. Mead: A Contemporary Examination of His Thought* (Cambridge, UK: Polity, 1985); Hans Joas, *Pragmatism and Social Theory* (Chicago: University of Chicago Press, 1993); and Axel Honneth, *The Fragmented World of the Social* (Albany: SUNY Press, 1995), 247–260.

12. For an excellent discussion, see Philip J. Ethington, "The Metropolis and Multicultural Ethics: Direct Democracy versus Deliberative Democracy in the Progressive Era," in *Progressivism and the New Democracy*, ed. Sidney Milkis and Jerome Mileur, pp. 192–225 (Amherst: University of Massachusetts Press, 1999), 209.

13. For a discussion, see Stephen Skowronek, *Building the New American State: The Expansion of Administrative Capacities, 1877–1920* (New York: Cambridge University Press, 1982), 248–284.

14. Dewey, "Future of Liberalism," 31.

15. Walter Weyl, *The New Democracy: An Essay on Certain Political and Economic Tendencies in the United States* (New York: Macmillan, 1912), 163–164.

16. The empirical literature here is enormous, and the consensus is clear. For different aspects of this phenomenon, see Edward Wolff, *Top Heavy* (New York: New Press, 1996); T. Piketty and E. Saez, "Income Inequality in the United States, 1913–1998," *Quarterly Journal of Economics* 118 (2003): 1–39; and William Julius Wilson, *The Bridge over the Racial Divide* (Berkeley: University of California Press, 1999).

17. Of course, there was reason to be skeptical of many of the internal aspects of American unionism, from corruption to racism and beyond. But this skepticism has been used rhetorically to devalue the idea of worker organization in toto. See Robert Fitch's important study, *Solidarity for Sale* (New York: Public Affairs Books, 2006).

18. The classic analysis of personality and the problem of freedom is Erich Fromm's *Escape from Freedom* (New York: Rinehart and Company, 1959), 240–276, and it is an analysis that retains its salience. For a more up-to-date analysis of this problem, see C. Fred Alford, *Rethinking Freedom: Why Freedom Has Lost Its Meaning and What Can Be Done to Save It* (New York: Palgrave Macmillan, 2005).

19. Eugene D. Genovese, *The Southern Tradition: The Achievement and Limitations of an American Conservatism* (Cambridge, MA: Harvard University Press, 1994), 8.

20. For more on the analysis of neoliberalism, see Gerard Dumenil and Dominique Levy, *Capital Resurgent: Roots of the Neoliberal Revolution* (Cambridge, MA: Harvard University Press, 2004); Gerard Dumenil and Dominique Levy, "Neoliberal Income Trends: Wealth, Class, and Ownership in the USA," *New Left Review* 30 (2004): 105–133; M. Fourcade-Gourinchas and S. Babb, "The Rebirth of the Liberal Creed: Paths to Neoliberalism in Four Countries," *American Journal of Sociology* 108 (2002): 533–579.

21. David Harvey, *A Brief History of Neoliberalism* (New York: Oxford University Press, 2005), 3.

22. In many ways, this reality was the fear of many liberals during the 1960s about the power of capitalist elites. As John Kenneth Galbraith argued in the closing pages of his book *The New Industrial State*, "The danger to liberty lies in the subordination of belief to the needs of the industrial system. . . . If we continue to believe that the goals of the industrial system—the expansion of output, the companion increase in consumption, technological advance, the public images that sustain it—are coordinate with life, then all of our lives will be in the service of these goals. What is consistent with these ends we shall have or be allowed; all else will be off limits. Our wants will be managed in accordance with the needs of the industrial system; the policies of the state will be subject to similar influence; education will be adapted to industrial need; the disciplines required by the industrial system will be the conventional morality of the community" (Boston: Houghton Mifflin, 1967), 398.

23. For an excellent analysis of the effort to repeal the wealth tax, see Michael J. Graetz and Ian Shapiro, *Death by a Thousand Cuts* (Princeton, NJ: Princeton University Press, 2005).

24. For a discussion, see C. B. MacPherson, *The Rise and Fall of Economic Justice and Other Essays* (Oxford: Oxford University Press, 1985), 101–119. Also see Michael J. Thompson, "What's the Matter with Capitalism?" *Logos: A Journal of Modern Society & Culture* (www.logosjournal.com/issue_5.1/thompson.htm), for a discussion of the depoliticization of economic life under capitalism. These analyses owe much to the insights of Georg Lukács; see his *History and Class Consciousness* and the discussion of "reification" (Cambridge, MA: MIT Press, 1971).

25. As Richard Sennett has argued, "A stereotype holds that Americans are aggressive competitors in business. Beneath this stereotype lies a different, more passive mentality. Americans of the middling sort I've interviewed in the past decade have tended to accept structural change with resignation, as though the loss of security at work and in schools run like businesses are inevitable: you can do little about such basic shifts, even if they hurt you." Richard Sennett, *The Culture of the New Capitalism* (New Haven, CT: Yale University Press, 2006), 9–10.

26. Walter Lippmann, *Public Opinion* (New York: Macmillan, 1960 [1922]), 248–249.

27. The idea of suburbia has always rested on ideas about domesticity and family life that can be seen as feeding into conservative ideas about family and community. Dolores Hayden persuasively argues that "[f]rom the beginning, the [suburban] dream conflated piety and gender-stereotyped 'family values.' . . . The single-family house was invested with church-like symbols as a sacred space where women's work would win reward in heaven. Catholic and Jewish immigrants also tied domesticity to religion." *Building Suburbia: Green Fields and Urban Growth, 1820–2000* (New York: Vintage, 2003), 6.

28. There has been excellent work done on this theme. See Margaret Kohn, *Brave New Neighborhoods: The Privatization of Public Space* (New York: Routledge, 2004), esp. 115–137. Also see Lizabeth Cohen, *A Consumer's Republic: The Politics of Mass Consumption in Postwar America* (New York: Knopf, 2003); and Susan Bickford, "Constructing Inequality: City Spaces and the Architecture of Citizenship," *Political Theory* 28., no. 3 (2000): 355–376.

29. Both Lizabeth Cohen and Dolores Hayden have done excellent work on this theme. As Hayden argues, "The postwar suburbs were constructed at great speed, but they were deliberately planned to maximize consumption of mass-produced goods and minimize the responsibility of the developers to create public space and public services." *Building Suburbia,* 128.

30. The excellent work on this theme from sociological as well as historical perspectives are, respectively, Douglas Massey and Nancy Denton, *American Apartheid: Segregation and the Making of the Underclass* (Cambridge, MA: Harvard University Press, 1993), and Thomas Sugrue, *The Origins of the Urban Crisis: Race and Inequality in Postwar Detroit* (Princeton, NJ: Princeton University Press, 1996).

31. Amy Maria Kenyon discusses the problem of the "detachment" that pervades modern suburban life. Her argument is that detachment comes in three simultaneous forms: detachment between suburb and city, between neighbors themselves, and, within the home itself, between individuals: "the triadic spaces of detachment from city, from neighbors, and from family members had to work in harmony to produce dream suburbanites in dream suburbs. The suburban subject had to move in a world in which detachment and avoidance could be reflected back as attachment or connection." *Dreaming Suburbia: Detroit and the Production of Postwar Space and Culture* (Detroit: Wayne State University Press, 2004), 46–47.

32. For a seminal discussion of the way urban environments affect mental life, see Georg Simmel's classic essay, "The Metropolis and Mental Life," in *The Sociology of Georg Simmel,* trans. and ed. Kurt H. Wolff, pp. 409–424 (New York: Free Press, 1964).

33. Richard Sennett, *The Uses of Disorder* (New York: Knopf, 1971).

34. For a discussion of this theme in relation to the support for regressive tax

cuts, see Larry M. Bartels, "Homer Gets a Tax Cut: Inequality and Public Policy in the American Mind," *Perspectives on Politics* 3, no. 1 (2005): 15–31.

35. Ethington, "Metropolis and Multicultural Ethics," 212.

36. See chapter 4 of Locke's *Second Treatise of Government.*

37. Robert Nisbet calls this "the new science of despotism." See his *The Twilight of Authority* (New York: Oxford University Press, 1975), 194–287.

Chapter 2

Cultural Rage and the Right-Wing Intellectuals

Philip Green

The proto-totalitarian moment in contemporary American politics has three key components: First, the takeover of democratic political institutions by a single party intent on establishing a permanent one-party state bent on world domination. It is seriously misleading to go on calling the United States a "representative democracy" when what it has become, with little effective opposition, is an oligarchy: a centralization of unchecked power that at this point in time looks like a way station on the road to an imperial tyranny.[1] Second, an all-out coercive assault on independent centers of knowledge and communication, including institutions of higher education; practitioners of scientific and medical research in or out of the public sector; and above all the mass media of communication. Third, a mass mobilization of voters and activists galvanized by the ideological doctrines of authoritarian populism and patriarchal Christian theocracy.

According to the classic literature of totalitarianism, its ideological assault is all-inclusive, waged throughout civil society, encompassing even such unlikely foci as the arts (in the Soviet Union and Nazi Germany). Although at first glance reference to such literature might seem at best suggestive, at worst hysterical, closer inspection shows that this program in one way or another is being carried out even in the contemporary United States. The restless reach of the proto-totalitarian drive is attested to by, to take just a few examples, the attacks that ensue whenever a center of artistic or scientific artifacts such as the Smithsonian Museum attempts to mount an exhibit containing elements critical of American history or practices or by the federal government's behavior in the cases of Terry Schiavo or California's medical marijuana law. "Authoritarian populism," an antidemocratic ideology masquerading as majoritarian democracy (unlike its predecessor, Fascism), gives ideological cover to the drive for total power. In truth, though, it is an ideology not of fairness but of exclusion, and it proceeds by stigmatizing as enemies all those who allegedly betray or seduce the otherwise virtuous "people": e.g., Jews, Communists, liberals, homosexuals, and so on.[2]

My primary purpose here is to discuss the ideological component of this moment: the centrality in our politics of what I call "cultural rage." How that rage came to be so central, and what are the intellectual forces behind it, is the main focus of this essay. What do I mean by "cultural rage"? It is the feeling, on the part of millions of people, that they are in some way *excluded* from culture in both standard senses of the word. They feel excluded from representation in the institutions that produce mass communications and from the content of those communications as well; the social order they feel excluded from is what anthropologists call the symbolic order. This felt exclusion manifests itself as rage (the classical sociological term is *ressentiment*). Politically, this sense of exclusion and consequent rage in turn generates and justifies the exclusionary ideology of authoritarian populism: the excluded excluding those who have excluded them, so to speak. But why this response?

Primarily, this state of being is felt not as a historical outcome, a technological inability or the like, but as the result of a conscious *conspiracy*. There is a very relevant documentary film from the 1980s called *Faces of the Enemy,* in which the filmmaker asks a man who had executed a Seattle family because they were "communists" why he thought they deserved to die. The man replies that he is a skilled welder who has been out of a job for two years, and "it must be somebody's fault." Analogously, at the center of cultural rage is an alienating sense of distance from the major sites of ideological communication, especially institutions of higher education and mass communication. To be sure, most of us do experience this alienation, but in the case of those who respond with authoritarian populist rage it is perceived as "somebody's fault" in a very special way. Alienation in its various forms can be perceived as one of the consequences, both intended and unintended, of the way our social institutions have come to be arranged, of the way capitalist "democracy" has developed historically, and the class and other dominations attendant to that development. In the case of cultural rage, though, the pattern of development as it affects individuals and their fates is primarily laid at the door of other, identifiable scapegoats, individuals, groups, or organizations: enemies.

In particular, the general state of belief on the Right, which is consistent with much of historical conservatism and radicalism, is that all mass communications are in any event manipulative; it is only a matter of who is to do the manipulating. For more than two decades a tendentious and politically charged answer to that question has been insistently promulgated by a coterie of so-called media watchdog organizations and individuals, lavishly financed by right-wing organizations such as Olin and Scaife.[3] Their answer to that question is that the conspirators are an *elite*—as of course they are, since there is no complex social institution that is not run by an elite, and the creation of cultural commodities or information streams, fictional or nonfictional, is a highly skilled process. Worse, this is an elite of a special kind, for as an elite based on possession of certain professional skills, it is open to participation from every recognizable social group *except* unskilled and semiskilled members of the working and lower-middle classes. That is crucial, in that the unavoidable class component of the elite makes it seem like more than just a skill elite but also or even instead like an elite the members of which actively disdain the many consumers of mass culture. Also, it is a *liberal* elite, the modifier being an amalgam of identifiers that is in some sense impossible to clarify but that explains to believers why, for example, the millionaire Yalie John Kerry belongs to it and the plutocrat Yalie George W. Bush does not. This aspect of cultural rage also carries over to such symbolic targets as gun control and gay marriage, which come to us courtesy of "activist judges," special interests with an "agenda," and so on—all easy to scapegoat as not being of "the people." So insistent has been the drumbeat of this propaganda campaign, and so reluctant the monopolized mass media have been to stand up to it, that during this period of precipitous liberal retreat on all fronts the big lie of "liberal control" has become the generally accepted "truth" at the heart of the culture wars.

There is a common theme in discussions of this contemporary variant of conservatism and its ideological triumph, best summed up in Thomas Frank's heartfelt outcry, *What's the Matter with Kansas?* The story is that Americans, buffeted for three decades by an economy that worsens the position of all but the well off, ought to be turning to the Left, to the politics of redistribution. Instead, though, a significant proportion of voters have turned rightward, as described in my analysis. Why should this be? In Frank's analysis, the organizational and propagandistic skills of the Right and the failure of the Democratic Party and neoliberalism are together responsible for this unexpected turn of events. Millions of voters are deluded by the well-financed and coordinated ideological onslaught of the

Right, but they succumb to delusion in part because Democrats offer no effective counterargument. As a later review of several books on the conservative triumph puts it, "They [the Democrats] bemoan the phenomenon of working-class voters getting suckered into voting for the GOP yet shy away from embracing a populist economic agenda that might win back their allegiance." Betrayed by a liberalism that has turned its back on their material needs, they have succumbed to the symbolic rewards of conservatism, its attacks on "liberal elites" and other class enemies. In Frank's oft-quoted litany of delusion,

> *Vote* to stop abortion; *receive* a rollback in capital gains taxes. *Vote* to make our country strong again; *receive* deindustrialization. *Vote* to screw those politically correct college professors; *receive* electricity deregulation. *Vote* to get government off our backs; *receive* conglomeration everywhere from media to meat-packing. *Vote* to stand tall against terrorists; *receive* Social Security privatization. *Vote* to strike a blow against elitism; *receive* a social order in which wealth is more concentrated than ever before in our lifetimes, in which workers have been stripped of power and CEOs are rewarded in a manner beyond imagining.[4]

This is a devastating indictment—although of what is not perfectly clear. After all, voting patterns (in Kansas, for example) are not that much different from what they have been historically. Indeed, only once since the end of World War II has a Democrat gained a majority of the popular vote in a presidential election. And of course there have always been periods of rage and *ressentiment* on the American scene.[5] But Frank is certainly correct that the resentful have never been so powerful as now. If one looks at social science analyses of the 1950s radical right, for example, the analysts are always talking about a population they clearly think of as marginalized, even though powerfully represented by such voices as Senator Joe McCarthy.[6]

What was marginal has become central, however, and the most obvious reason why this should be so is the historic collapse, over the past forty years, of the New Deal coalition that as a majority formed the bedrock of American politics, against which minority voices such as those on the radical right beat mostly in vain. The absence of that coalition, and most crucially of an organized industrial working class that was its center, together with its replacement in the Democratic Party by a neoliberal leadership with no genuine ties to the working class and the nonprofessional middle class, opened the way for the eventual success of the reaction that began with George Wallace and that has transformed the political identity of so many of the old coalition's descendants.

Still, cultural historical analysis is intended to explain not just "what has happened" but also what has happened instead of something else that might equally well have happened. Thus, it is appropriate to ask, as the Republican Party has moved farther and farther to the Right, why have there not been corresponding defections from its voting base, most of which is not composed of the millionaires and billionaires who are the chief beneficiaries of its economic policies? This question, though, applies equally well to Frank and those who share his viewpoint. Why should the Democratic Party need a "populist" agenda to attract votes from a class that is betrayed so decisively by the other party, a party that operates hand-in-hand with the union-busters of capital? What we have to understand, after all, is not merely the failure of the nonpopulist Democrats, which is obvious enough, but the corresponding success of the very anti-working-class Republicans. Here, the attribution of default to the Democrats is too simple.

It is undoubtedly the case that, originating in the mid-1970s, the longest-running decline of real wages since the founding of the American republic, orchestrated quite consciously by organized capital, has proceeded without significant resistance from the Democratic Party, and often with its collusion. It was Democrats, after all, who initiated deregulation and the latest round of "free trade," collaborated in the original initiative for privatizing Social Security, and succeeded in abolishing the minimal floor to the American welfare state. This argument, then, certainly explains some portion of working-class defection from the Democratic Party and thus from the betrayed promise of redistributive or simply welfarist politics; but it is not really satisfying. In the first place, it remains the case that ever since the New Deal period, and extending through the Clinton years, income growth among nonaffluent Americans has on average been proportionately much greater during Democratic than Republican administrations.[7] Why shouldn't this clear and unchanging historical tendency, that must be evident to anyone paying attention to his or her material circumstances, have more influence on voting patterns than it evidently has had?

The apparent defects of neoliberalism cannot explain this. But more crucially, what is missing from Frank's and similar analyses is the answer to a fundamental question that is rarely asked: what exactly is in it for the voters who welcome verbal attacks on network television newscasters, homosexuality, advocacy of abortion rights, and the separation of church and state as symbolized in the issues of school prayer and creationism? The apparent answer given by Frank is that Americans derive emotional satisfaction from this symbolic outrage on their behalf (and from the intensive propaganda barrage that has helped to produce it): *How Conservatives Won the Heart of America* is his subtitle. This is a double entendre, of course, conjuring up both the geographical and emotional cores of the nation. But what the analysis does not explain is why *this* outrage rings a bell. Why do people care about television? It hardly meets one of their fundamental needs. Why such anger among both men and women about other people's abortions, or "gay" marriages that apparently have no impact on their actual lives, or "gun control" proposals that will take nothing away from them but the chance to own lethal automatic weapons, or the other mantras of contemporary conservative rage? Most crucially, perhaps, why is the Right able to maintain at least some strength among women (the "gender gap" among white women virtually closed in the 2004 presidential election) while mobilizing around masculinist and pro-male politics? Have conservative intellectuals and politicians simply lucked into an accidental conjunction of popular attitudes with their own quest for power?

On the contrary, neoconservatism has succeeded by intelligently exploiting real needs. The Democratic Party might secure more votes in the short run by abandoning neoliberalism for a second New Deal, but those real needs will not readily go away. Moreover, the obstacles in the way of redistributive politics are in their own right as substantial as the desires to which contemporary conservatism appeals. In the ideological realm, what has happened over the past three decades is that the neoconservative intellectuals and activists have crafted a right-wing package, a compromise of standpoints and issues from which every party to the compromise both gains something and gives up something. There are several items in this package (I separate them for the sake of convenience; they cannot easily be disentangled), chief among them being the recovery of traditional Christianity and its repressive approach to female sexuality. But we must also take account of white racial *ressentiment,* militant nationalism, the all-out attack on "liberal media elites" (the *kulturkampf*), and antitax ideology, which leftists and liberals tend to misunderstand as an issue, though Democratic Party leaders do not.[8]

Each of these components of the right-wing package deserves explication. Race especially is consistently underrated as a component of the American social order. Ever since the coming of the New Deal, few domestic policies have been put into place in the United States that were not meant to either include or, more often, exclude African Americans in some important way.[9] As the federal government's initial nonresponse to Hurricane Katrina made clear, and the disappearing "reconstruction" effort makes even clearer, in the hands of a regime strongly committed to putting the needs of wealthy white people before all other social needs, and to abolishing the constitutional mandate of promoting "the general welfare," public policy is now more unbalanced racially than it has been since a long time past.

If this resegregation goes unopposed, one reason is that the former slave states are now the core of so-called red/blue polarization (voting patterns within them being even more one-sided than those of the Great Plains states), and within those states virtually all politics is racial. What has happened since the apotheosis of the civil rights movement is that "angry white men," especially those who no longer experience the solidarity of trade unionism, and including especially the descendants of those who lost the War Between the States, now have an explicable account for what feels like the relative falling behind of many working-class and middle-class males in the social order during the general social transformation of the past forty years. "Quotas" as a demonizing term for "affirmative action" is the alleged account of the cause—except when the quotas favor white men, as they so often do. In addition, the very nonsymbolic issue of "gun control" is shorthand for a perceived shift of racial authority—"coddling" the crimes of blacks who are envisioned as pouring out of the "inner cities" to rampage through the lily-white suburbs, while penalizing the anticrime stance of whites as though it was racism. (In this respect Michael Moore's *Bowling for Columbine* could unfortunately be an ad campaign for the NRA.)

That the administration's class war is thus also or even more a race war should not be overlooked; the attempt by some Republican-controlled state legislatures to suppress African American voting rights is the advance guard of that war. However, the key to understanding where Frank's analysis and similar analyses come up short is to focus on the question of taxes and specifically the so-called tax revolt that began in the late 1970s in California. From the standpoint of those who wish in some way to revive the decayed welfare state—usually zeroing in on health care as the central issue arena—the question of taxation is an immense and in the short run insuperable obstacle. To begin with, the macroeconomic argument that higher taxes can be used to provide needed social services is just that—an argument, greatly complicated, with economists on either side of it; it cannot compete with a slogan that apparently matches lived experience.

Beyond that, the complexity of the argument is matched or even exceeded by the complexity of the material facts, in that the apparently negative impact of increased taxes, and the supposedly positive impact of decreased taxes, are instantly apparent; whereas the benefits supposed to flow from the former, and painful fiscal shortfalls from the latter, are well in the future and in any event quite suppositious. Will single-payer health ultimately pay for itself in the United States as it has done in Canada? Nobody knows, but everybody knows that it will be very expensive and difficult to implement. Perhaps average individuals will pay less for their health care ultimately, but averages are only that, and individuals cannot be satisfied with an identification of their costs and needs as "average." As Michael J. Graetz and Ian Shapiro have pointed out in their important case study of the inheritance-tax repeal movement, *Death by a Thousand Cuts,* the paralysis of Democrats in the face of antitax ideology left them unwilling or unable to defend the one tax that truly affects only the wealthy. Its positive effects are too abstract to constitute a rallying point; the only thing the "death tax" promises surely to do is redistribute levels of income in a rarely visible way, and with little apparent impact on the Left's target audience for populist rhetoric.[10]

In other words, even a populist appeal is not at all guaranteed to overcome the built-in obstacles to any revival of the welfare state—including most prominently the overwhelming debt that conservative fiscal strategists have deliberately built up in order to "strangle government." And the effects of the fiscal strangulation of the state are exacerbated by the decay of American trade-unionism. Furthermore, as trade-union membership has dwindled drastically along with the decomposition and in many cases virtual disappearance of industrial labor, and as the once predominantly white male work force fragments into gendered, aged, and racial components, unionism becomes more and more concentrated in the public sector. Even the traditional working class often feels little identification with public service workers outside of police and fire departments.[11] The consequent shrinking of the space for traditional class consciousness has in turn increased the salience of militarized nationalism, which provides the sense of a common identity that liberal pluralism cannot match and that a fragmented working-class identity can no longer provide.[12] Moreover, nationalist ideology dovetails with the antigovernment strategy that undergirds the antitax movement. In the name of "national security," the Keynesian multiplier of massive government expenditure, without which no administration could make any claim on working-class affections, can be maintained while the rest of the state withers away.

There is also an additional, little-appreciated consequence of the political divide between so-called symbolic issues and the class-based economic concerns that its Left critics wish the Democratic Party to focus on. The former—gun control, gay marriage, abortion, school prayer, smashing of "liberal" media monopolies, abolition of "quotas," etc.—are unique in that a conservative resolution of them can be achieved *without costing taxpayers anything.* In this context, unfortunately, oligarchical conservatism, even with its built-in tendency to tyranny, can be *more* representative than less-oligarchical liberalism. In recent times more and more voters have learned —with considerable pedagogical help from political leaders and "opinion makers"—to think of themselves as "taxpayers" rather than as members of this class or that class. Democratic Party leadership, most especially President Bill Clinton, not only did very little to forestall that "classless" identification but actively promoted the idea of the United States as an agglomeration of "middle-class taxpayers." Given that in this key realm the Democratic Party has indeed, as Frank alleges, decisively rejected its New Deal heritage, then even the unmitigated plutocracy of the GOP becomes not wholly unrepresentative: at least Republicans are paying attention to *something.*

This very simple version of a cost-benefit analysis makes the relative success of what I would argue is the core of neoconservatism—patriarchal religiosity and the assault on the media—easier to comprehend. With respect to the former, we might begin with Marx's pronouncement, in his *Critique of Hegel's* Philosophy of Right, that "[m]aterial force can only be overthrown by material force, but theory itself becomes a material force when it has seized the masses." The theory he had in mind was "the *positive* abolition of religion," but apparently today the shoe is on the other foot. The recrudescence of religion has seized enough of the masses to make a significant difference in the calculus of American politics—even to *be* the difference, since the Republican Party has adopted the totalizing politics of authoritarian populism, between a one-party and a two-party state.

What is this contemporary "material force"? In brief, the most important material basis of cultural rage is the decline of patriarchy, and the decline of traditional religion, as *institutions authoritatively organizing and governing the collective lives of Americans*. It needs to be emphasized that these cannot be reduced to mere components of social class. Frank's argument, to paraphrase, is that the people of Kansas have sold their pottage for a mess of souls. But patriarchy and institutionalized religion can also undergird the material conditions of life; they are also a form of pottage. Moreover, the legitimacy or even existence of class hierarchy has never been assumed in the United States, where the myth of equal opportunity has been paramount and commercial mass culture counters the pains of inequality by continually assuring us that lower is better. Hierarchies of sex, gender, race, and religion are rather what Americans mostly obsess about; class enters the fray mostly as a matter of *style*, as John Kerry learned to his dismay and as George W. Bush thoroughly understands.

How do religiously inflected preoccupations with sex and gender become a "material force"? To exaggerate only slightly, that force is the very real fear of imaginary events: the fear of parents living in, say, Kansas, that their daughter will run off to San Francisco, get pregnant by a black man, have an abortion, find a lesbian partner, and go to Berkeley, where she will learn defiance of traditional authority—perhaps by reading Mill's *On Liberty* or learning about the separation of church and state in constitutional law class.[13] Seen in this light, what seems to be the inane or even imbecilic fanaticism with which the religious Right pursues such chimeras as school prayer or creationism makes at least some sense. These are not merely symbolic issues; they are tokens of respect for the authority that makes patriarchy possible, and the rejection of all alternative authorities that would undermine it. The reader who doubts the material salience of this ideological complex could benefit by looking at them the other way around for a moment. Suppose, for example, the reader has or had a teenage daughter who became pregnant; would it be a "purely symbolic" or "religious" issue whether or not she could have a safe and legal abortion? The genuinely material consequences for her, after all, will potentially be at least as great as the question of what wage she will be paid if she gets a clerical job at Wal-Mart.

The hysteria that clings to all contemporary discussions of these issues, then, is that new rules for resolving them—or at least proposals about new rules for resolving them—represent the passing of the mantle of authority from one subculture to another. More specifically, the mantle of authority is passing from parents and the (male) church leaders they look up to, who together attempt to exercise authoritative control over female sexuality, to unchurched peers and (as it seems to them) libertine intellectuals who uphold—even if only rhetorically—the "liberation" of that sexuality.

This is the core of what traditional authority has always been about. The late-twentieth-century assault on that core, unprecedented in its strength, has been revolutionary and thus deeply upsetting, regardless of how limited its results might seem to be from the standpoint of its advocates and protagonists.[14] Of course, as a structure of beliefs patriarchy remains strong, especially in some areas of the country (again led by the white South). But this renascence disguises the extent of what has happened over the past four decades.

As a structure of authoritative institutions, patriarchy has disintegrated and like Humpty-Dumpty can never be put back together—though the hope of doing so is the main driving force behind the Right's attempt to take over the Supreme Court. But as *rules* about how men behave toward women, how women behave toward men, how men take care of women and women take care of men, what men and women can do or cannot do, what a man can count on and what a woman can count on, what used to be genuine if often informal requirements are now nonexistent. What once could have seemed to be steadfast and reliable expectations—they never were, of course—have vanished, to become instead pious hopes that may be fulfilled, are sometimes more likely to be fulfilled than not, but can never be counted on in the ordinary, nonsectarian social world. Not only does no one know his place (or hers), but no one even knows what it is supposed to be. As for *power and authority,* though there is still a long way to go and the glass ceiling remains where it counts the most, more and more they are subjects of competitive struggle, especially at the middle levels and especially where gender is concerned. More and more, that is, the sense of entitlement men carry around with them is separated from actual entitlements. And more crucially for the conduct of the culture wars, in working-class or semiprofessional occupations in which male bastions built around masculine camaraderie and often actual physical strength have been invaded (the military and police and fire departments, for example), sexual harassment has become a concept and even a legal doctrine, and *ressentiment* has grown in consequence. This is the territory where Rush Limbaugh and his like most avidly pursue their feminist prey. (My own guess would be that at the core of the ideological construct of "political correctness," or "PC," is a counterattack against the very notion of "sexual harassment.")

It is a territory, furthermore, that has become the most crucial terrain of struggle with the carefully orchestrated remasculinization of the polity in the wake of 9/11. Whereas before September 11, 2001, the neoconservative cabal within and outside the state apparatus linked Middle East policy primarily to an ideology of American world supremacy and Israeli national interests, immediately after the attack on the World Trade Center key figures in the administration, including the president himself, seized on that event as an opportunity to restructure American *domestic* politics. The key to this restructuring, which has succeeded more than one might have believed possible, has been to recast the Republican Party as the Party of Masculinity and a president who deserted his military post as a masculine leader. The invasion of Iraq was the final answer to the question, What can a strong leader do to reassure us that our situation is under control? Democrats have not understood this; indeed, it is probably no exaggeration to say that John Kerry's fate was sealed the moment he bounded onstage to accept his nomination with a floppy salute and the words, "Lieutenant Kerry reporting for duty." In times of crisis, real or imagined, imposed by enemies or constructed by alleged victims, people in search of a strong leader, women as well as men (if not even more so), do not want a lieutenant; they want a commander-in-chief. That President Bush has been perhaps the worst commander-in-chief in American history does not change the fact that he was willing to assume that role. In the moment of crisis, a militantly nationalist *fear* of the Other has become the mobilizing emotion beyond all else. It is the one emotion to which liberalism and feminism are so far unable to respond—unless they too transform themselves into their own variety of nationalism.

The social significance of 9/11, in other words, is that in justifying what is an essentially masculinist nationalism, it also thereby reinvigorated patriarchy in the continuing struggle for ideological supremacy. Even as it has lost its grip on the social world, patriarchy has never been counted out ideologically. That is because the drastic social change that the feminist revolution began is not only not a net gain for everyone; it is not necessarily even a net gain, or at least is not necessarily perceived as a net gain, for all women or even for the great majority of women. If it were, the "gender gap" would be much greater than it actually is.

To understand a reactionary patriarchy's pull on women, one has to read such works of sympathetic understanding as Andrea Dworkin's *Right-Wing Women* or Kristin Luker's *Abortion and the Politics of Motherhood* or, from the other side of the coin, Barbara Ehrenreich's *The Hearts of Men*; or contemplate the hatred of Hilary Clinton or the campaign against the movie *Kinsey*.[15] What is done in the name of concepts such as "equality" and "freedom of choice" is of only ambiguous value to many people, men and women both, and they are not suffering from some version of false consciousness in internalizing that ambiguity. That is, the uncertainties and pains of an only halfway achieved "equality," or "freedom of choice," very often is about all we manage to get out of social change. This partial accomplishment may quite reasonably be seen by many people as failing to outweigh the certainties that allegedly can be counted on by retaining the earlier (patriarchal) ways, thus creating a politics of obsessive nostalgia. And even though the main targets of hostility and fear may seem, as I have characterized them, to be only "symbolic," consciousness is not "false" where the symbolic target is truly related to the unspoken material target. Thus, for example, the mobilizing hysteria over gay marriage *is* truly related to the egalitarian assault on patriarchy. And the barely concealed glee with which Left cultural critics (e.g., Frank Rich of the *New York Times*) note the continued decay of the normative family, as though this were proof of conservative hypocrisy, simply further inflames those Americans who blame liberal elites for that decay in the first place.

Frank is wrong, then, in supposing that conservative voters in Kansas get nothing for their support of religious projects such as creationism or school prayer. These projects are part of the package deal that promises to restore the traditional patriarchal authority that has been lost— the authority of (especially male) parents, of (male) religious leaders, of the morally authoritative masculine State—rather than what is targeted as the feminized welfare state. In the process they may not get single-payer health insurance, but even if a Democratic Party leader promised it, what conceivable reason would there be, in the present and foreseeable state of the economy, to believe that the promise could be kept? Better to get what you can while the getting is good.

Moreover, institutionalized religion is not just a locus of belief and communal organization but is also a political structure—as I have noted, a structure of authority and thus of discipline and control, rewards and punishments. In large parts of the United States churches indeed dispense concrete material rewards, operating as semipublic welfare ministates, and even informal law courts, for their communicants.[16] The United States is not the only modern nation in which churches are still vying with the state in those areas of life, but it is probably the only one in which the church's failure to triumph is viewed by large parts of the population not as a welcome aspect of modernization but as a loss. We are, perhaps uniquely, two peoples living together in an asynchronous social formation. The struggle over creationism, for example, is largely a struggle between parents (more often than not mothers) and (mostly male) expert authorities—curriculum designers, school administrators, and scientists. It is a struggle not for psychological reward or status but for actual social power, and this struggle replicates itself throughout the arena where fundamentalist religions and secular authority or rationality come into contact and conflict.

Once we see this conflict as genuine, we can also see that there is a common misunderstanding about the relationship of religious authoritarianism to modernist culture. Among Left intellectuals, it is often said that if only secularists could understand their limitations and be more generous to their religious opponents relations between the two groups would improve to everyone's benefit. I doubt that this is true. The real philosophical issues raised in the debate around secularism are mostly of interest to intellectuals themselves, having to do with questions of ontology, scientific method, and the like. To most advocates of toleration, liberal neutrality, and cultural modernity in the United States, however, the real enemy is not religion in general but religious authoritarianism in particular. And the authoritarians proclaim their enmity toward "secular humanism" only as "the best possible shell" for their true goal, which is an all-out *institutional* war, not merely an ideological war. This is a war not merely against Enlightenment secularism but against *all forms* of *nonsectarianism*.

The latter is different from pure secularism. It actually encompasses many varieties of religious belief but merely denies, or agrees to the denial of, ultimate truth value in any one of them. Thus, the only substantial disagreement over matters of value between myself and my religious friends on the Left is that I am an atheist and they are not—an insubstantial difference, since almost nothing rides on it. On the other hand, everything, including potentially the entirety of the way social institutions are organized, does ride on the distinction between public sectarianism and public nonsectarianism. The existence of influential persons or institutions in the public world who (or which) categorically deny that there is ultimate truth value or even any truth value in the word of Jesus Christ is critically important, along with the decline of patriarchy, in defining cultural rage (and is also often identical with patriarchy, abortion and homosexuality being the flash points that unite the two). So the truth of beliefs, of ideologies, is in one sense the ultimate issue—but only because, as Marx said, they have "seized the masses," or at least those among the masses (and their self-anointed leaders) who see skepticism about the rightness of social hierarchies and hierarchies of religious value as intellectual and social treason.

The alleged center of this treason is, of course, the mass media. This might seem self-evident, but we must remember that the occasionally plausible perception of the media as "liberal" (to which I shall return) has been heightened by the multimillion-dollar output of a one-sided propaganda machine that had no equal in the past century. This machine, financed by immense subventions from a few right-wing foundations, has been a crucial part of a political effort that has finally captured the heights of power in a one-party state. This accomplishment has been dependent on being able to caricature all holdouts as belonging to a disloyal minority; "liberal" is the word used to capture the meaning of that disloyalty. Ronald Reagan's first Secretary of the Interior, James Watts, famously said that he had once used to think that the American people were all either Democrats or Republicans; now he thought that they are all either Americans or liberals. This was just one of many steps in a one-sided cultural war that began with George Wallace and Spiro Agnew and developed its own dynamic, even outside the central drive for political power.

The story of liberal control at the heart of this *kulturkampf* is not just a myth but a lie—one of the big lies of the late twentieth century. However, it has not been countered by any organized effort from the Left or the Center. As an oft-repeated lie without much substantial denial to be found in the mass media themselves, it is thus an attribution that prevails because in part it is superficially plausible and no one with the same resources and access counterattacks it. At the present moment, to be sure, since the mass media tend to follow power, the institutionalization of the one-party state has dragged them firmly to the Right.[17] Still, only on issues of nationalism are the institutions of mass visual culture safely in the same ideological camp as the right wing, and even in that case network television's preference for "balance" in news and entertainment often prevents it from getting fully on board. In any event, for many years prior to the recent collapse of corporate media in the face of an aggressive and ruthless oligarchy, the mobilizing attack on "liberal elitist media" met the response it did because its basis in a half-truth enabled it to maintain the appearance of plausibility.

Since feelings about the social world usually stem at least partially from real exposure to concrete manifestations of that world, and since even the most insidious propaganda cannot work in the absence of a minimally plausible correspondence to the material world, the obvious question is, What was and is the material reality that has nourished and still sustains the myth of liberal dominance of, especially, the commercial television networks, so that the propaganda machine has something substantial to work with? The answer cannot be simple. Anyone who has not noticed the obvious truth about television's worldview—the predominant police-world orientation of law-and-order TV, both fictional and pseudo-nonfictional; the familialism of family dramas and sitcoms; the nationalism of adventure shows; the flamboyant patriotism of sports coverage; the cynical competitive individualism of reality TV; the obsequiousness to higher authority of most news coverage; and the class complacency about economic issues of most news coverage—clearly has not been watching television.[18]

What is crucial here, however, is the difference between "ideology" and "propaganda." To simplify, ideology is always recognizable by its absence; propaganda, by its presence. The key to the distinction is the presence or absence of a visible narrator, presenting himself (usually) as morally authoritative, telling a story with an overt moral lesson. Put another way, propaganda is didactic; ideology is subliminal. Both on mainstream network news (including public television's version) and entertainment television, ideology is considered preferable to propaganda as a narrative framing device. This statement, which treats information and entertainment television as similar, may therefore sound puzzling at first hearing, since presentation of "news" is obviously always imbued with propaganda of one kind or another, compared with any single episode of, say, *Desperate Housewives*. However, outside of a few cable news channels, the effort by most television journalists (and by most print journalists who seek a nationwide audience) to be or at least seem to be "objective" drives their presentations of information away from the realm of visible propaganda. Its anchor then becomes a kind of putatively neutral ideological frame that attempts to be inclusive within certain broad parameters, excluding only obvious public and foreign enemies and the like. Moreover, the corporate orientation of news media means that with the exception of outright propagandists such as Rupert Murdoch, the owners of Clear Channel, and a few others, they have no sympathy with any populist program, Left or Right, unless it can help them advance their corporate goals. An "objectivity" that excludes populism, however, is a limited form of neutrality at best.

This distinction links up with the general imperatives that drive the mass media, especially television, wholly aside from class consciousness. There are many, but the most important is this: commercial television is a competitive, profit-making, oligopolistic enterprise, with a universal consumer base consisting of a nation of individuals consuming as individuals (nowadays often even a worldwide consumer base). As in all oligopolies, innovation is risky, so that generally speaking what works or does not work for one works or does not work for all, with only minor variations. If there is to be innovation, then as with the American automobile industry it can only come from outside, in this case the world of film production (e.g., HBO) or abroad ("reality television"). Moreover, television (and the press as well) has followed the bell-curve trajectory of many innovations —discovery, introduction, expansion to a peak, and then decline, as both market saturation and competition from substitutable industries (e.g., the Internet) set in. Commercial network television reached the point of decline quite some time ago, and it now fights a desperate rear-guard action, like the Red Queen running faster and faster just to stay in place. Its potentially mortal enemy is not ideological revanchism but boredom. Thus, it must keep up with what is happening, whatever that may be, and please its most important audience, which can make or break its particular efforts: the purveyors not of morality or ideology but of professional standards. This general condition puts great emphasis on three of the system's central features: its need to stay abreast of social change; to stay abreast of technological and aesthetic innovation, to the extent that any occurs, in communications content and techniques; and to be as socially inclusive as possible, even on a worldwide basis.

To return then to the distinction between ideology and propaganda, propaganda is always based on the exclusion of someone who is not following the authoritative moral rules. Ideology, contrarily, works by incorporation, as the dissenter, whoever that might be, is finally reintegrated into the social whole. (*Casablanca,* conceived as it happens by people of the Left, is the most well-known and beloved example of this kind of inclusive ideology at work.) But formally, what theorists would call narratologically, the presentation of dissent is usually necessary before it is recuperated, or else there is no story, just a lecture (or, on the news, nothing but official communiqués from the party in power). Only nationalist, military-oriented narratives can take on the aura of propaganda without suffering as stories; even they will often highlight the initial defection and reintegration of some central character in order to make the narrative interesting (this was the use made of dissenting Democrats by TV pundits in both Iraq wars). Family dramas or soap operas, to take a contrary case, demand the forefronting of some kind of sexual misbehavior to be dramatically compelling. Sitcoms, since the days of Aristophanes or Shakespeare, have gender-role reversal as their mainspring. Law-and-order narratives, which for the most part are quite satisfactorily politically conservative in their ideological orientation, usually originate in some kind of credible violence or threat of violence that has to be met with a credible response.

The problem for the mass media is that over time categories such as "sex" and "violence" completely change their meaning. In 1925 an Agatha Christie detective story could be based on the premise that illegitimacy of birth was a sufficient motive for murder; by 2000, when *Lady Chatterley's Lover* had become the all-time Penguin fiction bestseller, the premise would be laughable. "Sex" on television competes with newsstands where erotic promise abounds, and "women's" magazines may feature tips on love-making that would have been considered horrifyingly deviant fifty years ago. "Violence," often hideous violence, is a visual fact of life everywhere, and any adventure or law-and-order show that did not show it openly would soon be surpassed in popularity by video games that make no bones about it. So the "descent into sleaze" that animates right-wing critics is a descent of the social order itself, not of "liberal media elites." It is, however, real enough to enrage millions of real citizens as well.

Furthermore, the would-be universal appeal of television is to an audience of consumers who are presumed to agree on some abstractly stated basic propositions, while often disagreeing on the precise content of those propositions—what is sometimes called "Americanism." But at least in the United States and perhaps everywhere, "universalism" is always *liberal* universalism—there is no such thing as conservative universalism, except perhaps the universalism of conquest. In the United States, to be sure, this liberal universalism is totally compromised by its affiliation with corporate capital, in that by and large its protagonists in the media accept the agenda of *capital* as the universal agenda—precisely as Marx demonstrated. At the same time, though, this universalism is also consistently *pluralist,* both by necessity and by conviction. Especially for network television news and entertainment, not skepticism but a simple-minded version of liberal neutrality is their goal, to include everyone and offend no one. But of course they offend the religious sectarians, living in a different world and to some extent, as I have suggested, in a different time. Such persons see this behavior as antireligious, as well they might. Furthermore, this specifically American pluralism is not just a matter of incorporating previously excluded groups but also even, to a minimal degree, dissenting groups. Incorporating, of course, is not the same as forefronting—most often it winds up as co-opting. But it is a lot compared to its traditionalist opposite; and it can be truly offensive to those who live by the traditional rules.

Moreover, and above all, liberal universalism for better or worse has contemporaneously become almost indistinguishable from liberal *feminism*, at least to the extent that the latter does not on the whole challenge the corporate agenda of profit-maximization and imperial outreach. This is true not only of entertainment television, on which women ranging from female district attorneys, judges, and surgeons to housewives lead frankly sexual lives. It is also true, and to its opponents again offensively so, in the news divisions of television: not so much in hiring practices but in the presentation of what journalists call "social issues." (Alterman admits this quite readily in his *What Liberal Media?*) Moreover, liberal universalism is also, for reasons that I think are obvious, largely indistinguishable from modernity and the turn away from traditionalism. Thus, on what might be called matters of style, as of sex, gender, and religion—with which they are intertwined—the mass media are always vulnerable to the perception that they are on the wrong side, even while they bend over backward to accommodate the populism of cultural rage. These are the grounds on which Fox News, dissenting from this conventional liberalism, has carved out a place for the disaffected (and is now more and more imitated by the other cable news purveyors, MSNBC and CNN).

Thus, the profit-making imperative of the commercial television system has both formal and substantive components. Together, in both information and entertainment media they add up to something that, the unspoken capitalist agenda aside, looks very much like the kind of liberal neutrality that political theorists such as John Rawls and Ronald Dworkin are often accused of advocating. Another way of putting this is that within understandable limits mass media in general are accommodationist above all. But to the contemporary right wing, neutrality can look like anything from immorality to treason, and accommodation is surrender. The dedicatedly nonpartisan PBS becomes the subject of an attempted takeover: only right-wing partisanship is acceptable. "News" must be plainly propaganda, making no room for "feminazis" and their ilk; and entertainment is acceptable only if it too looks like sectarian propaganda. The latter requirement especially is incompatible with the way Hollywood has learned to tell a story—which is why Fox's version of entertainment, as opposed to news, is indistinguishable from that of the other networks in its predilection for "sex and violence" and its pluralist gesturings to stigmatized groups.

The Right, however, wants either its own version of socialist realism, with happy peasants and workers being replaced by God-fearing small-town Americans, or tales about right versus wrong, which like the reverse side of pornography are boring monomania posing as narrative. So while generally speaking no one is really represented in the mass media, which are truly sites of alienated discourse, the Right has an additional source of exclusion, and it is a self-inflicted, incurable wound. The "cultural war" is a real enough war, but it is fought against a self that estranges itself. The hated Other is only a stand-in, well chosen for the pursuit of political power but futilely chosen as an enemy if the actual goal of the war is to change the dominant culture rather than just to harass it. Since 9/11, network television particularly has been working hard to appease the *enrages*, especially in accepting an imperial, macho-inflected foreign policy as the American norm and treating the president's constant lies as merely the other side of the coin of Democratic criticism, a preference for truth, reason, civil liberties, and such being treated as "the other extreme." But still the conservative cultural rage, based on the felt need for total control of an uncontrollable world, is essentially unappeasable. For although the neoconservative program exploits real needs, in no way can it or does it truly address them. Skepticism about the "natural" supremacy of men over women, whites over nonwhites, normative sexuality over nonnormative sexuality, and believers over nonbelievers eventually turns into public or semipublic *policies* that tend to overthrow or diminish the traditional institutional structures of that supremacy; and the damage is irreparable. So the stage is set. Mobilized by the Right's well-funded propaganda machine, and given muscle by a party that is willing to use any means to bend all independent institutions, including the mass media, to its own total will, the *kulturkampf* yet genuinely appeals to those for whom belief in that supremacy, and the instantiation of it, are thought to be properly the underlying condition of social life.

Here we return, finally, to the title of this essay. The *kulturkampf* has to be propagated. Even enraged people with real and unmet material needs do not spontaneously believe nonsense and lies, do not necessarily think of themselves as the victims of nonexistent conspiracies, without having been encouraged to do so.[19] That encouragement has been all too forthcoming. Thus, although his political analysis may be open to question, the main thrust of Frank's sociological critique is certainly correct. The way in which the highly educated intellectuals and theocrats of the Right (a category that does not, to be sure, include the president himself) cloak their bid for total power by posing as representatives of the popular will would be a comic spectacle worthy of a Molière, were the results of their activities not so destructive. Perhaps the pit of this faux-populist spectacle is the sight of prominent Jewish intellectuals passing themselves off as supporters of fundamentalist Protestants and reactionary Catholics with whose lives they have no genuine contact—and who carry a long history of anti-Semitism in their wake. Indeed, the unanimous silence (in a few cases even endorsement) with which Jewish neoconservatives greeted the odiously anti-Semitic *Passion of the Christ* has no parallel that I can think of in recent times. One has to suspect that if they thought it would help their credentials as spokespersons for "the silent majority," they would chummy up to Holocaust deniers.

We must remember that Christianity, after all, is not inherently authoritarian. But along with the power-seeking leaders of religious revolt, the neoconservative intellectuals, Jews and non-Jews alike, also have done everything in their power to turn it in that direction. In this respect, their tacit—sometimes explicit—embrace of the Christian Right has been a serpent's kiss. For centuries serious Roman Catholic theologians have struggled to find a place for reason and science within a tradition that ordains belief in a divinely ruled universe. Now, mouthing hypocritical pieties, the neoconservative intellectuals (shielded by reactionary theologians like Michael Novak and Richard Neuhaus) look away while know-nothing Protestantism, in the guise of such intellectual buffoons as Jerry Falwell, discards serious thought and replaces it with dogmatic ignorance, prejudice, and ideological rant. Nor are they discomfited by the neo-Nazi ravings of Ann Coulter or the assaults on intellectual freedom by such idols of the enraged as Limbaugh or Bill O'Reilly, not to mention the vice president. Neither does the Bush administration incur any criticism from them as, led by the president, it returns us to the days of Lysenkoism in the Soviet Union and Aryan blood science in Nazi Germany, deliberately substituting lies for scientific knowledge on any and every occasion where the truth might be politically inconvenient.[20] This is the end result of intellectual neoconservatism. It is the ultimate *trahison des clercs*, who make speeches and write books about "values" and "standards" but will acquiesce in any lie at all, bow down to any mass hysteria or cultural demand, as long as it takes them where they want to go. The anonymous policymaker who notoriously told reporter Seymour Hersh that only power is what matters and that "truth" is made by whomever has the power was apparently speaking for them all.

In sum: the power of ideologues and propagandists who have been allowed to seize (or been given) the space of public discussion, the aspects of popular consciousness and material interests that they have come to represent, and the fatal malleability of American political institutions together make a devastating fit at this point in time. This is not to say that resistance to the coming of the one-party oligarchical state is futile. But we need to be clear about the possibilities. The most common way of looking at this picture on the Left is the one I described earlier: there is a potential class divide in the United States, and the Left can be on the winning side of this divide if only it—or anyone—can find a way to mobilize a potential working-class majority. For all the reasons given here, this strategy in and of itself is unlikely to succeed. In fact, if we ask why the one-party state has come into existence, the answer is not simply that working-class white males have defected from the Democratic Party because it does not offer them a populist economic program. White racism, militarized nationalism, and sexual anxiety are real too; they cannot be wished away. The right wing's bid for total power hinges on these issues and cannot be derailed by a strategy of avoidance or by marginal repairs to a demolished welfare state. The civil rights and antiwar movements of the 1960s and, above all, the feminist movement of the 1970s brought about a massive social dislocation that, though incomplete, has been genuinely revolutionary. Tremendous gains in individual and cultural freedom emerged from that revolution; but if we are unwilling to affirm them openly, they will certainly disappear.

NOTES

This essay grew in part out of conversations with Judith Ezekiel, who also read an earlier version of it; I am grateful for her valuable comments and suggestions. In thinking about this topic I have also benefited greatly from conversations with and discussions by Drucilla Cornell, Carol Gould, Peter Marin, Alyson Cole, Stephen Eric Bronner, John Ehrenberg, Rick Fantasia, Judith Grant, Steven Lukes, Ellen Willis, Rick Wolff, Norman Rush, Leonard Quart, and Dorothy Green.

1. For an elaboration and fuller discussion of "representative oligarchy," see Philip Green and Drucilla Cornell, "Rethinking Democratic Theory: The American Case," *Journal of Social Philosophy* 36, no. 4 (winter 2005): 517–35.

2. See especially the well-known text of Carl J. Friedrich and Zbigniew Brzezinski, *Totalitarian Dictatorship and Autocracy,* 2nd rev. ed. (Cambridge, MA: Harvard University Press, 1965). On authoritarian populism, a concept explicated most notably by the British sociologist Stuart Hall, see Green and Cornell, "Rethinking Democratic Theory," 529–30.

3. For an analysis of this movement, see my *Primetime Politics: The Truth about Conservative Lies, Corporate Control, and Television Culture* (Lanham, MD: Rowman and Littlefield, 2005), esp. chs. 3–5. Among the most prominent contributors to this "research" project are L. Brent Bozell III, Reed Irvine, Stanley Rothman, Michael Medved, and S. Robert Lichter.

4. Thomas Frank, *What's the Matter with Kansas? How Conservatives Won the Heart of America* (New York: Henry Holt, 2004), 7. The review-essay is by Eyal Press, in the *Nation,* January 2, 2006, p. 31.

5. See, e.g., the essays in Daniel Bell, ed., *The New American Right* (New York: Criterion, 1955).

6. See, e.g., the essays in ibid.

7. See Larry M. Bartels, "Is the Water Rising? Reflections on Inequality and American Democracy," *Political Science and Politics* 39, no. 1 (January 2006): 41, fig. 2. Income in the bottom quintile, for example, has grown more than five times as much under Democratic administrations; Jimmy Carter's is the only Democratic administration during which inequality did not decrease.

8. I have omitted from this list the historically determinative phenomenon of "consumerism." As Rick Wolff has demonstrated, this has always been at the heart of an informal social contract by which American workers learned to accept uniquely high levels of exploitation at the workplace, in return for uniquely high wage levels and thus levels of consumption. See Richard D. Wolff, "Ideological State Apparatuses, Consumerism, and U.S. Capitalism: Lessons for the Left," *Rethinking Marxism* 17, no. 2 (April 2005): 223–35. I think that Wolff is entirely correct in his emphasis on the historical power of consumerism in determining the American working class's relative political conservatism. However, although it may help undergird the package I am discussing here, the "new social contract" (which operates by being no contract at all), it is not part of that package as crafted by today's neoconservative intellectuals.

9. It would require much more than another essay to elaborate fully on this point. The definitive account is Douglas S. Massey and Nancy A. Denton, *American Apartheid: Segregation and the Making of the American Underclass* (Cambridge, MA: Harvard University Press, 1993).

10. Michael J. Graetz and Ian Shapiro, *Death by a Thousand Cuts* (Princeton, NJ: Princeton University Press, 2005).

11. This was made evident, for example, by Channel 1's "man in the street" interviews during the Christmastime transit strike of 2005.

12. On the importance of militarism in forming an American national identity, see John Ehrenberg's invaluable account of the contemporary Right's intellectual origins, *Servants of Wealth: The Right's Assault on Economic Justice* (Lanham, MD: Rowman and Littlefield, 2006), ch. 2. On the inability of liberal pluralism—or its successor, "multiculturalism"—to provide a satisfying narrative about "the nation" and its potential satisfactions, see Rogers M. Smith, *Civic Ideals: Conflicting Visions of Citizenship in U.S. History* (New Haven, CT: Yale University Press, 1997). On the symbiosis between nationalism and the return of patriarchy, see my discussion later in this essay.

13. It is worth recalling that in the movie *Basic Instinct,* that neoclassical compendium of gynophobia, the most terrifying thing about Catherine Trammel/Sharon Stone is that she has "a B.A. in Psychology from Berkeley." Scriptwriter Joe Esterhasz knew exactly where the pulse of the mass audience beats most feverishly. So did the casting director: Stone, with her famously high IQ, perpetually raised eyebrows, and extracurricular dedication to worthy liberal causes, personifies the liberal feminist "elite" that the Right has turned into an American nightmare.

14. This case has been made very forcefully by Ellen Willis, in "Escape from Freedom: What's the Matter with Tom Frank (and the Lefties Who Love Him)?" *Situations: Project of the Radical Imagination* 1, no. 2 (2006) (available at http://ojs.gc.cuny.edu/index.php/situations/issue/view/3), and also by Judith Ezekiel in a private communication.

15. Andrea Dworkin, *Right-Wing Women* (New York: Coward, McCann and Geoghegan, 1983); Luker, *Abortion and the Politics of Motherhood* (Berkeley: University of California Press, 1984); and Barbara Ehrenreich, *The Hearts of Men: American Dreams and the Flight from Commitment* (New York: Doubleday/Anchor, 1983).

16. For a detailed description of such activities, see Barbara Ehrenreich's "The Faith Factor," *Nation,* November 29, 2004.

17. On the nature and extent of the big lie, see Green, *Primetime Politics* and, especially, Eric Alterman's *What Liberal Media? The Truth about Bias and the News* (New York: Basic Books, 2003). Alterman's weekly column in the *Nation* continues to expose the self-regenerating lie. See, e.g., his "Never Mind the Truth," *Nation,* February 6, 2006, p. 10, which demonstrates the framing by almost all television newscasters of the Alito Supreme Court nomination hearings as a face-off between Republican reasonableness and Democratic obduracy.

18. See Green, *Primetime Politics,* ch. 4, "The Real World of Television."

19. On the changing concept of "victim" in the American social order, and the intellectuals and political leaders who have helped bring that change about, see Alyson Cole, *The Cult of True Victimhood: From the War on Welfare to the War on Terror* (Palo Alto, CA: Stanford University Press, 2006).

20. It seems redundant to offer citations to a statement that merely sums up what is known by everyone who has been paying any attention at all. Still, diehard doubters of sweeping generalizations might want to look at, say, David Corn's *The Lies of George W. Bush: Mastering the Politics of Deception* (New York: Crown, 2003), or Eric Alterman and Mark Green's *The Book on Bush: How George W. (Mis)leads America* (New York: Penguin, 2004). The lies come in such profusion that both books were dated before they hit the bookstores, but they serve as useful reminders.

Chapter 3

Considerations on the Origins of Neoconservatism
Looking Backward

Stanley Aronowitz

Old-fashioned conservatism in America is a fairly large tent containing, uncomfortably, many tendencies. Its general theme is consistent with Adam Smith's portrait of the state as a "night watchman" whose fundamental task is to protect property and otherwise maintain law and order against a rabble that would tear society apart in the wanton pursuit of its self-interest. Most conservatives regret the New Deal—government aid to the poor, public goods, and a publicly sponsored national pension system for the employed. But in the interest of securing social peace some, like the writer Peter Viereck, were prepared to support government intervention into the economy to alleviate suffering and even approved of the creation of public institutions to secure the lives of the poorest Americans. Responding to the acute postwar shortages in 1950, Robert Taft, the Senate's leading conservative, introduced legislation to create tens of thousands of public housing units, a proposal that was superceded by a deft maneuver to shift public support to new private, mostly suburban housing through low-interest federal loans. And in 1945 isolationists, often identified with the conservative camp, signed on to a bipartisan internationalist foreign policy whose main weapon was the Marshall Plan, to prevent the spread of communism if Western Europe's economic viability was not restored with U.S. help. But as the American economy partially recovered from its economic slump, by the 1950s many conservatives, while unable to reverse the entire legacy of the New Deal, successfully repealed many aspects of business regulation, restricted the scope of the welfare state, opposed and successfully thwarted a national health scheme through public financing, privatized the housing boom, and expressed dismay that the Kennedy and Johnson administrations opted to address the still stubborn phenomenon of poverty through federal programs and when in power eliminated most of these programs. When in power the conservatives in the White House, whose most relentless champion was Ronald Reagan, resolved to reduce federal spending for income support (except for the rich), education, health, and housing and tried, but failed, to privatize Social Security even as they successfully privatized almost everything else.

Neoconservatism stems, chiefly, from the disillusionment with radicalism of a relatively significant number of intellectuals. Many, if not most, neocons had some background in the socialist movements of the 1930s and 1940s and moved slowly to the Right, largely under the impetus of the Cold War. Neoconservatism's relationship to the old conservatism is entirely strategic and does not necessarily share Smithian doctrines such as neoliberal economics, budget balancing, and slashed welfare programs, the signature policies of the old conservatism. In fact, its leading protagonists in the Bush administration may be described as spend, but not tax, bureaucrats. They have gone along with steep tax restructuring that favors the wealthy, but their heart is not in it. For the real neocons, foreign policy is the arena that will determine the fate of the American empire, which is now, after the collapse of the Soviet Union, the main project of government. Their task is to oppose every sign of postcolonial political autonomy in Latin America, Asia, and, most urgently, the Middle East. Replacing the War on Communism with the War on Terror, they have spearheaded a revival of the historical nuclear threat by labeling Iran, Libya, and North Korea "rogue" states and, following the dictum of the philosopher Leo Strauss—an éminence grise of the movement—will forfeit no deceit, no calumny, no subterfuge to advance their cause. Neocons, often against their own political philosophy, support domestic conservative proposals because they have forged an alliance that, in their view, is necessary to win agreement on foreign policy. And contrary to conventional belief, neoconservatism crosses party lines. It may be argued, for example, that Daniel Patrick Moynihan, Nathan Glazer, and Daniel Bell, Democrats all, were key players in the neoconservative insurgency.

Neoconservatism's roots lie deep in what one of its leading protagonists, Daniel Bell, calls "the failure of American Socialism." Even as, after 1935, the Communists were able to smell the coffee and swing behind the New Deal, albeit, according to Bell, for their own selfish and entirely dishonest ends, Socialists and Trotskyists refused to abandon their radical and revolutionary rhetoric and consigned themselves permanently to irrelevance. Writing these comments in 1949–50, Bell was a lonely advocate of a socialism, later to be adopted by others, notably Michael Harrington and Irving Howe and the readers of *Dissent*, that would, in effect, adopt the Communist Party's popular front program of binding with liberals without its Stalinist foreign policy or dictatorial methods of political organization. But as we shall see, neoconservatism stems also from the weariness of intellectuals who spent a considerable period of their lives on the outside and eventually found New Deal liberalism wanting for its pervading tendency to compromise with an "authoritarian" Left, including, on occasion, Soviet Russia. Neocons were particularly disenchanted with the New Left and the broader student movement, which, in their collective "innocence" (a word frequently invoked by Bell) tended to support Communist-inspired and led revolutionary "national liberation movements" in Africa, China, Vietnam, Cambodia, and Cuba. The term "innocence" connoted the New Left's refusal to acknowledge that these regimes were not only undemocratic but totalitarian.

The flight of many neocons from liberalism was accelerated by the shift of some of its leading lights, notably George McGovern, Eugene McCarthy, and Robert Kennedy, from the precepts of the Atlantic anticommunist alliance to a stance that opposed U.S. military interventions against revolutionary regimes, notably Vietnam. World communism had to be contained by any means necessary, and its satellite states and subservient nationalist movements had to be crushed. For the hawks of all ideological stripes, what was at stake in the Vietnam War was nothing less than the preservation of democracy and freedom. One neocon strain, that of former leftists Irving Kristol and Daniel Bell, viewed with trepidation the rise of Black Power movements at home, the serious decline of the work ethic, especially among the young, and, God forbid, the emergence of feminist thought and action, especially its radical intransigent wing that called for a profound transformation in relations among the sexes, in the home as well as the workplace, in the bedroom as well as the streets. Alarmed by any evidence that cultural as much as prevailing political authority was being questioned—and make no mistake, authority and discipline are among their major concerns—it was a relatively short step for "economic" liberals like Bell and his friend Nathan Glazer to move to the Right.

According to conventional wisdom, Irving Kristol is the grandfather of neoconservatism. Arguably his transformation from a socialist to a liberal during the early 1960s and to a leader of a fairly large group of intellectuals who became Nixon supporters, then to a full-blown "neoconservative" in the 1970s, is the most ubiquitous example of what has become a significant ideological and political tendency in the United States today. One might claim that Norman Podhoretz occupies similar stature. Surely the evolution of his magazine, *Commentary,* from its liberal origins to its current standing as the movement's pioneer publication might qualify. In 2004, writing the epitaph for the *Public Interest,* which he and Daniel Bell had founded in 1966, Kristol himself described the relationship between the two magazines as a division of labor between foreign (*Commentary*) and domestic politics and policy (*Public Interest*), but he made no substantive distinctions to connote perspectival differences. In my view neither Kristol nor Podhoretz made major intellectual contributions to the movement; few of their respective writings may be singled out as key texts in the main rightward drift of important segments of their generation. It was their role as editors and publishers, as publicists and public intellectuals of their movement that elevated them to prominence. Since neoconservatism was, and remains, chiefly an intellectual movement whose policy effects are grounded in a small cluster of ideas—chiefly the urgency of advancing the interests of the American empire—the mantle of conceptual and ideological leadership belongs instead to two very different, but strangely convergent, figures in American social and political theory: Daniel Bell and Leo Strauss.

Bell, a self-professed lifelong socialist, began his career as a journalist, notably as editor of the *New Leader,* a left-liberal weekly in the 1940s, and then was a staff writer for *Fortune.* In his late thirties he turned sociologist, first at Columbia and finally—after the student rebellion and the politics that accompanied the occupations and strikes at Columbia, which like many intellectuals of his generation he repudiated—at Harvard, where he finished his career and, mistakenly, hoped for academic peace. His works in social theory were widely read and were extremely influential on a small but important group of academics and intellectuals precisely during the period of the 1960s and 1970s when the movement of ideas and politics among intellectuals seemed to be turning leftward. He was among the leading detractors of the student movement and of the New Left, but even as he railed against the indiscipline and irresponsibility of the new radicalism, Bell remained a political liberal and a social conservative. In fact, during the turbulent period of the formation of the neoconservative movement, Bell's writings bear the indelible mark of his Marxist beginnings.

Bell all but dismissed American Marxian socialism as hopelessly mired in its European inspiration. Yet despite his decisive turn away from Marxism in the late 1940s, he is a shining example of the old slogan, You can take the theorist out of (Marxism) but you can't take (Marxism) out of the theorist. Taking a right turn, he nevertheless remained intensely interested in questions of class, the changing social relations during the transition between industrial and "post"-industrial society, and remained a scholar of the various interpretations of Marx and Marxism.

Although later works are better known, his 1952 book *Marxian Socialism in the United States* marks Bell's definitive deradicalization. It is a work that carefully avoids the important debates about Marxist theory, even those, like Sidney Hook's contributions, that might be considered close to his own predilections. The reason? For Bell there was no significant theoretical Marxism, if by that term we mean theory that is linked to viable practice. Instead, *Marxian Socialism* is a survey of the Left parties and movements from the late nineteenth century to the immediate postwar period, at once admiring of Socialist standard bearer Eugene V. Debs, whose political intransigence he was prone to forgive, but also sharply critical of the Socialist Party's 1930s refusal to come to terms with the practicalities of American politics. In his account of the rise of the ultra-left, he betrays utter contempt for the small Trotskyist sects that called themselves revolutionary "vanguard" parties but, like the Socialists, remained sects largely out of touch with any real American politics. Particularly irksome was the Socialist Party's leftist stance during the Roosevelt years and the unrelenting pacifism of its leader, Norman Thomas, which resulted in the party's isolation from the mainstream. From this period, Bell becomes an unapologetic supporter of modern liberalism, at least on economic issues, while remaining a critical ally of organized labor—critical because he is an implacable opponent of the corruption that remains rife in some major unions, particularly on the East Coast waterfront and the Teamsters.

Bell's signature work, *The End of Ideology: On the Exhaustion of Political Ideas in the 1950s,* is really a loose collection of essays containing disparate and sometimes contradictory themes. First published in 1960, it remains a key text in the deradicalization of an entire generation of once leftist, anticommunist intellectuals. The essays range from the rather empirical discussion of the emerging radical Right and various forms of crime including labor union corruption, to his justly famous essay "Work and Its Discontents," to social theory—notably on class and class politics in

America—and to a final, philosophical section entitled "The Exhaustion of Utopia," whose bookends are "The Failure of Socialism in America" and "The End of Ideology in the West." In between is perhaps the most revealing meditation in the entire volume, "The Mood of Two Generations."

It is in this final section of the book that one may detect one of the roots of what Michael Harrington first termed "neoconservatism" a decade later. Although Harrington was responding to the rightward swing of the *Public Interest* in the early 1970s, a careful reading of Bell's earlier migration from intellectual radicalism speaks eloquently of the changes that overcame two generations of American-Left intellectuals, beginning in the 1950s. Born at the turn of the twentieth century, most from immigrant Jewish parents, the first generation that played a key role in shaping American intellectual politics was, most famously, the group that started and nurtured the "little magazine"—the term refers to a cluster of small-circulation publications that cropped up in the 1920s and early 1930s—*Partisan Review (PR)*. *PR*'s earliest incarnation was as the voice of the John Reed Clubs, the early 1930s federation of Communist-inspired intellectual organizations, of which Richard Wright, James T. Farrell, and a host of others were among the most notable adherents. *PR* counted among its number some of the luminaries of intellectual radicalism of the late 1920s and early 1930s. Edmund Wilson, James T. Farrell, and many other later famous writers frequented its pages. Among them were Lionel Trilling, later to play a crucial role in helping to shift many critics and literary historians from the Left to Cold War liberalism; Dwight Macdonald, a journalist whose brief sojourns in the Communist Party and the Trotskyist movement barely disguised his essential anarchism; and the chief ideologue of intellectual anticommunism, Sidney Hook, to whom Bell dedicates *End of Ideology.*

Hook was not only one of the most brilliant of the entire cohort—his two books on Marxism, *Towards an Understanding of Karl Marx,* published in 1933, and *From Hegel to Marx,* published three years later, are among the best produced by any American—but he was a serious political actor who understood the importance of political organization and did not hesitate to join parties and movements with which he generally agreed. *Towards an Understanding of Karl Marx* attempts to fuse two traditions: American pragmatism and the independent Marxism of Karl Korsch, himself a defector from the German Communist Party and the Communist International but who remained a lifelong Marxist. For his heresy Hook was taken to task, not only by his Communist reviewers, who objected vehemently to his argument against the universal validity of the dialectic, but by Earl Browder, the party's leader from 1933 to 1945. By 1934 Hook was affiliated with the short-lived American Workers Party (AWP), an independent Marxist organization begun a few years earlier by A. J. Muste, an ordained Methodist minister with a long record of labor radicalism. Like his comrades, Muste was suspicious of the much larger Communist Party, particularly its close relationship with Moscow, but worked with its trade union and unemployed organizations. But the AWP was simply too small to survive on its own, so it responded affirmatively to overtures tendered by an even smaller Trotskyist sect to merge. In the wake of the merger of AWP with the Trotskyist Communist League to make the Socialist Workers Party, Hook gravitated briefly to the Trotskyist Left but was disappointed with its ideological rigidity and small membership and influence. By the end of World War II, having become persuaded that the West, with all its warts, was severely threatened by its two main totalitarian rivals, Nazi Germany and Stalin's regime, Hook had affiliated with an international group of intellectuals who in retrospect might be considered prefigurative of neoconservatism. The Committee for Cultural Freedom, which Hook headed, was formed in the late 1940s to combat international communism's powerful cultural offensive and linked itself with leading intellectual figures of European-Left anticommunism, notably Stephen Spender, Ignacio Silone, Nicola Chiaromonte, Arthur Koestler, and Maurice Cranston, the editor of the British journal *Encounter.* Hook was a lifelong militant, by which I mean that he was an organizer and an ideologue. His alliance with the Western powers, indicated by acceptance of CIA and other U.S. government funds to fuel his organizational and literary/political work, was motivated entirely by the conviction that the United States and its allies held in their collective hands the hope that the terroristic dictatorships of the Communist World could be contained and ultimately defeated. For most of his activist years in behalf of empire he remained, like Bell, an avowed democratic socialist, but unlike Bell he was a social liberal and a distinctly humanistic philosopher in the American pragmatist vein. Like many of his generation he became an open-throated advocate of American global hegemony.

Edited chiefly by William Phillips and Phillip Rahv, *PR* separated from the Communist Party in the late 1930s, on the heels of the Moscow trials of some of the leading Bolsheviks, and turned anticommunist in 1939, when Stalin signed a nonaggression pact with Hitler. Its editors and their circle, many recent migrants from Trotskyism, found themselves torn by World

War II. In two famous essays, "The Failure of Nerve" and "The Failure of the Left," Hook admonished his comrades to reverse their decision to oppose U.S. entrance into the war, to hold their nose, and, despite its atrocities and betrayals, accept the strategic alliance with the Soviet Union. Writing under a pseudonym, the art historian Meyer Shapiro replied, repeating the well-known radical thesis that the war was an instance of interimperialist rivalry from which the working class—and the Left—could derive no comfort. Shapiro's intervention proved somewhat futile as Hook's appeal carried the day not only among the inner circle of *PR* but among its growing readership. Although it can be argued that given the severity of the Nazi threat, the Left had little choice but to support the Allied side in World War II, the resignation of a large cohort of the first generation of independent Left intellectuals to the proposition that in a bipolar world the interest of freedom demanded that they make a choice between the contending blocs was to fundamentally alter the character of the Left for its own and a second generation. Anticommunism became the cutting edge of all politics and trumped the unity of the labor movement and the working class in its struggle against capital. Now the fault lines were defined differently: the working class would have to wait until the external threat was either annihilated or neutralized.

Although *PR* emerged from the war with the decision to leave national and international politics to others, it remained a major player in the cultural cold war until, in the 1960s, its fervent anticommunism pushed it increasingly into the shadows of a debate that was dominated by antiwar fervor. There were defections, of course. Farrell objected to Trilling's and others' efforts to construct an antirealist literary canon and, more to the point, was incensed by his tendency to virtually identify the realists like Theodore Dreiser and Farrell himself with the cultural enemy. During the war, Macdonald split on the issue of pacifism and what he perceived to be the editors' retreat from radicalism. In 1943 he started the independent radical magazine *Politics* and hired the Schactmanite Trotskyist Irving Howe as assistant editor and tried to recruit a young contributor, C. Wright Mills—an independent sympathizer—to help run the magazine. This was the period when Bell's intellectual generation was divided between those who embraced America as a beacon of hope and a smaller group that declared the utopian horizon of a "third camp" as a protest not only to the American celebration and Soviet Communism but also to many nonparty radicals who aligned with Stalinism on various grounds.

But for twenty years after the war, the writings of Trilling, Hook, and

Arthur Schlesinger Jr., whose 1950 book, *The Vital Center,* was perhaps the veritable manifesto of the Cold War liberals, including the leading writers in *PR,* dominated the intellectual imagination. Only Norman Mailer, once a darling of its editors, Susan Sontag, the designated successor to Mary McCarthy—once a *PR* stalwart—whose early writings intrigued its editors and readers, and C. Wright Mills, whose anticommunist credentials were impeccable until the late 1950s, dissented from the emerging consensus that, as Trilling so ably noted, "[the intellectual] has become aware of the virtual uniqueness of American security and well being. Perhaps for the first time in his life he has associated his native land with the not inconsiderable advantages of a whole skin, a full stomach and the right to wag his tongue as he pleases." Thus, "[f]or the first time in the history of the modern American intellectual, America is not be conceived of *a priori* the vulgarist and stupidest nation of the world. And this is not only because other nations are exercising as never before the inalienable right of nations to be stupid and vulgar. The American situation has changed in a way that is not merely relative. There is an unmistakable improvement in the present American cultural situation over that of, say, thirty years ago. . . . against the state of affairs of three decades ago we are notably better off" ("Our Country and Our Culture," May-June 1952, 319). Therefore, concluded the editors in an introductory statement to the 1952 symposium "Our Country and Our Culture," from which this excerpt from Trilling's contribution is derived, "The American artist and intellectual no longer feels 'disinherited' . . . or 'astray.' We have obviously come a long way from the early rejection of America as spiritually barren, from the attacks of Mencken on the 'booboisie' and the Marxist picture of America in the thirties as a land of capitalist reaction" (ibid., 283). These comments were made at the height of the McCarthyite hysteria and the Korean War. As the joke goes, "Aside from that, Mrs. Lincoln, how did you enjoy the play?" So the *PR* circle, aside from Mailer and Mills, whose contribution comes sometime later, invents a new wrinkle to what Mills termed "the American celebration." We were alienated, hungry, disaffected, but now, except for mass culture, we embrace our country and its culture.

That Bell, Kristol, and (more ambiguously) Nathan Glazer became exemplary figures in the neoconservative movement by no means encompassed their entire generation's response. Mills, the novelist and critic Harvey Swados, and Mailer were among a relatively small minority who stayed, in different degrees, outside the consensus. Irving Howe was a centrist figure among the anticommunist intellectuals of his generation.

While choosing the West in the Cold War, he and the writers for *Dissent* tried to retain a more or less vigorous critique of the dominant tendencies of capitalism and, after the beginning of the disintegration of the Communist movement, encouraged contributions from some of those who came to embrace liberal democracy even as they remained socialists. Bell saves a soft spot for Howe and his associate, the sociologist Lewis Coser, and their magazine, *Dissent,* but argues that they are participants in, rather than dissenters from, the exhaustion of political ideas and even the most practical utopias. Bell insists that the erstwhile radical intellectual had been overcome by a certain "disenchantment," not particularly with really existing Communism—that was for most an old story associated with the generation of Hook and Trilling—but with political ideas themselves. The intellectual recognizes the simplism of all manner of the "old" Left but has no utopias to replace it: "Ours a twice born generation finds its wisdom in pessimism, evil, tragedy and despair. So we are both old and young 'before our time.'"[1] Bell is about forty when these words were written, and we can hear the echoes of the antiradicalism of Friedrich Nietzsche, for whom the Paris Commune was an abomination because it signaled the rise of the "masses."

Strauss, who died in 1973, was a political philosopher, a designation he carefully distinguished from political science, whose guide is the methods of natural science and whose purview is the inductive study of contemporary politics by means of empirical methods. He also said his work was not political theory, which, however dedicated to concepts, remains tied to value neutrality, which to this day is characteristic of all the social sciences. Strauss was a philosopher because he insisted that values constituted the core of politics and reflections on politics. The task of political philosophy is to determine the best society and system of social rule. Therefore, it is a moral and ethical endeavor, not a branch of science. For the *ought* cannot be derived from the *is.* As we shall see, it can only be arrived at by going back to ancient Greek philosophy and a special reading of the Jewish religious tradition. Thus, a large portion of Strauss's corpus is devoted to the reinstatement of ancient Greek philosophy to contemporary politics. And not insignificantly, Strauss invoked his own reading of Kabbalistic Judaism to the study of politics.

Like many European Jewish intellectuals, Leo Strauss was forced to leave his native land. First settling in Paris, he struck up a friendship with Alexandre Kojeve, for among other reasons their mutual admiration for and their affiliation with the existential philosophy of Martin Heidegger.

Kojeve famously taught Hegel to a generation of French intellectuals, including Sartre and Merleau-Ponty, first as a Marxist and later as a Hegelian deeply influenced by Heidegger's ontology. Kojeve's magisterial *Introduction to a Reading of Hegel* (bowdlerized and abridged in English translation by Strauss follower Allan Bloom) stands as among the three or four great commentaries on the Master-Slave dialectic in the *Phenomenology of Spirit* (the others include Herbert Marcuse's habilitation *Hegel's Ontology* and Jean Hippolyte's *Genesis and Structure of Hegel's Phenomenology of Spirit*). Strauss and Kojeve had an extensive correspondence, during which they vigorously disagreed, not only about their respective interpretations of Hegel but also about Plato and Aristotle, one of Strauss's main specializations. Throughout Kojeve's intellectual itinerary, and even as he was influenced by Heidegger, he adhered to concepts such as historicity, if not historicism, and especially the dialectic of history. Although Strauss admired Hegel's invocation of the absolute, he believed Hegel went wrong in his reliance on history and his development of the dialectic to arrive at the absolute, his critical refusal of ethical philosophy, and, most tellingly, notions such as progress and change.

When Strauss migrated to the United States and took up a post at the University of Chicago, his constant polemic against these concepts served as the basis of his reading of politics. Strauss's readings of ancient Greek philosophy, and not only of its two great exemplars, focused sharply on the transhistorical values that emerged from his readings. Selectively, Strauss emphasizes natural law as the foundation of any possible "best" political order. According to Plato and Aristotle, the best political order can only be run by superior "men" who are freed from the burdens of labor and other aspects of everyday life. While conceding that in modern times, whose characteristic perspective is "liberalism," the consent of the masses is necessary for the reproduction of political rule, it is important to recognize that the best political order requires the formation of a political elite that can administer justice on the basis of the eternal verities as enunciated by the ancient Greeks. Like his teacher, Martin Heidegger, Strauss views modernity with alarm, if not terror. Strategically, he cannot credibly renounce "democracy" as a mode of rule, but for him it must be a democracy of equals among the superior categories. In this respect Strauss is not a proponent of the rule of capital. His best political order is ruled by philosophers—or to be more exact, those trained in nonmodern political philosophy—and those political operatives trained in their value systems. Indeed, one of Strauss's achievements during his thirty years at the University of Chicago was to train two groups: teachers of legislators and some of the legislators themselves, where "legislators" signifies not necessarily elected officials but high-level state bureaucrats. These bureaucrats were to be trained to identify the common or public interest, against the particular interests of contending groups, and employ their wisdom to promulgate high values against the mundane conflicts that fill up political life.

What are these essential values? In the main they are based on highly abstract antinomies: superior and inferior, good and evil, elite and mass, from Nietzsche the critique of the idea of history and with it the idea of progress, and consequently the passionate advocacy of transhistorical values and against change, which in any case is always chimerical. First, in the struggle against relativism—a concomitant of the dogma of natural science as well as historicism—Strauss argues that the attempt to derive politics from scientific principles, that is, the positivist methodologies of the social sciences, can only illuminate what is but not what ought to be. Political philosophy will never completely dominate existent politics, but Strauss insists that it is an ethical discipline.

I cannot here provide an extensive analysis of Strauss's most glittering achievements but can only suggest the extent of his influence: Allan Bloom's best-selling diatribe *The Closing of the American Mind* became a manifesto for those who would permanently subvert the postwar program to broaden access to higher education for the working class, particularly people of color. Beginning with a caustic but essentially accurate indictment of colleges and universities—notably that they had become diploma mills that lowered the quality of teaching and learning—Bloom concludes that only a handful of American institutions are capable of providing a classical education to a select coterie of students. All the rest should be consigned to vocational training. We may also cite the powerful influence of Straussianism during the whole canvas of the Reagan revolution and the virtual dominance of the first term of the Bush administration by Straussian "legislators"—notably Paul Wolfowitz, Condoleezza Rice, and other top officials at the Pentagon and the State Department who, despite some reversals of fortune, remain in power during the second term—and Strauss's important intellectual influence on the erstwhile radical intellectuals around *Commentary,* the *Public Interest,* and the *Weekly Standard,* edited by William Kristol, especially of Strauss's insistence on the crucial role of Jewish mysticism's critique of conventional rationalism in the shaping of contemporary as well as ancient Greek value systems. Needless to say, American academic philosophy and political theory, though still mainly overcome with scientistic illusion, is today laden with Straussians; Strauss has become perhaps the leading referent for those who are interested in Heidegger, Nietzsche, and others coded as practitioners of "continental" philosophy. Perhaps more salient is the spread of Strauss's ideas among political theorists and historians of political philosophy, particularly those who, like Bloom, became harsh critics of American education and social policy and fervent supporters of U.S. global reach. What they find attractive is his antirelativist and antipositivist arguments, his return to "classical" as opposed to modern political philosophy, his strong endorsement of Nietzsche and especially Heidegger, who himself had written extensively on ancient Greek philosophy, especially his ground-breaking work on Parmenides, a "pre-Socratic" who anticipates many of Platonic and Straussian themes. The Straussians are ensconced in the University of Chicago, even after Bloom's passing, and Strauss has influenced many political theorists weary of the incessant repetition of commentaries on the English canon.

Perhaps the key concept that demarcates neoconservatism from conventional liberalism and the old conservatism is that of the absolute necessity of preserving at all costs the Western social order under the leadership of the United States. At least putatively the United States stands as the most stable political order; as opposed to Western Europe, its elites are prepared to build and sustain the empire of reason, even at the cost of waging a permanent war against the infidels who challenge Judeo-Christian traditions from secular as well as religious premises. For the neocons, there can, at most, be only temporary compromises with these challengers to our quest for the best political order. In the long run, under the banner of the War on Terror (anyone who is not with us is against us and can be classified as "evil") and the universalism of democracy (but only in the restricted sense I outlined earlier) they must be vanquished or subordinated. Otherwise, the crisis of values in which mass democratic and revolutionary politics have obscured our vision and brought constant disaster to the West since the French and Bolshevik revolutions will result in disintegration or, worse, the apocalypse.

It would be a grave mistake to interpret the end of communism as a prelude to the dawning of a new era of reconciliation. For the neocons have largely succeeded in conjuring new demons to sustain their binary worldview. In forging their alliance with the old conservatism they have set the agenda for the new parameters of Empire. And their program remains bipartisan insofar as there are few Democratic "legislators" either in Congress or in various public bureaucracies prepared to challenge neoconservative precepts. Moreover, it is arguable that the Clinton administration was, and the Democratic establishment remains, in their thrall. We are at the stage of intellectual combat. We have yet to set the conditions, nor have we laid out the fundamental philosophical underpinnings for challenging the new imperialism, the Empire.

Finally, what distinguishes neoconservatism from its liberal and conservative competitors is its proposal to change the world based on principle and replace the doctrine of compromise with one of absolute truth. Thus, its policy prescriptions—for example, no diplomatic conversations with members of the "axis of evil"—appear to its critics as doctrinaire and inflexible. Precisely. As a political philosophy, neoconservatism is the sworn opponent of one of the sacred cows of pluralism: compromise with one's opponents. In this sense, neoconservatism is a kind of right-wing Jacobinism, even bolshevism. In its quest for absolute power there is no violence that it will refuse to impose on civil liberties, especially those enjoyed by the Empire's opponents. Thus, in contrast to the period when the U.S. State Department encouraged cultural exchanges with the Soviet Union and its member states, even admitted foreign radicals to U.S. shores for lectures and sanctioned academic appointments, an administration successfully infiltrated by neoconservative apparatchiks will bend every effort to preserve the purity of our culture, by cynically evoking the War on Terror to perpetrate such exclusions. And if, as was the case of Paul Wolfowitz, the political heat is turned up against them, the affected neocon is not left to fry but is transferred, arguably to a more influential position in global economic policy, the presidency of the World Bank.

Make no mistake, neoconservatism in both its ex-socialist and its reactionary philosophical guises is not the latest flavor in the unending flow of ideologies and doctrines. It has made a conservative reading of Aristotle and of Hegel into an original paradigm that justifies empire building. It is an assault against the infidels of all varieties whose purpose is to overcome the contradictions of global capitalism, by waging permanent war on critics at home and afar. Its strategy is to define dissidence as unpatriotic and terroristic, even if not a single bomb is thrown. Wrapping itself in the banner of the ancient Judeo-Greek traditions, neoconservatism seeks nothing less than to force a race back to the future. Its defeat would be a condition for developing a new paradigm of global social and political relations, one that would share Strauss's critique of relativism and scientism and would adopt the contrary readings of classical political philosophy to show the ways they may contribute to a democratic future.

NOTES

1. Daniel Bell, *The End of Ideology,* 2nd rev. ed. (New York: Macmillan, 1962), 300.

Chapter 4

The New Political Right in the United States

Reaction, Rollback, and Resentment

Chip Berlet

Barry Goldwater was the ultraconservative's dream candidate for president in 1964. Goldwater was for small government and against big labor. He wanted to reduce taxes while expanding the American military. He was willing to fight communism by any means necessary. He stood for God and country, the American way of life, and he actually could ride a horse and shoot a rifle.

The American voters smashed an electoral pie in his face. Goldwater won only six states against Democratic Party opponent Lyndon Baines Johnson.[1]

In less than forty years, the American-as-apple-pie ultraconservatives not only regrouped but also seized political power in the United States. When the new millennium dawned, they finished the task of asserting control over all three branches of government. Back in 1964, Goldwater told the Republican convention, "Extremism in defense of liberty is no vice. . . . moderation in the pursuit of justice is no virtue."[2] Before he died in 1998, Goldwater called for moderation and said that some of the activists in the New Right who had taken over the Republican Party in the 1980s were too extreme, especially in their opposition to abortion and gay rights.

What happened? The answers are rooted in the broad reactionary forces of social, political, and cultural ultraconservatism in the United States, the coalition to roll back the New Deal policies of Franklin D. Roosevelt, and the resentment that was mobilized against the social liberation movements of the 1960s and 1970s.[3]

Roots of Reaction

The political Right has always mobilized people and resources to sway the electoral and social scene in the United States, but as John B. Judis observes, "In the early twentieth century, there was no such thing in American politics as a conservative movement. The right was an unwieldy collection of anti-Semites, libertarians, fascists, racists, anti–New Dealers, isolationists, and Southern agrarians who were incapable of agreeing on anything."[4]

Following a large railway strike in 1877, the Reverend Henry Ward Beecher, a popular and widely known preacher, suggested that alien ideas from Europe were being imported into the United States. As M. J. Heale observed, Beecher "thought 'un-American' the idea that government should provide for the welfare of its citizens, described collectivist theories as destructive of that 'individuality of the person' that alone preserved liberty, and unabashedly insisted that 'God has intended the great to be great and the little to be little.'"[5] To meet this challenge of ungodly collectivism, right-wing industrial and business interests organized a series of national networks and institutions between the late 1800s and Roosevelt's New Deal in the 1930s.

In 1895, the National Association of Manufacturers (NAM) was founded with a special interest in stopping labor organizing in the South. It was no coincidence that the "influential Southern newspaper, *The Dixie*," rallied support for the group.[6] NAM "tended to represent small businessmen, was fiercely antiunion and strongly endorsed the 'open shop' crusade to ban union influence in industrial plants."[7]

NAM swam in the common currents of white racial supremacy and solidarity prevalent in the 1930s. The *New York Times,* for example, editorialized that one aid to NAM president John E. Edgerton and his associates "in their effort to maintain the open shop [was] the racial and language unity of [employees] and employers in the South, and the pressure of long custom."[8]

Edgerton proclaimed that southern wage earners "are almost wholly of one blood, one God, and one language. . . . No people on earth love individual liberty, or will make greater sacrifices for it, than . . . those proud Anglo-Saxon elements who constitute the working army of this homogeneous section of the nation."[9]

To oppose President Franklin Roosevelt's New Deal proposals, in 1934,

NAM launched a huge thirteen-year $15 million public relations campaign "for the dissemination of sound American doctrines to the public." These doctrines included blasting labor unions while calling for reductions in the size of government and the number of government regulations. NAM still brags about how it distributed "leaflets, movie shorts, radio speeches, films for schools, reprints of articles by economists, and other public relations efforts. A daily NAM column appeared in 260 newspapers with a circulation of more than 4.5 million persons in 1936. The NAM's movie shorts were seen by six million persons in 1937."[10]

NAM saw labor unions as a threat to American democracy and the free-enterprise system. In 1955 one steel company official warned NAM that employers needed to show some solidarity of their own and organize to defend the free-enterprise system against a powerful attack from the AFL-CIO and other unions.[11] "Red scare tactics were frequently employed in attempts to halt the surge of unionization," with NAM issuing one pamphlet titled "Join the CIO and Help Build a Soviet America."[12]

NAM claims credit for having "helped launch the National Council of Commerce in 1907."[13] This predecessor group became the United States Chamber of Commerce in 1912.[14] The Chamber of Commerce primarily represented small-business interests, although a few big businesses were also members; and the Chamber reflected these sectors in its "periodic imprecations against the New Deal, labor unions, and anything resembling socialism," according to Heale.[15]

The United States Business and Industry Council (USBIC) was even further to the political Right than NAM and the Chamber. John E. Edgerton, the former president of NAM, became the first president of the Council. Originally established in 1933 as the Southern States Industrial Council, the organizing conference attracted "presidents and secretaries of Southern state manufacturers' associations."[16]

Council founders sought to undermine the New Deal approach to the Depression, "as well as to the political challenges posed to business by the Roosevelt Administration."[17] This was unremarkable, since up until the New Deal, laissez-faire economic polices were the "conventional wisdom" taught at major universities and business schools.[18] Therefore, Heale notes, it was a widely held belief across much of America in the late 1800s and early 1900s that "workers benefited from the free enterprise of the capitalist, that trade unions were potential monopolies that disrupted the free market, and that labor actions like strikes were offenses against society."[19]

Rolling Back the New Deal

Many activists on the political Right, especially secular and religious libertarians, see the way Roosevelt pushed through the National Labor Relations Act during the New Deal as greasing the slippery slope toward tyran-
nical collectivism.[20] To this day they argue that labor disputes were pulled
out of the court system and handed over to faceless bureaucrats in a federal agency, the National Labor Relations Board (NLRB). In 1975, these actions by Roosevelt still angered rightists, including Hans F. Sennholz, who
claimed the NLRB "became prosecutor, judge, and jury, all in one. Labor
union sympathizers on the Board further perverted this law, which already
afforded legal immunities and privileges to labor unions. The U.S. thereby
abandoned a great achievement of Western civilization, equality under the
law."[21]

As soon as the National Labor Relations Act was passed, conservatives
began writing legislation to gut key sections of the law, with a big push between 1938 and the start of World War II.[22] The National Association of
Manufacturers and the U.S. Chamber of Commerce lobbied Congress to
add a clause about "coercion" that Gilbert J. Gall argues was essentially designed to allow employers to undermine union organizing drives.[23]

Fanning Fears of Subversion

Rollback of the New Deal was the specific aim of the ultraconservatives,
but they pursued a broader agenda as they fanned fears of a domestic
threat of communism to justify "entirely smashing the labor movement
and the New Deal" and "rooting out the subversives who supposedly
infested Hollywood, the Ivy League, the State Department, and Wall
Street."[24] This is the essence of the term *ultraconservative*—not just conservative political ideology but an aggressive approach to eliminating collectivism, immorality, external threats, or subversion that undermine an
idealized vision of the American Dream.

Why do so many ultraconservatives imply, or state outright, that Roosevelt was a tool of a vast subversive communist conspiracy? This tendency, called "countersubversion," dates back to the late 1700s, when an
early reactionary movement pushed through the Alien and Sedition Acts.
Later, in the mid- to late 1800s, some xenophobic activists launched "nativist" anti-Catholic and anti-immigrant movements, using fears of sub-

version to mobilize a mass reaction.[25] Fear of communist subversion "was being developed as a weapon to isolate labor organizations and control the untamed urban masses," writes Heale. This worked in a way that "legitimated the use of strong-arm tactics and the expansion of police powers."[26]

In the 1900s the most prevalent form of countersubversion was "Red Scares" such as those that promoted the Palmer Raids of 1919–20 and the trial of Sacco and Vanzetti in 1921. In the 1930s, according to Leo P. Ribuffo, it was no surprise to find conservatives adapting these "venerable countersubversive themes" and deeming "Roosevelt's program un-American as well as unwise."[27] And by 1934, "critics routinely compared the whole New Deal to 'Russianized' government."[28]

Ultraconservative business and industrial leaders "saw the New Deal as proof of a sinister alliance between international finance capital and communist-controlled working-class organizations to destroy free enterprise."[29] This sector of the U.S. political Right became known as "business nationalists," and today their views are represented by ultraconservative political figures such as Pat Buchanan.[30] Back in the mid-1930s, it was firebrand orator Gerald L. K. Smith who carried the banner for the business nationalists, many of whom were isolationist and would later oppose the entry of the United States into World War II.[31]

Smith received public and financial support from wealthy businessmen who were "concentrated in nationalist-oriented industries." These included "the heads of national oil companies Quaker State, Pennzoil, and Kendall Refining; and automakers Henry Ford and John and Horace Dodge." Two business nationalists who networked other ultraconservatives were J. Howard Pew, president of Sun Oil, and William B. Bell, president of the American Cyanamid, a chemical company.[32]

Pew and Bell were on the executive committee of the National Association of Manufacturers.[33] Pew also funded the American Liberty League, Sentinels of the Republic, and other groups that flirted with fascism prior to World War II.[34] After World War II, Pew funded conservative Christian evangelicals such as the Reverend Billy Graham.

Old Christian Right of the 1930s and 1940s

Leaders of what Ribuffo calls the "Old Christian Right" mobilized large groups of people in the United States into searching for subversives during the 1930s and 1940s.[35] The fear of the Red Menace in some ultraconservative Protestant circles was fueled by apocalyptic biblical prophecy. The term *apocalypse* simply means the idea that there is an approaching confrontation of epic proportions after which the world will be changed forever and hidden truths will be revealed. A number of Protestant evangelicals and fundamentalists have historically connected apocalyptic prophecies in the Bible's book of Revelation to current political and social events.[36] Robert C. Fuller notes that trying to match real-life political figures with the evil Antichrist (prophesied as the sidekick of Satan in Revelation) became something of an "American obsession" in certain circles.[37]

For many Christian evangelicals and fundamentalists, communism and anarchism were literally tools of the devil. According to Frank Donner, "Bolshevism came to be identified over wide areas of the country by God-fearing Americans as the Antichrist come to do eschatological battle with the children of light," as prophesied in Revelation. Although based in Christianity, this apocalyptic anticommunist worldview developed a "slightly secularized version," explains Donner, and it was "widely shared in rural and small-town America," where leaders of evangelical and fundamentalist groups regularly "postulated a doomsday conflict between decent upright folk and radicalism—alien, satanic, immorality incarnate."[38]

Red Scares Revisited

Apocalyptic biblical prophecy played a major role in right-wing Protestant movements between World War I and World War II and helped frame the rhetoric used by the leading spokesmen for what Ribuffo calls the "Protestant Far Right": William Dudley Pelley, Gerald B. Winrod, and Gerald L. K. Smith.[39] President Roosevelt was seen not only as promoting "modernist" ideas such as collectivism but also as sliding down "a slippery slope from liberalism to atheism, nudism, and Communism," quips Ribuffo.[40]

Claims about a vast conspiracy to subvert America could remain focused on communism or involve suggestions that Jews were "responsible for the New Deal," with a few even claiming "to have uncovered Roosevelt's Jewish ancestry."[41] Elizabeth Dilling is but one example.[42] Her most famous work is *The Roosevelt Red Record and Its Background.*[43]

Most conservative Protestants, however, avoided obvious anti-Semitism and were more in tune with the National Association of Evangelicals, founded in 1942, which "assailed the 'revolutionary' activities of the New Deal and the infiltration of government, the unions, and churches by 'reds.' "[44] Catholic church leaders, including Francis Cardinal Spellman and Bishop Fulton J. Sheen, were also outspoken anticommunists.[45]

After the end of World War II, the 1946 "general elections were greatly influenced by the onset of the Cold War."[46] In 1947 the passage of the Taft-Hartley Act was eased by what would become a new Red Scare that eventually morphed into the McCarthy Period. Among the supporters of Joseph McCarthy's 1946 Senate campaign were those who framed the issue as anticommunism, but as one admitted, the real reason for their support of McCarthy was "to force Congress to crack down on militant industrial unionism."[47] The Taft-Hartley Act facilitated the linkage of antiunion right-to-work organizing by explicitly allowing employers to target their employees with antiunion materials.[48] Booklets, reports, and flyers linked labor unions with subversion by communists, and the Chamber of Commerce developed a huge "propaganda campaign . . . alleging extensive Communist penetration of government and of the labor unions."[49]

Congressional committees, the FBI, and private watchdog groups cooperated both publicly and privately to monitor and "expose" communist influences in film, radio, television, and the theater.[50]

Fraternal and veterans organizations published warnings about subversion.[51] The Minute Women organized ultraconservative women to combat subversion.[52] The American Security Council began tracking names of communist sympathizers for use by employers screening job seekers.[53] The right-wing Church League of America also kept a huge collection of files on subversives. For a fee, employers could have the files searched to see if a prospective employee was a troublemaker or radical.[54] The Church League of America also attacked mainline Protestant denominations for their doctrinal and political liberalism and issued reports claiming the National Council of Churches was infested with subversives and communists. The "internal subversion thesis and the view of liberalism as merely a soft form of communism provided the logic for Christian Rightists' attacks on reputable Church bodies," explains Sara Diamond.[55]

The messages of militant anticommunism continued to be circulated well into the 1950s by NAM, the Chamber of Commerce, and USBIC, as well as early think tanks such as the Hoover Institution at Stanford University and the Foreign Policy Research Institute, founded with assistance from the University of Pennsylvania. Conservative media led by the ubiquitous *Reader's Digest,* with its huge reader base, spread the messages. A variety of chapter-based grassroots fraternal and religious groups carried the anticommunist alerts into the hands of members across the land.[56]

Postwar Fusionism

After World War II and the Truman administration, a moderate Republican, Dwight D. Eisenhower, was elected president in 1952. The political
Right in the Republican Party (called the "Taft wing" after the former
president, Robert Taft) had been eclipsed. Three strategists, Frank Meyer,
M. Stanton Evans, and William F. Buckley Jr., decided it was time to carve
a conservative movement out of the fractured remains of the political
Right, in part by specifically rejecting the legacy of overt white supremacy
and anti-Semitism. Buckley had gained attention writing for the libertarian journal *Freeman* but secured his niche when in 1955 he founded the influential *National Review* magazine.[57]

Buckley, Evans, and Meyer sought a working coalition—a fusion—
bridging three tendencies: economic libertarianism, social traditionalism,
and militant anticommunism.[58] According to Jerome L. Himmelstein,
"The core assumption that binds these three elements is the belief that
American society on all levels has an organic order—harmonious, benefi-
cent, and self-regulating—disturbed only by misguided ideas and policies,
especially those propagated by a liberal elite in the government, the media,
and the universities."[59] This coalition plan became known as "Fusionism."

Among the libertarian ideologues were old-timers including former
presidents Herbert Hoover and Robert Taft; classical liberal (laissez-faire)
economists including Ludwig von Mises, Friedrich Hayek, and Milton
Friedman; "and a variety of iconoclastic individualists and objectivists like
Albert Jay Nock and Ayn Rand."[60]

Social traditionalist ideologues included Leo Strauss, Eric Vogelin, Robert Nisbet, Russell Kirk, and Richard Weaver.[61] They contributed ideas
with "arguments rooted in natural law, Christian theology, and nineteenth-century European conservatism and its notions of tradition," reports Himmelstein.[62]

During this same period, a number of industrial interests repackaged
their opposition to labor unions and in 1955 helped form the National
Right to Work Committee (NRTWC). Fred A. Hartley—the same Hartley
who cosponsored the antiunion Taft-Hartley Act in 1947—became the
first president of the NRTWC. According to Gall, unions feared an "organized assault by a coalition of the National Association of Manufacturers,
the U.S. Chamber of Commerce," and the new national group.[63] The
NRTWC reframed the issue, shifting away from anticommunism and the
claims of subversion used during the New Deal and early Cold War period

to the theme of greedy and thuggish union bosses denying the rights of workers their freedom to choose their employer and terms of employment.[64] This reframing would not be used by the forces that built the Goldwater campaign but later would influence the messages crafted by the New Right.[65]

The collapse of the McCarthyist form of anticommunism sent some ultraconservatives in another direction. In 1959 the John Birch Society (JBS) was founded to continue to combat the communist conspiracy and its liberal handmaidens. The JBS launched a campaign to get the United States out of the United Nations, and this project peaked in the early 1960s. For Birch members, there was still the threat of communist subversion aided by liberal internationalists and collectivists. Another group, the Liberty Lobby, continued the tradition of weaving anti-Semitic allegations into the conspiracy theories.[66]

When John F. Kennedy was elected in 1960, ultraconservatives sought to build a broad coalition to retake the presidency from the Democrats and install a real Republican, unlike President Dwight D. Eisenhower, a moderate whose Republican administration from 1952 to 1960 was seen as an unmitigated disaster by ultraconservatives.

In 1963 William A. Rusher, publisher of the ultraconservative magazine *National Review,* "urged fellow conservatives to take a risk" in order to "break the New Deal Coalition's lock on the presidency," Schoenwald reports.[67] Rusher predicted, "It will take courage; it will take imagination; it will compel the GOP to break the familiar mould that has furnished it with every presidential nominee for a quarter of a century—but it can be done."[68]

It was done when "the right wing of the party . . . seized control of the G.O.P. in the early 1960s." According to Ferguson and Rogers, this was "supported strongly by such protectionist and nationalistically inclined figures as National Steel's George Humphrey, textile magnate Roger Milliken, and independent oil men John Pew and Henry Salvatori." As the Republican Party was tugged to the right, there was a flotilla of multinational businesses (including a portion of the high-technology sector) that sailed from the Republican Party to the Democratic Party.[69]

The Goldwater campaign attracted support from ultraconservative and Christian Right activists who were worried about subversive conspiracies, including those who feared international treaties and U.S. participation in the United Nations. While the Liberty Lobby remained marginal, many JBS activists helped secure the 1964 Republican Party nomination for Goldwater and went on to help build the New Right in the 1970s and 1980s.[70] The Goldwater campaign also elevated Phyllis Schlafly to a high-profile role in ultraconservative organizing that lasted more that forty years, as she built the Eagle Forum and led the successful blocking of the Equal Rights Amendment.[71]

Lucy Williams observes that the Old Right rhetoric behind the Goldwater campaign focused on messages stressing the "confluence of poverty, race, labor unions, violence and communism. In this way, the Old Right was able to promote its agenda of lower taxes and reduced government."[72] Williams notes that during the Goldwater campaign, "rightist publications attacked the welfare state for undermining rugged individualism and private property, fostering immorality and non-productive activity, contributing to crime (particularly associated with urban riots and the Civil Rights Movement), and ultimately leading to Communism."[73] This frame did not propel Goldwater to victory in the general election, but it did begin a process that eventually altered the way ultraconservatism presented itself to appeal to a wider audience.

When Goldwater's presidential campaign wiped out on Election Day 1964, political conservatism was dismissed as a quaint relic of earlier political turmoil. Mason explains that "[d]espite the birth of a modern movement of conservative thought in the 1950s and its growth in the 1960s, conservative ideas remained relatively marginal to intellectual and wider public debate" throughout most of the 1960s.[74]

Transition: From Old Right to New Right

Instead of bemoaning the failure of Goldwater to attract voters, ultraconservatives repackaged themselves as populists and reframed their messages. To the middle class, they offered tax reductions, which also served their goal of reducing the size of federal and state budgets and meddling government programs. To the emerging Christian Right, they promised to restore America to its proper status as a Christian nation built on "family values" and to defend the idealized Christian family against the sinful feminist, homosexual, secular humanist, and socialist subversives.[75]

The subtext in this campaign of reframing was race.[76] Ultraconservative strategists began to "use welfare and the War on Poverty to capture the increasing racial fears of much of white America at a time when African Americans were asserting their rights in new ways," explains Williams.[77]

William Rusher set the tone of the new frame, pitting populist produc-
ers against parasitic liberal elites:

> new economic division pits the producers—businessmen, manufacturers,
> hard-hats, blue-collar workers, and farmers—against the new and powerful
> class of nonproducers comprised of a liberal verbalist elite (the dominant
> media, the major foundations and research institutions, the educational es-
> tablishment, the federal and state bureaucracies) and a semipermanent wel-
> fare constituency, all coexisting happily in a state of mutually sustaining
> symbiosis.[78]

These new frames were designed to build a mass base and increase
voter turnout. Some analysts claim that it involved an intentional plan to
"mobilize resentment" through populist rhetoric and convince portions
of the electorate to vote against their economic self interest in favor of
hot-button social issues.[79] In addition to rhetorical populism and pro-
ducérism, different sectors of the political Right (and different players in
specific sectors) also use dualism and the demonization of opponents,
conspiracist narratives, and an apocalyptic frame that raises the stakes of
political struggle to a cosmological level.[80]

To implement the plan, conservatives began constructing a network of
social movements and social movement organizations and institutions
that would feed people into their political operation. As Doug McAdam
and David A. Snow explain, social movements consist of groups of people
who act with "some degree of organization and continuity outside of institutional channels for the purpose of promoting or resisting change in
the group, society, or world order of which it is a part."[81] Just as the civil
rights movement pulled the Democratic Party to the political Left, the
new conservative movement, energized and trained in the Goldwater campaign, would pull the Republican Party to the Right.

Articles in the *Freeman, National Review,* and other ultraconservative
publications demonized liberals as wealthy, arrogant elitists destroying
America. In 1965, M. Stanton Evans wrote a book titled *The Liberal Establishment Who Runs America . . . and How.* Conservatives, therefore, needed
to set up a "counterestablishment" to give America back to the people.[82] At
the time a political strategist close to the Republican Party, Kevin Phillips
outlined a plan for building an "emerging Republican majority" in a 1969
book.[83] President Nixon, elected in 1968, began to implement Phillips's
plan, which became known as the "Southern Strategy." After meeting with

Phillips, Nixon's aide H. R. Haldeman wrote a note to use "Phillips as an analyst—study his strategy—don't think in terms of old-time ethnics, go for Poles, Italians, Irish, must learn to understand Silent Majority. . . . don't go for Jews & Blacks."[84]

A series of conservative institutions that helped build social movements were either established or refocused during this period. For example, in 1969 the National Taxpayers Union was founded, and in 1970 the Religious Roundtable was founded by another Christian Right activist, Ed McAteer, who became an important architect of the New Right. In 1971 Karl Rove (later a key strategy adviser to President George W. Bush) became the executive director of the national College Republicans, which began a transition into more aggressive political activism, especially on college campuses.

Nixon, responding to pressure from conservatives to stop funding government programs where they claimed liberals and progressives were on the federal gravy train pursuing social engineering, appointed conservative activist Howard Phillips to dismantle the Office of Economic Opportunity. Phillips had been active with the conservative youth group Young Americans for Freedom (YAF), and other YAF activists and allies from the American Conservative Union joined in the effort.[85]

Following a similar theme of defunding the Left, corporate attorney Lewis F. Powell Jr. wrote a 1971 memo claiming that there was an organized "[a]ttack on [the] American Free Enterprise System." To counter this attack, Powell suggested a coordinated campaign to reshape the ideological debate in the media, on college campuses, and in the political and legal arenas. The memo was widely circulated among business and political leaders and reached the White House. Within a few months, Powell was named by Nixon to a seat on the U.S. Supreme Court.[86]

The New Right

The 1971 Powell memo picked up on long-standing complaints about statism, collectivism, and big government, as well as a defense of a laissez-faire model of political economy. All of this had previously been aired in the *Freeman* and *National Review*. This time, however, a number of wealthy ultraconservatives such as Richard Mellon Scaife and Joseph Coors and many others began funding right-wing organizations and institutions in a strategic manner to help build a national and state network of think tanks, training centers, watchdog groups, opposition research groups, magazines, and endowed chairs for professors at universities.[87]

One example was the formation of the Heritage Foundation in 1973 to represent ultraconservative interests in Washington, DC. Paul Weyrich was the first president of Heritage, and initial funding came from Joseph Coors.[88] Another is the Conservative Caucus (TCC), founded in 1975 and run by Howard Phillips with fundraising support from direct-mail fundraising guru Richard Viguerie and ideological support from Jesse Helms, an ultraconservative former senator from North Carolina with whom Phillips briefly worked. For a time, Ed McAteer also worked as the field director at the Conservative Caucus.[89]

Richard Viguerie built his conservative direct-mail empire by collecting names from the 1964 Goldwater campaign and from the 1972 presidential campaign of George Wallace and entering them into a computer database.[90] Viguerie originally envisioned a new conservative third party and, with William Rusher of *National Review,* Howard Phillips of the Conservative Caucus, and Paul Weyrich of the Free Congress Foundation, tried to establish control over Wallace's American Independent Party in 1976. When this failed, they turned their attention to gaining control over the Republican Party.[91]

In the 1976 election cycle, the National Conservative Political Action Committee (NCPAC) and the Committee for the Survival of a Free Congress (CSFC) joined other conservative political PACs in raising more than $3.5 million for conservative candidates for public office.[92] In 1977 Paul Weyrich took his experience with CSFC and established the Free Congress Foundation, which spearheaded the idea of "cultural conservatism" as the bulwark for defending family values and helped launch what became known as the Culture Wars.[93]

In 1978 Howard Jarvis led a "taxpayer revolt" in California, Proposition 13, that garnered national headlines and was replicated in many other states.[94] Grover Norquist, who later served as the executive director of the National Taxpayers Union, worked on "Proposition 13 in California and similar tax cutting initiatives in other states that year."[95] The ultraconservative Arlington House, publishers of the first edition of the Phillips book, produced a user guide on how to run a state initiative targeting the progressive income tax.[96]

It was the 1978 national election that gave the "first indication that the new conservative movement was nationally viable," states John B. Judis. Among Republican candidates elected were half a dozen governors, a dozen members of the House of Representatives, three senators, and over three hundred representatives on the state level. According to Judis, Republican conservatives made the "most impressive gains."[97]

William Simon, an ultraconservative ideologue, chose election year 1978 to renew the call to bolster public support to defend the free-enterprise system. Simon urged that money "generated by business (by which I mean profits, funds in business foundations and contributions from individual businessmen) must rush by multimillions to the aid of liberty . . . to funnel desperately needed funds to scholars, social scientists, writers, and journalists who understand the relationship between political and economic liberty."[98]

The Christian Right

Christian nationalism was reinvigorated in the 1970s, and a key organization was the now-defunct Christian Freedom Foundation (CFF), which was for "twenty years the most influential of the 'old' Christian right organizations."[99] In 1974, the Pew Freedom Trust contributed $300,000 to the group, and the president of Amway Corporation, Richard M. DeVos, gave $25,000.[100] The next year, according to John S. Saloma III, a group of wealthy ultraconservative businessmen began to change the work of CFF toward more aggressive political activism. The group included DeVos, "John Talcott of Ocean Spray Cranberries and Art De Moss, board chairman of the National Liberty Insurance Corporation."[101]

The purpose of taking over CFF, reports Saloma, was "to use the foundation's tax-exempt status to further religious right organizing efforts and to channel funds" into a publishing project, including *One Nation Under God*, a text that provided "a political rationale for the religious right." Saloma writes that "Art De Moss admitted publicly that the purpose of CFF was to elect Christian conservatives to Congress in 1976."[102] DeMoss himself explained that "[t]he vision is to rebuild the foundations of the Republic as it was when first founded—a 'Christian Republic.' We must return to the faith of our fathers."[103]

In the mid-1970s, CFF sponsored seminars "on government and politics in Washington," where Christian Right activists were trained. Among those attending was Robert Billings, who later set up shop in the nation's capital "monitoring legislation that had implications for Christian schools." Billings's group evolved into the National Christian Action Coalition, "and its mission broadened to include lobbying," according to Jeffrey K. Hadden and Charles E. Swann, in *Prime Time Preachers*. Billings reached out to ultraconservative televangelists such as Jerry Falwell.[104]

McAteer worked closely with Paul Weyrich, founder of the Free Congress Foundation. McAteer at various times worked for both the Christian Freedom Foundation and the Conservative Caucus, which had been formed by Howard Phillips with help from Richard Viguerie. In 1979 McAteer founded the Religious Roundtable, an influential Christian Right networking group.

Given their interaction as conservative movement activists, the next move for these men was a natural step forward: they became the godfathers of a new ultraconservative brainchild: the New Right. This movement was born at a meeting in 1979 where Billings, Falwell, McAteer, Phillips, Viguerie, and Weyrich discussed a way to link political activism with the growing evangelical subculture being networked through televangelism. Abortion was singled out as a wedge issue that could mobilize a voter base and split the Democratic Party. What emerged was the idea of a "Moral Majority," which became the name of an organization under the leadership of Falwell. Billings became executive director of the Moral Majority. Another activist who had been thinking along the same lines, Tim LaHaye, became a board member of the Moral Majority, along with D. James Kennedy of Coral Ridge Presbyterian Church in Florida.[105]

LaHaye went on to help found the Council for National Policy (CNP), which Billings, McAteer, Falwell, Weyrich, Phillips, and Viguerie also joined. In 1979 Beverly LaHaye, wife of Tim (and for many years more well known as a conservative movement activist), established Concerned Women for America, which became a large and effective national institution mobilizing grassroots political activism.[106]

In the early 1980s, another member of the CNP, Richard M. DeVos, (who had funded the Christian Freedom Foundation in its move into political activism in the 1970s) continued to network religious and fiscal conservatives as finance chairman of the Republican National Committee.[107] Christian conservatives played a significant role in helping to elect Reagan.[108] Billings, for example, joined the 1980 Reagan presidential campaign as the liaison to the religious community and then assumed that post in the Reagan White House.[109]

Reagan was influenced by conservative Christian theologian Francis A. Schaeffer and pediatrician C. Everett Koop, who in the late 1970s and early 1980s had organized Protestants to be concerned about the issues of abortion and the rise of secular humanism.[110] Schaeffer and Koop later helped Reagan write a tract opposing abortion. Koop was appointed U.S. Surgeon General by Reagan.[111] Reagan also adopted and echoed the framework of apocalyptic millennialism common among evangelicals and fundamentalists active in the Christian Right.[112]

The New Wave

Ronald Reagan took office as president in 1981, and his administration was immediately presented with over one thousand pages of detailed policy recommendations assembled into a book by the Heritage Foundation. Titled *Mandate for Leadership: Policy Management in a Conservative Administration,* the text was written by conservative activists with input from dozens of right-wing think tanks, political advocacy groups, and social movement organizations that lined the streets around the White House, congressional office buildings, and the Capitol building in Washington, DC.[113]

The "New Conservative Labyrinth" is what John S. Saloma III called this interlocking network that also reached out to journalists, academics, students, and grassroots activists. Saloma, a moderate Republican, warned about the "ominous politics" being promoted by the growing New Right infrastructure.[114]

One ongoing New Right elite networking group that at first received little public attention was the Council for National Policy, founded in 1981. The CNP brings together "a broad array of top right-wing evangelicals, secular activists, government officials, retired military and intelligence officers, journalists, academicians, and business leaders," writes Matthew N. Lyons.[115] CNP membership is by invitation only, and it is pricey since "several thousand dollars a year" are expected as dues.[116]

Tim LaHaye, a well-known conservative Christian family counselor and author, became the first president of the CNP.[117] According to Russ Bellant, LaHaye was working with the Moral Majority when he contacted T. Cullen Davis and Nelson Bunker Hunt for assistance in setting up the CNP.[118] At the same time, LaHaye, Paul Weyrich, and Richard Viguerie had been discussing the idea of such a group.[119] As a result, there are conflicting stories about the origins of the CNP, although it was clearly a group effort.

By the mid-1990s, Bellant reports that the Council for National Policy was essentially run by a "triumvirate" composed of Paul Weyrich, chair of the Free Congress Foundation; Reed Larson of the National Right to Work Committee; and Morton Blackwell of the Leadership Institute, who also served as executive director of the CNP.[120]

The CNP meetings "are so secretive that the press is not allowed, and no public announcements of the meetings are ever made," writes Skipp Porteous, who adds that "[p]lainclothes security guards carefully watch who comes and goes at the hotels where the meetings are held."[121] The CNP was once described in a *New York Times* political column as "a few hundred of the most powerful conservatives in the country," who meet "behind closed doors at undisclosed locations for a confidential conference" where they "strategize about how to turn the country to the right."[122]

The Neoconservatives

Whereas the Christian Right was an original part of the Old Right that morphed into the New Right, there is also a relatively new player on the scene. In the late 1960s and early 1970s the student, feminist, and antiwar movements caused alarm in the ranks of a group of Cold War liberals who promptly wrote about their misgivings in publications, especially *Public Interest* and *Commentary*. As they shifted to the political Right, they began to be known as the "neoconservatives" because they were new to conservatism.[123] Neoconservatives "attacked feminism, gay rights, and multiculturalism," but they "often placed less emphasis on social policy issues, and many of them opposed school prayer or a ban on abortion."[124] Neoconservatives are uneasy coalition partners with the Christian Right and other ultraconservatives.

Neoconservatives' concern over the spread of communism and the power of the Soviet Union mobilized them into forming the Committee on the Present Danger, and their emphasis on foreign policy included "aggressive anticommunism, U.S. global dominance, and international alliances."[125] Gary J. Dorrien profiled several neoconservative leaders in a series of chapters in which he described, in turn, Irving Kristol as an ideological warrior; Norman Podhoretz as opposing the "culture of appeasement," first toward communism and later toward other forms of moral corruption; Michael Novak as encouraging the "renewal of Whiggery";

and Peter Berger as exploring how religion and capitalism had to face up to the influences of modernity.[126]

Throughout the late 1970s and 1980s, neoconservatives developed an impressive collection of policy and strategy documents.[127] Yet it was not until the presidency of George W. Bush that neoconservative strategists emerged into public awareness for their central role in shaping an aggressive interventionist U.S. foreign policy.[128] Many of their ideas predated the George W. Bush administration and were published by the neoconservative Project for a New American Century (PNAC), founded in 1997.[129] PNAC itself is part of a larger network of foreign-policy hawks that carry on a long-standing tradition begun by anticommunist think tanks such as the Hoover Institution (founded 1919), Cold War cheerleaders such as the American Security Council and its Coalition for Peace through Strength, and PNAC's close forerunner, the Committee on the Present Danger.[130]

A number of early neoconservative ideologues came out of Jewish intellectual traditions, leading some analysts to hyperbolize this into anti-Semitic stereotyping.[131] Obviously, most Jews are not neoconservatives, many neoconservatives come from secular viewpoints or other ethnoreligious traditions, and there are several high-profile Catholic neoconservative intellectuals. Some critics of neoconservatism claim that it is influenced by the elitist and manipulative theories promulgated by University of Chicago philosopher Leo Strauss.[132] Strauss was one of the intellectuals whose ideas were used to build conservative Fusionism in the 1950s.[133]

What actually unites the neoconservatives as a group, however, are three "common themes," write Stefan A. Halper and Jonathan Clarke: a dualistic worldview, a focus on using military power, and the threat of non-Western cultures, especially Islam.

The dualism is based on a set of beliefs "deriving from religious conviction that the human condition is defined as a choice between good and evil and that the true measure of political character is to be found in the willingness by the former (themselves) to confront the latter."[134] This is especially dangerous when merged through coalition with the apocalyptic and messianic aspects of President Bush's alliance with the Christian Right.[135] Neoconservatives also claim that "the fundamental determinant of the relationship between states rests on military power and the willingness to use it," according to Halper and Clarke. The final portion of the triad is a "primary focus on the Middle East and global Islam as the principal theater for American overseas interests."[136]

Christian Nationalism and Dominionism

The melding of ultraconservative political activism and right-wing evangelicalism that became so significant during the New Deal and Cold War periods continued during the Reagan years. Recruitment across boundaries and coalition projects were common.[137]

For example, as Rick Henderson and Steven Hayward note, while anti-tax advocate Grover Norquist was earning his Harvard MBA, one of his papers "outlined a plan for the national College Republicans to switch from a resume-padding social club to an ideological, grassroots organization." In the early 1980s, he helped implement his plan with the help of the group's executive director, recent University of Georgia graduate Ralph Reed.[138] Norquist was the executive director of the National Taxpayers Union when the Reagan White House asked him to run another project, Americans for Tax Reform.[139]

Reed went on to assist Pat Robertson in his failed 1988 presidential bid, then helped transform the campaign apparatus into Robertson's Christian Coalition, with Reed ending up as that group's policy director.[140] Reed later became a Republican strategy consultant and the party's leader in Georgia.

As the millennial year 2000 approached, excitement built in some evangelical and fundamentalist circles over the potential significance of the date and its possible connection to the End Times prophesied in the Bible's book of Revelation. Groups such as the Promise Keepers sprang up and then faded after the date passed and Jesus did not return.[141] Yet the millennial excitement seemed to transfer into renewed energy for "restoring" a Christian Nation, a phenomenon called "dominionism" by critics.[142] This dominionist trend was based in part on the influence of Christian Reconstructionism and other forms of the small doctrinaire tendency called "dominion theology."[143]

The Christian Right exerted considerable pressure on Republican administrations since 1980, and by the new millennium, there was substantial evidence that they played a major role in shaping domestic and foreign polices.[144]

Paul Boyer advises that political analysts need to understand the "shadowy but vital way that belief in biblical prophecy is helping mold grassroots attitudes toward current U.S. foreign policy," especially concerning the Middle East.[145] In particular, a tendency called Christian Zionism pushes the United States to side with the most aggressive and intransigent forces within Israel, based on a reading of biblical prophesy that requires Jews to control Jerusalem and rebuild the Temple in order for Jesus to return.[146] These political sentiments about foreign and domestic policies are echoed in the Left Behind series of twelve novels by Tim LaHaye and Jerry B. Jenkins, with more than seventy million copies in circulation.[147] The series is rife with conspiracy theories and violence aimed at non-Christians. As Gershom Gorenberg complains, the books "demonize proponents of arms control, ecumenicalism, abortion rights and everyone else disliked by the Christian right; and they justify assassination as a political tool. Their anti-Jewishness is exceeded by their anti-Catholicism. Most basically, they reject the very idea of open, democratic debate."[148]

It is easy to stereotype Christian evangelicals and the more militant subgroup, the fundamentalists. There is tremendous diversity under those labels, however. As a self-identified group, evangelicals and those who consider themselves "born again" comprise somewhere between 25 and 50 percent of the U.S. population, depending on how the questions are phrased. Some 15 percent of voters identify with the Christian Right.[149] Many white evangelicals vote Republican, but some are independents and even Democrats. Black evangelicals historically have voted overwhelmingly for Democrats. It is more useful to see the Christian Right as a social movement built around a set of shared theological and moral beliefs mobilized in support of the Republican Party.

Conclusions

How did the political Right take power in the United States?[150] Since the early 1970s conservatives have invested more than $2 billion in their plan to take power in the United States.[151] Jean V. Hardisty argues in *Mobilizing Resentment* that the victory of the New Right was assisted by a confluence of factors unique in American history:

- a well-funded network of conservative institutions;
- religious revitalization and apocalyptic fervor among large numbers of conservative Christian evangelicals;
- economic contraction, restructuring, and redistribution—people worry about their future;

- race resentment and bigotry, often cloaked in rhetoric about taxes and welfare;
- backlash and social stress caused by fear of the social liberation movements of the 1960s and 1970s.[152]

The discussion of the types of close ties, relationships, and job switches throughout this chapter is not meant to suggest a "vast right-wing conspiracy."[153] They illustrate that the political Right consciously recruits young activists into a social movement and grooms the most promising for a career as social movement professionals. They can choose to remain in a particular topical movement, switch movements, or choose to become political activists embedded inside the Republican Party.[154] This dense social movement network also allows for transitions involving religious ideologues and activists moving into secular posts and vice versa. There are hundreds of right-wing social movement institutions, past and present, not mentioned in this article, such as the Business Roundtable, the Intercollegiate Studies Institute, and the Christian Anti-Communism Crusade. The political Right has a large and vibrant network with a rich and varied ideological palette from which to draw.

The intellectual roots of the type of ultraconservative thinking that helped build the New Right involve elitist forms of Protestant Calvinism, a reliance on theories of social and economic Darwinism, and the theme of rugged individualism. These ideas are woven into American culture and reappear repeatedly in ultraconservative rhetoric.

Claude A. Putnam, president of the National Association of Manufacturers, sought to roll back the New Deal when in 1950 he wrote, "If we do not cut big government down to the relative size and shape the founding fathers intended—then government eventually will dominate our lives, destroy our freedom and kill the spirit of individual enterprise and initiative which has made America great." Putnam sought to "restore the historic balance of power between central and state governments" by "transferring back to the states various service responsibilities which they can and should assume."[155]

The legacy of the New Deal was the target of tax-reduction warrior Grover Norquist when he said he wanted to starve the federal government to the size where it "could be drowned in a bathtub."[156] He once called all recipients of federal funds "cockroaches" and said that he wanted to "crush labor unions as a political entity."[157]

Ultraconservatives have learned to play the same melody but with interchangeable lyrics. If the unadorned libertarian argument for small government is not persuasive, then the rhetoric is carefully rewritten to appeal to the southern-based states'-rights movement and white racist baggage. The Christian Right is mobilized through appeals to social issues and "family values." Thus, fears about communism, collectivism, statism, unionism, states' rights, race, gender, sexual identity, abortion, and sin can all be mobilized to protect power, privilege, and wealth.

In response, the Democratic Party has shifted to the right, and along with liberal and progressive advocacy groups and other organizations on the political Left, it relies on a strategy featuring direct-mail and advertising campaigns warning of "religious political extremists" and the "radical right" but does not mobilize social movement participation or effective grassroots political activism.

Colin Greer argues that this is "emblematic of what has happened with a whole range of civil-rights issues in the United States. The original base has been cut off by professional advocacy organizations. Meanwhile, the right has built its own base, which is activist-oriented, risk-taking, and has a strategic long-term focus."[158]

The irony is that the model used by the political Right to gain power in the United States is based on earlier campaigns by organized labor, the civil rights movement, and other social movements of the political Left. Until that legacy is reclaimed by a new series of progressive social movements emerging from the grassroots and demanding political change outside established institutional channels, the ultraconservative coalition will continue to dominate the political scene in the United States.

Appendix: Sectors of the U.S. Political Right

Conservatives

Corporate Internationalists—Nations should control the flow of people across borders but not the flow of goods, capital, and profit. Sometimes called the "Rockefeller Republicans." Globalists.

Business Nationalists—Multinational corporations erode national sovereignty; nations should enforce borders for people but also for goods, capital, and profit through trade restrictions. Enlists grassroots allies from Patriot Movement. Antiglobalists. Generally protectionist and isolationist.

Economic Libertarians—The state disrupts the perfect harmony of the free-market system. Modern democracy is essentially congruent with capitalism.

National Security Militarists—Support U.S. military supremacy and unilateral use of force to protect perceived U.S. national security interests around the world. A major component of Cold War anticommunism.

Neoconservatives—The egalitarian social liberation movements of the 1960s and 1970s undermined the national consensus. Intellectual oligarchies and political institutions preserve democracy from mob rule. The United States has the right to intervene in its perceived interests anywhere in the world.

Religious Right

Religious Conservatives—Play by the rules of a pluralist democratic republic. Mostly Christian, with a handful of conservative Jews and Muslims and other people of faith. Moral traditionalists. Cultural and social conservatives.

Christian Nationalism (Soft Dominionists)—Biblically defined immorality and sin breed chaos and anarchy. America's greatness as God's chosen land has been undermined by liberal secular humanists, feminists, and homosexuals. Purists want litmus tests for issues of abortion, tolerance of gays and lesbians, and prayer in schools. Overlaps somewhat with Christian Theocracy.

Christian Theocracy (Hard Dominionists)—Christian men are ordained by God to run society. Eurocentric version of Christianity based on early Calvinism. Intrinsically Christian ethnocentric, treating non-Christians as second-class citizens. Implicitly anti-Semitic. Includes Christian Reconstructionists.

Xenophobic Right

Patriot Movement (Regressive Populists)—Secret elites control the government and banks. The government plans repression to enforce elite rule or global collectivism. The armed militias are one submovement from this sector. Americanist. Often supports Business Nationalism due to its isolationist emphasis. Antiglobalist yet support unilateralist national security militarism. Repressive toward scapegoated targets below them on socioeconomic ladder.

Paleoconservatives—Ultraconservatives and reactionaries. Natural financial oligarchies preserve the republic against democratic mob rule. Usually nativist (White Nationalism), sometimes anti-Semitic or Christian nationalist. Elitist emphasis is similar to the intellectual conservative revolution wing of the European New Right. Often libertarian.

White Nationalism (White Racial Nationalists)—Alien cultures make democracy impossible. Cultural Supremacists argue different races can adopt the dominant (white) culture; Biological Racists argue the immutable integrity of culture, race, and nation. Segregationists want distinct enclaves; Separatists want distinct nations. Americanist. Tribalist emphasis is similar to the race-is-nation wing of the European New Right.

Extreme Right (Ultra Right)—Militant forms of revolutionary right ideology and separatist ethnocentric nationalism. Reject pluralist democracy for an organic oligarchy that unites the homogeneic nation. Conspiracist views of power that are overwhelmingly anti-Semitic. Home to overt neofascists, neo-Nazis, Christian Identity, Creativity (Church of the Creator), National Alliance.

For more information on the U.S. political Right, visit http://www.public eye.org.

NOTES

Portions of this chapter reflect research first done for "Following the Threads: A Work in Progress," in Amy E. Ansell (ed.), *Unraveling the Right: The New Conservatism in American Thought and Politics* (Boulder, Colo.: Westview, 1998), 80–102. Much of my work in this area was conducted jointly with Matthew N. Lyons, with whom I coauthored *Right-Wing Populism in America,* from which I expropriated (with permission) ideas and smidgens of text. Some research into the history of ultraconservative networks was funded by a grant to Political Research Associates (PRA) from American Rights at Work. Without the ongoing support of the staff and board of PRA, my research would not be possible.

1. Rick Perlstein, *Before the Storm: Barry Goldwater and the Unmaking of the American Consensus* (New York: Hill and Wang, 2001).

2. Cited in Perlstein, *Before the Storm,* 391.

3. Jean V. Hardisty, *Mobilizing Resentment: Conservative Resurgence from the John Birch Society to the Promise Keepers* (Boston: Beacon, 1999), 9–36.

4. John B. Judis, *The Paradox of American Democracy: Elites, Special Interests, and the Betrayal of the Public Trust* (New York: Pantheon, 2000), 142.

5. M. J. Heale, *American Anticommunism: Combating the Enemy Within, 1830–1970* (Baltimore: Johns Hopkins University Press, 1990), 28.

6. NAM, "NAM Historical Highlights," http://www.nam.org/s_nam/doc1.asp?CID=22&DID=201891 (accessed on June 14, 2006).

7. Heale, *American Anticommunism*, 44.

8. "Labor in the South," editorial, *New York Times*, August 10, 1930, E1; also cited in John E. Edgerton, "A Labor Policy for the South," pamphlet, reprinted from *American Industries*, NAM 31:1 (August 1930).

9. Edgerton, "Labor Policy," from a speech before the Institute of Public Affairs of the University of Virginia at Charlottesville (August 5, 1930); quotation from p. 6.

10. NAM, "NAM Historical Highlights."

11. Gilbert J. Gall, *The Politics of Right to Work: The Labor Federations as Special Interests, 1943–1979*, Contributions in Labor Studies 24 (New York: Greenwood, 1988), 73.

12. Heale, *American Anticommunism*, 117.

13. NAM, "NAM Historical Highlights."

14. Ibid.; U.S. Chamber of Commerce, "The U.S. Chamber's History," http://www.uschamber.com/about/history/default (accessed on June 14, 2006).

15. Heale, *American Anticommunism*, 139.

16. William H. Wynn, John J. Sweeney, Robert A Georgine, and John J. Barry, *A Report on the Board of Directors of the National Right to Work Committee* (Washington, D.C.: Ad Hoc Committee on Restrictive Legislation: AFL-CIO Executive Council, August 1988), 18, n. 115, citing *New York Times*, December 20, 1933, 8.

17. USBIC, "USBIC Educational Foundation," http://www.usbusiness.org/i4a/pages/index.cfm?pageid=13 (accessed on June 14, 2006).

18. Heale, *American Anticommunism*, 28.

19. Ibid.

20. Friedrich A. Hayek (ed.), *Collectivist Economic Planning: Critical Studies on the Possibilities of Socialism* (includes Ludwig von Mises as contributor) (London: Routledge, 1935); Friedrich A. Hayek, *The Road to Serfdom* (Chicago: University of Chicago Press, 1944); John T. Flynn, *As We Go Marching* (Garden City, N.Y.: Doubleday, Doran, 1944); Ludwig von Mises, *Omnipotent Government: The Rise of the Total State and Total War* (New Haven, Conn.: Yale University Press, 1944); Ludwig von Mises, *Planned Chaos* (Irvington-on-Hudson, N.Y.: Foundation for Economic Education, 1947); Ludwig von Mises, *The Anti-Capitalistic Mentality* (Princeton, N.J.: Van Nostrand, 1956).

21. Hans F. Sennholz, "The Great Depression," *The Freeman* (April 1975): 212–213; quoted in Lawrence W. Reed, "Great Myths of the Great Depression: Phase IV: The Wagner Act," Mackinac Center for Public Policy, http://www.mackinac.org/article.asp?ID=4020 (accessed on June 14, 2006).

22. Gall, *Politics of Right to Work*, 14.

23. Ibid., 14–15.

24. Chip Berlet and Matthew N. Lyons, *Right-Wing Populism in America: Too Close for Comfort* (New York: Guilford, 2000), 165.

25. David Brion Davis (ed.), *The Fear of Conspiracy: Images of Un-American Subversion from the Revolution to the Present* (Ithaca, N.Y.: Cornell University Press, 1971); David H. Bennett, *The Party of Fear: The American Far Right from Nativism to the Militia Movement,* rev ed. (New York: Vintage, 1995 [1988]).

26. Heale, *American Anticommunism,* 28.

27. Leo P. Ribuffo, *The Old Christian Right: The Protestant Hard Right from the Great Depression to the Cold War* (Philadelphia: Temple University Press, 1983), 15.

28. Ibid.

29. Berlet and Lyons, *Right-Wing Populism in America,* 163. See also Ellen Schrecker, *The Age of McCarthyism: A Brief History with Documents* (Boston: Bedford/St. Martin's, 1994).

30. Matthew N. Lyons, "Business Conflict and Right-Wing Movements," in Amy E. Ansell (ed.), *Unraveling the Right: The New Conservatism in American Thought and Politics* (Boulder, Colo.: Westview, 1998), 80–102. On Buchanan, see Berlet and Lyons, *Right-Wing Populism in America,* 279–281.

31. Ribuffo, *Old Christian Right,* 128–177; Glen Jeansonne, *Gerald L. K. Smith: Minister of Hate* (New Haven, Conn.: Yale University Press, 1988), 64–79.

32. Berlet and Lyons, *Right-Wing Populism in America,* 163. See also Jeansonne, *Gerald L. K. Smith,* 65; Ribuffo, *Old Christian Right,* 147.

33. Berlet and Lyons, *Right-Wing Populism in America,* 163. See also George Seldes, *1000 Americans: The Real Rulers of the U.S.A.* (New York: Boni and Gaer, 1947), 38–56.

34. Seldes, *1000 Americans,* 297.

35. Ribuffo, *Old Christian Right.*

36. Paul Boyer, *When Time Shall Be No More: Prophecy Belief in Modern American Culture* (Cambridge, Mass.: Belknap/Harvard University Press, 1992); Robert Fuller, *Naming the Antichrist: The History of an American Obsession* (New York: Oxford University Press, 1995).

37. Fuller, *Naming the Antichrist.*

38. Frank J. Donner, *The Age of Surveillance: The Aims and Methods of America's Political Intelligence System* (New York: Knopf, 1980), 47–48.

39. Ribuffo, *Old Christian Right,* 2–24, 58–72, 83–116, 175–177.

40. Ibid., 110.

41. Ibid., 113. See also 59–60, 72–74.

42. Ibid., 16–17, 167, 196–197, 211; Bennett, *Party of Fear,* 269.

43. Elizabeth Dilling, *The Red Network: A "Who's Who" and Handbook of Radicalism for Patriots* (Chicago: self-published, 1934); Elizabeth Dilling, *The Roosevelt Red Record and Its Background* (Chicago: self-published, 1936).

44. Heale, *American Anticommunism,* 139.

45. Bennett, *Party of Fear,* 287–288; Heale, *American Anticommunism,* 139.

46. David M. Oshinsky, *Senator Joseph McCarthy and the American Labor Movement* (Columbia: University of Missouri Press, 1976), 52.

47. Ibid., 54.

48. Sara Diamond, *Roads to Dominion: Right-Wing Movements and Political Power in the United States* (New York: Guilford, 1998), 52, citing in n. 78, Alan F. Westin, "Anti-Communism and the Corporations," *Commentary* (December 1963): 479–487.

49. Heale, *American Anticommunism,* 136. See also Bennett, *Party of Fear,* 287.

50. Victor S. Navasky, *Naming Names* (New York: Viking, 1980); Ellen Schrecker, *Many Are the Crimes: McCarthyism in America* (Boston: Little, Brown, 1998).

51. Heale, *American Anticommunism,* 138–140.

52. Abby Scher, "Cold War on the Home Front: Middle-Class Women's Politics in the 1950s," Ph.D. diss., New School for Social Research, 1995.

53. Donner, *Age of Surveillance,* 422–424.

54. Ibid.

55. Diamond, *Roads to Dominion,* 102.

56. Russ Bellant, *Old Nazis, the New Right, and the Reagan Administration: The Role of Domestic Fascist Networks in the Republican Party and Their Effect on U.S. Cold War Policies* (Boston: South End Press/PRA, 1991), 33–38. Christopher Simpson, *Blowback: America's Recruitment of Nazis and Its Effects on the Cold War* (New York: Macmillan/Collier, 1988), 219.

57. Jerome L. Himmelstein, *To the Right: The Transformation of American Conservatism* (Berkeley: University of California Press, 1990), 43–44.

58. Ibid., 14.

59. Ibid. Himmelstein's discussion of how the three strands were woven into a conservative movement is illuminating, 43–60.

60. Ibid., 46.

61. Ibid. Himmelstein cites their key works in n. 26 on p. 220.

62. Ibid., 49.

63. Gall, *Politics of Right to Work,* 72.

64. Marc Dixon, "The Politics of Union Decline: Business Political Mobilization and Restrictive Labor Legislation, 1938 to 1958," paper presented at the annual meeting of the Social Science History Association, Baltimore, Maryland, 2003.

65. George Lakoff, *Moral Politics: How Liberals and Conservatives Think,* 2nd ed. (Chicago: University of Chicago Press, 2002 [1996]). On framing, see Erving Goffman, *Frame Analysis: An Essay on the Organization of Experience* (Cambridge, Mass.: Harvard University Press, 1974).

66. On the John Birch Society, see Berlet and Lyons, *Right-Wing Populism in America,* 177–185. On the Liberty Lobby, see Frank P. Mintz, *The Liberty Lobby and the American Right: Race, Conspiracy, and Culture* (Westport, Conn.: Greenwood,

1985); Berlet and Lyons, *Right-Wing Populism in America*, 185–192. On the legacy of militant anticommunism, see Berlet and Lyons, *Right-Wing Populism in America in America*, chaps. 9 and 10, esp. 201–202; Chip Berlet and Margaret Quigley, "Theocracy and White Supremacy: Behind the Culture War to Restore Traditional Values," in Chip Berlet (ed.), *Eyes Right! Challenging the Right-Wing Backlash* (Boston: South End Press, 1995), 15–43; Scher, "Cold War on the Home Front," 300–301.

67. Jonathan M. Schoenwald, *A Time for Choosing: The Rise of Modern American Conservatism* (New York: Oxford University Press, 2001), 258; citing to Rusher, "Crossroads for the GOP," *National Review*, February 12, 1963, 110.

68. Ibid.

69. Thomas Ferguson and Joel Rogers, "Labor Law Reform and Its Enemies: Anti-Union Alliance," *Nation*, January 6–13, 1979, 1, 17–20, quotation from 18.

70. Hardisty, *Mobilizing Resentment*; Berlet and Lyons, *Right-Wing Populism in America*; Michelle Goldberg, *Kingdom Coming: The Rise of Christian Nationalism* (New York: Norton, 2006).

71. Hardisty, *Mobilizing Resentment*, 74–79. Donald T. Critchlow, *Phyllis Schlafly and Grassroots Conservatism: A Woman's Crusade*, Politics and Society in Twentieth-Century America (Princeton, N.J.: Princeton University Press, 2005).

72. Lucy A. Williams, *Decades of Distortion: The Right's 30-Year Assault on Welfare* (Somerville, Mass.: Political Research Associates, 1997), available online at http://www.publiceye.org/welfare/Decades-of-Distortion.html (accessed on June 14, 2006).

73. Ibid.

74. Robert Mason, *Richard Nixon and the Quest for a New Majority* (Chapel Hill: University of North Carolina Press, 2004), 115–116, cited and discussed by William Rusher, "The Long Detour," review of Mason, *Richard Nixon*, in *Claremont Review of Books* (summer 2005), http://www.claremont.org/writings/crb/summer2005/rusher.html (accessed on June 14, 2006).

75. Berlet and Lyons, *Right-Wing Populism in America*; Diamond, *Roads to Dominion*; Hardisty, *Mobilizing Resentment*.

76. Michael Kazin, *The Populist Persuasion: An American History* (New York: Basic Books, 1995), 246; Dan T. Carter, *The Politics of Rage: George Wallace, the Origins of the New Conservatism, and the Transformation of American Politics* (New York: Simon and Schuster, 1995), 379. See also Dan T. Carter, *From George Wallace to Newt Gingrich: Race in the Conservative Counterrevolution, 1963–1994* (Baton Rouge: Louisiana State University Press, 1996).

77. Williams, *Decades of Distortion*.

78. William Rusher, *Making of a New Majority Party* (New York: Sheed and Ward, 1975), 14. See also Berlet and Lyons, *Right-Wing Populism in America*, esp. 6–13.

79. Alan Crawford, *Thunder on the Right: The "New Right" and the Politics of*

Resentment (New York: Pantheon, 1980); Hardisty, *Mobilizing Resentment*; Berlet and Lyons, *Right-Wing Populism in America*; Thomas Frank, *What's the Matter with Kansas? How Conservatives Won the Heart of America* (New York: Metropolitan Books, 2004).

80. Berlet and Lyons, *Right-Wing Populism in America,* 4–13. On apocalypticism, see Boyer, *When Time Shall Be No More*; Charles B. Strozier, *Apocalypse: On the Psychology of Fundamentalism in America* (Boston: Beacon, 1994); Stephen D. O'Leary, *Arguing the Apocalypse: A Theory of Millennial Rhetoric* (New York: Oxford University Press, 1994); Lee Quinby, *Anti-Apocalypse: Exercises in Genealogical Criticism* (Minneapolis: University of Minnesota Press, 1994); Fuller, *Naming the Antichrist*; Didi Herman, *The Antigay Agenda: Orthodox Vision and the Christian Right* (Chicago: University of Chicago Press, 1997); Berlet and Lyons, *Right-Wing Populism in America*; Carol Mason, *Killing for Life: The Apocalyptic Narrative of Pro-Life Politics* (Ithaca, N.Y.: Cornell University Press, 2002); Brenda E. Brasher and Chip Berlet, "Imagining Satan: Modern Christian Right Print Culture as an Apocalyptic Master Frame," paper presented at the Conference on Religion and the Culture of Print in America, Center for the History of Print Culture in Modern America, University of Wisconsin–Madison, September 10–11, 2004.

81. Doug McAdam and David A. Snow, "Introduction—Social Movements: Conceptual and Theoretical Issues," in Doug McAdam and David A. Snow (eds.), *Social Movements: Readings on Their Emergence, Mobilization, and Dynamics* (Los Angeles: Roxbury, 1997), xviii.

82. M. Stanton Evans, *The Liberal Establishment Who Runs America . . . and How* (New York: Devin-Adair, 1965).

83. Kevin P. Phillips, *The Emerging Republican Majority* (New Rochelle, N.Y.: Arlington House, 1969).

84. Carter, *Politics of Rage,* 380, citing Haldeman notes from Nixon presidential archives.

85. Diamond, *Roads to Dominion,* 116.

86. Lewis F. Powell Jr., "Attack on American Free Enterprise System," available online at http://www.mediatransparency.org/story.php?storyID=22 (accessed June 14, 2006). An early report mentioning the importance of the memo appeared in 1993 in Alliance for Justice, *Justice for Sale: Shortchanging the Public Interest for Private Gain* (Washington, D.C.: Alliance for Justice, 1993), http://www.alliancefor justice.org/images/collection_images/Justiceforsale.pdf (accessed June 14, 2006).

87. Berlet and Lyons, *Right-Wing Populism in America*; Diamond, *Roads to Dominion*; Hardisty, *Mobilizing Resentment*; People for the American Way, *Building a Movement: Right-Wing Foundations and American Politics* (Washington, D.C.: People for the American Way, 1996); Sally Covington, *Moving a Public Policy Agenda: The Strategic Philanthropy of Conservative Foundations* (Washington, D.C.: National Committee for Responsive Philanthropy, July 1997).

On targeting of college campuses, see Ellen Messer-Davidow, "Manufacturing the Attack on Liberalized Higher Education," *Social Text* (fall 1993): 40–80; Ellen Messer-Davidow, "Who (Ac)Counts and How," *MMLA* (The Journal of the Midwest Modern Language Association) 27:1 (spring 1994): 26–41; Lawrence C. Soley, *Leasing the Ivory Tower: The Corporate Takeover of Academia* (Boston: South End Press, 1995).

88. Russ Bellant, *The Coors Connection: How Coors Family Philanthropy Undermines Democratic Pluralism* (Boston: South End Press/PRA, 1991).

89. Crawford, *Thunder on the Right*, 39–40; John S. Saloma III, *Ominous Politics: The New Conservative Labyrinth* (New York: Hill and Wang, 1984); 54–56; Jeffrey K. Hadden and Charles E. Swann, *Prime Time Preachers: The Rising Power of Televangelism* (Reading, Mass.: Addison-Wesley, 1981), 138, http://religiousbroadcasting.lib.virginia.edu/primetime/home.html (accessed June 14, 2006); Flo Conway and Jim Siegelman, *Holy Terror: The Fundamentalist War on America's Freedoms in Religion, Politics, and Our Private Lives* (New York: Delta, 1984), 88, 286.

90. Stephan Lesher, *George Wallace: American Populist* (Reading, Mass.: Addison-Wesley, 1994), 463–464; Richard Viguerie, *The New Right: We're Ready to Lead* (Falls Church, Va.: Viguerie Co., 1980), 26–27.

91. Himmelstein, *To the Right*, 80–94; Diamond, *Roads to Dominion*, 127–138; Kazin, *Populist Persuasion*, 255–260; William Martin, *With God on Our Side: The Rise of the Religious Right in America* (New York: Broadway Books, 1996), 88; Lesher, *George Wallace*, 463–464; Bellant, *Coors Connection*, 16, 44; Viguerie, *New Right*, 116.

92. Diamond, *Roads to Dominion*, 133.

93. Bellant, *Coors Connection*, 15–35; Berlet and Lyons, *Right-Wing Populism in America*, 228–242; Jeff Krehely, *Funding the Culture Wars: Philanthropy, Church and State* (Washington, D.C.: National Committee for Responsive Philanthropy, February 2005); Mark Schapiro, *Who's Behind the Culture Wars? Contemporary Assaults on Freedom of Expression*, report (New York: Nathan Cummings Foundation, 1994). See also Free Congress Research and Education Foundation (FCF), *Cultural Conservatism: Toward a New National Agenda* (Washington, D.C.: Institute for Cultural Conservatism (FCF), 1987); William S. Lind and William H Marshner (eds.), *Cultural Conservatism: Theory and Practice* (Washington, D.C.: Free Congress Foundation, 1991).

94. Clarence Y. H. Lo, *Small Property versus Big Government: Social Origins of the Property Tax Revolt* (Berkeley: University of California Press, 1995); Howard Jarvis with Robert Pack, *I'm Mad as Hell: The Exclusive Story of the Tax Revolt and Its Leader* (New York: Times Books/Quadrangle, 1979).

95. Bernard Chapin, "Grover's Charge: An Interview with Grover Norquist," Enter Stage Right Web site (September 1, 2003), http://www.enterstageright.com/archive/articles/0903/0903norquistinterview.htm (accessed June 14, 2006).

96. Sheldon D. Engelmayer and Robert J. Wagman, *Tax Revolt 1980: A How-To*

Guide (Westport, Conn.: Arlington House, 1980), originally published under the title *The Taxpayer's Guide to Effective Tax Revolt* (New York: Dale Books, 1978). See also Alan Brinkley, "Reagan's Revenge: As Invented by Howard Jarvis," *New York Times Magazine,* June 19, 1994, 36–37.

97. Judis, *Paradox of American Democracy,* 149.

98. Alliance for Justice, *Justice for Sale,* 1, citing Jill Abramson, "Right Place at the Right Time," *American Lawyer* (June 1986): 100.

99. Hadden and Swann, *Prime Time Preachers,* 135.

100. Saloma, *Ominous Politics,* 53–54.

101. Ibid., 54.

102. Ibid.

103. DeMoss, quoted in Saloma, *Ominous Politics,* 54.

104. Hadden and Swann, *Prime Time Preachers,* 135.

105. Sara Diamond, *Spiritual Warfare: The Politics of the Christian Right* (Boston: South End Press, 1989), 60.

106. Hardisty, *Mobilizing Resentment,* 79–84. On conservative women generally, see Rebecca E. Klatch, *Women of the New Right* (Philadelphia: Temple University Press, 1987); Elinor Burkett, *The Right Women: A Journey through the Heart of Conservative America* (New York: Touchstone, 1998).

107. Saloma, *Ominous Politics,* 53–54.

108. Diamond, *Roads to Dominion,* 208–209, 233.

109. Hadden and Swann, *Prime Time Preachers,* 130, 135.

110. Berlet and Lyons, *Right-Wing Populism in America,* 212. See Francis A. Schaeffer and C. Everett Koop, *Whatever Happened to the Human Race* (Old Tappan, N.J.: Fleming H. Revell, 1979); Francis A. Schaeffer, *A Christian Manifesto* (Westchester, Ill.: Crossway Books, 1981).

111. C. Mason, *Killing for Life,* 114–118. See Ronald Reagan, *Abortion and the Conscience of the Nation* (Nashville, Tenn.: Thomas Nelson, 1984).

112. Frances FitzGerald, "The American Millennium," *New Yorker,* November 11, 1985, 105–196. See also Susan Harding, "Imagining the Last Days: The Politics of Apocalyptic Language," in Martin E. Marty and R. Scott Appleby (eds.), *Accounting for Fundamentalisms,* vol. 4, *The Fundamentalism Project,* 57–78 (Chicago: University of Chicago Press, 1994); Susan Friend Harding, *The Book of Jerry Falwell: Fundamentalist Language and Politics* (Princeton, N.J.: Princeton University Press, 2000).

113. Charles L. Heatherly (ed.), *Mandate for Leadership: Policy Management in a Conservative Administration* (Washington, D.C.: Heritage Foundation, 1981).

114. Saloma, *Ominous Politics.* Saloma had been the head of the Ripon Society, a national group of moderate Republicans.

115. Lyons, "Business Conflict and Right-Wing Movements," 91.

116. David D. Kirkpatrick, "Club of the Most Powerful Gathers in Strictest Privacy," *New York Times,* August 28, 2004, 10, online archive.

117. Russ Bellant, "The Council for National Policy: Stealth Leadership of the Radical Right," *Front Lines Research* (Planned Parenthood) 1:2 (August 1994), online archive.

118. Bellant, *The Coors Connection,* 26–27.

119. Jeremy Leaming and Rob Boston, "Behind Closed Doors: Who Is the Council for National Policy and What Are They Up To? And Why Don't They Want You to Know?" *Church and State* (Americans United for Separation of Church and State) (October 2004), http://www.au.org/site/News2?page=NewsArticle&id=6949 &abbr=cs_ (accessed June 14, 2006).

120. Bellant, "Council for National Policy."

121. Skipp Porteous, "Clandestine Council Meets in Virginia," *Freedom Writer* (June 1995), online archive.

122. Kirkpatrick, "Club of the Most Powerful."

123. Mark Gerson, *The Neoconservative Vision: From the Cold War to the Culture Wars* (Lanham, Md.: Madison Books, 1997); Berlet and Lyons, *Right-Wing Populism in America,* 243–244.

124. Berlet and Lyons, *Right-Wing Populism in America,* 243.

125. Ibid.

126. Gary J. Dorrien, *The Neoconservative Mind: Politics, Culture, and the War of Ideology* (Philadelphia: Temple University Press, 1993).

127. For early writings, see Mark Gerson, *The Essential Neoconservative Reader* (Reading, Mass.: Addison-Wesley, 1996).

128. Jim Mann, *Rise of the Vulcans: The History of Bush's War Cabinet* (New York: Viking, 2004); Tom Barry and Jim Lobe, "U.S. Foreign Policy: Attention, Right Face, Forward March," *Policy Report* (Foreign Policy in Focus) (April 2002), online archive; Khurram Husain, "Neocons: The Men behind the Curtain," *Bulletin of the Atomic Scientists* 59:6 (2003), http://www.thebulletin.org/issues/2003/nd03/nd03husain.html (accessed June 14, 2006).

129. Stefan A. Halper and Jonathan Clarke, *America Alone: The Neo-Conservatives and the Global Order* (Cambridge: Cambridge University Press, 2004), 14, 103–105, 198, 205–206.

130. Robert Scheer, *With Enough Shovels: Reagan, Bush, and Nuclear War* (New York: Random House, 1982); Bellant, *Old Nazis, the New Right, and the Reagan Administration,* 29–88; Bellant, *Coors Connection,* 47–49. Much writing on PNAC is awash with conspiracism and sometimes anti-Semitic motifs, memes, and tropes (especially material from the LaRouche network). An excellent resource that avoids these problems is "Project for the New American Century," Right Web Profiles (Silver City, N.M.: International Relations Center, June 2006), http://rightweb.irc-online.org/profile/1535 (accessed June 14, 2006).

131. Joshua Muravchik, "The Neoconservative Cabal," *Commentary* (September 2003), online archive. Materials circulated by the LaRouche Network, for example,

employ a coded form of anti-Semitic conspiracism to criticize neoconservatives. See, for example, LaRouche in 2004, *Children of Satan: The "Ignoble Liars" behind Bush's No-Exit War,* http://larouchein2004.net/pdfs/pamphletcos.pdf; *Children of Satan II: The Beast-Men,* http://larouchein2004.net/pdfs/pamphleto4o1cos2.pdf; *Children of Satan III: The Sexual Congress for Cultural Fascism,* http://larouchein 2004.net/pdfs/040614beast3.pdf; all published in Leesburg, Virginia, by the author (all accessed February 17, 2006).

132. Anne Norton, *Leo Strauss and the Politics of American Empire* (New Haven, Conn.: Yale University Press, 2004); Shadia B. Drury, *Leo Strauss and the American Right* (New York: St. Martin's, 1997).

133. Himmelstein, *To the Right,* 49.

134. Halper and Clarke, *America Alone,* 11.

135. Michael Northcott, *An Angel Directs the Storm: Apocalyptic Religion and American Empire* (London: I. B. Tauris, 2004); Robert J. Lifton, *Superpower Syndrome: America's Apocalyptic Confrontation with the World* (New York: Thunder's Mouth Books/Nation Books, 2003); Matthew Rothschild, "Bush's Messiah Complex," *Progressive* (February 2003), http://progressive.org/node/1344 (accessed March 15, 2006); Anatole Lieven, "Bush's Choice: Messianism or Pragmatism?" Open Democracy Web site, February 22, 2005, http://www.opendemocracy.net/articles/ViewPopUpArticle.jsp?id=3&articleId=2348 (accessed March 15, 2006); Hugh Urban, "Bush, the Neocons, and Evangelical Christian Fiction: America, 'Left Behind,'" *Journal of Religion and Society* 8 (2006), http://moses.creighton.edu/JRS/2006/2006-2.html (accessed March 15, 2006).

136. Halper and Clarke, *America Alone,* 11.

137. Sara Diamond emphasizes the importance of tactical and strategic projects on the political Right, in part because they allow for different levels of participation, nonparticipation, or even opposition without fracturing the broader coalition.

138. Rick Henderson and Steven Hayward, "Happy Warrior," interview, *Reason* magazine (February 1997), http://reason.com/9702/fe.int.norquist.shtml (accessed June 14, 2006).

139. People for the American Way, "National Taxpayers Union," profile, Right Wing Watch, http://www.pfaw.org/pfaw/general/default.aspx?oid=10235 (accessed June 14, 2006).

140. Diamond, *Roads to Dominion,* 249–250.

141. Berlet and Lyons, *Right-Wing Populism in America,* 323–338.

142. Diamond, *Roads to Dominion,* 246–249; Sara Diamond, "Dominion Theology," *Z Magazine* (February 1995), http://zena.secureforum.com/Znet/ZMag/articles/feb95diamond.htm (accessed June 14, 2006); Berlet and Lyons, *Right-Wing Populism in America,* 247–264; Goldberg, *Kingdom Coming.*

143. Bruce Barron, *Heaven on Earth? The Social and Political Agendas of*

Dominion Theology (Grand Rapids, Mich.: Zondervon, 1992); Diamond, *Roads to Dominion*, 246–249; Frederick Clarkson, *Eternal Hostility: The Struggle between Theocracy and Democracy* (Monroe, Maine: Common Courage, 1997).

144. Esther Kaplan, *With God On Their Side: How Christian Fundamentalists Trampled Science, Policy, and Democracy in George W. Bush's White House* (New York: New Press, 2004); Chris Mooney, *The Republican War on Science* (New York: Basic Books, 2005); Kevin Phillips, *American Theocracy: The Peril and Politics of Radical Religion, Oil, and Borrowed Money in the 21st Century* (New York: Viking, 2006).

145. Paul Boyer, "John Darby Meets Saddam Hussein: Foreign Policy and Bible Prophecy," *Chronicle of Higher Education,* supplement, February 14, 2003, B10–B11; William Martin, "The Christian Right and American Foreign Policy," *Foreign Policy* 114 (spring 1999): 66–80.

146. Duane Oldfield, "The Evangelical Roots of American Unilateralism: The Christian Right's Influence and How to Counter It," Foreign Policy in Focus (March 2004), http://www.fpif.org/papers/2004evangelical.html (accessed February 11, 2006); see also D. Wagner, "Evangelicals and Israel: Theological Roots of a Political Alliance," *Christian Century,* November 4, 1998, archived at http://www.publiceye.org/christian_right/zionism/wagner-cc.html (accessed February 17, 2006). See also Chip Berlet and Nikhil Aziz, "Culture, Religion, Apocalypse, and Middle East Foreign Policy," IRC Right Web (Silver City, N.M.: Interhemispheric Resource Center, 2003), http://rightweb.irc-online.org/analysis/2003/0312apocalypse.php (accessed February 11, 2006); Chip Berlet, "U.S. Christian Evangelicals Raise the Stakes (The Threats to Haram al Sharif/Temple Mount)," *BitterLemons* 2:34 (2004), http://www.bitterlemons-international.org/inside.php?id=226 (accessed February 11, 2006).

147. Tim LaHaye and Jerry B. Jenkins, *Left Behind: A Novel of the Earth's Last Days,* Left Behind Series, vol. 1 (Wheaton, Ill.: Tyndale House, 1995), through vol. 12, *Glorious Appearing: The End of Days* (2004). Visit the Web site at http://www.leftbehind.com (accessed February 17, 2006).

148. Gershom Gorenberg, "Intolerance: The Bestseller," book review of Left Behind series by LaHaye and Jenkins, *American Prospect,* September 23, 2002, http://www.prospect.org/print/V13/17/gorenberg-g.html (accessed February 17, 2006). See also Brasher and Berlet, "Imagining Satan."

149. Chip Berlet, "Religion and Politics in the United States: Nuances You Should Know," *Public Eye* (Political Research Associates) 17:2 (summer 2003): 13–16, adapted online, http://www.publiceye.org/magazine/v17n2/evangelical-demographics.html (accessed June 14, 2006).

150. In addition to the works cited in other notes, the following books offer important insights: Amy Elizabeth Ansell (ed.), *Unraveling the Right: The New Conservatism in American Thought and Politics* (Boulder, Colo.: Westview, 1998);

Daniel J. Balz and Ronald Brownstein, *Storming the Gates: Protest Politics and the Republican Revival* (Boston: Little, Brown, 1996); Earl Black and Merle Black, *The Rise of Southern Republicans* (Cambridge, Mass.: Belknap/Harvard University Press, 2002); Mary C. Brennan, *Turning Right in the Sixties: The Conservative Capture of the GOP* (Chapel Hill: University of North Carolina Press, 1995); Nina J. Easton, *Gang of Five: Leaders at the Center of the Conservative Crusade* (New York: Simon and Schuster, 2000); Susan Faludi, *Backlash: The Undeclared War against American Women* (New York: Doubleday, 1992); Thomas Ferguson and Joel Rogers, *Right Turn: The Decline of the Democrats and the Future of American Politics* (New York: Hill and Wang, 1986); Godfrey Hodgson, *The World Turned Right Side Up: A History of the Conservative Ascendancy in America* (Boston: Houghton Mifflin, 1996); Clarence Y. H. Lo and Michael Schwartz (eds.), *Social Policy and the Conservative Agenda* (Malden, Mass.: Blackwell, 1998); Lisa McGirr, *Suburban Warriors: The Origins of the New American Right* (Princeton, N.J.: Princeton University Press, 2001); John Micklethwait and Adrian Woodridge, *The Right Nation: Conservative Power in America* (New York: Penguin, 2004).

151. On the influence of think tanks, see Jean Stefancic and Richard Delgado, *No Mercy: How Conservative Think Tanks and Foundations Changed America's Social Agenda* (Philadelphia: Temple University Press, 1996); Philip H. Burch Jr., *Reagan, Bush, and Right-Wing Politics: Elites, Think Tanks, Power, and Policy,* Part A, *The American Right Wing Takes Command: Key Executive Appointments,* and Part B, *The American Right Wing at Court and in Action: Supreme Court Nominations and Major Policymaking,* supplement 1 in two volumes, Paul Zarembka (ed.), Research in Political Economy 16 (Greenwich, Conn.: JAI, 1997).

On strategic funding by right-wing foundations, see People for the American Way, *Building a Movement;* Covington, *Moving a Public Policy Agenda;* David Callahan, *$1 Billion for Ideas: Conservative Think Tanks in the 1990s* (Washington, D.C.: National Committee for Responsive Philanthropy, March 1999); Jeff Krehely, Meaghan House, and Emily Kernan, *Axis of Ideology: Conservative Foundations and Public Policy* (Washington, D.C.: National Committee for Responsive Philanthropy, March 2004).

152. Hardisty, *Mobilizing Resentment,* 9–36.

153. This assertion stands despite the hyperbolic statements of Democratic Party loyalists including Hillary Clinton, who made the phrase famous.

154. Pam Chamberlain, *Deliberate Differences: Progressive and Conservative Campus Activism* (Somerville, Mass.: Political Research Associates, 2004).

155. Claude A. Putnam, foreword to Harley L. Lutz, *Bring Government Back Home!* (New York: National Association of Manufacturers, 1950), iv.

156. Norquist's "crush" quotation from Henderson and Hayward, "Happy Warrior"; Norquist's "bathtub" quotation from Ed Kilgore, "Starving the Beast: If President Bush Keeps Listening to Grover Norquist, Republicans Won't Have a

Government to Kick Around Anymore," *Blueprint Magazine* (Democratic Leadership Council [DLC]), June 30, 2003, http://www.ndol.org/ndol_ci.cfm?kaid=127& subid=170&contentid=251788 (accessed June 16, 2006).

157. Kilgore, "Starving the Beast."

158. Colin Greer, "The Politics of Calm," Open Democracy, June 6, 2006, http://www.opendemocracy.net/democracy-americanpower/politics_calm_3617 .jsp (accessed June 16, 2006).

Part II

The New Conservatism at Home

Chapter 5

From Neoconservative to New Right
American Conservatives and the Welfare State

Charles Noble

When the neoconservative movement first emerged on the American political scene at the end of the 1960s, its leading lights did not oppose the welfare state in principle. To fellow conservatives who were succumbing to that heady brew of free-market ideology and antitax zeal that would so excite the New Right, neoconservatives counseled caution. Just as likely to be (or have been) Democrats as Republicans, neoconservatives believed that it was necessary, even proper, for government to aid the most vulnerable, not just the elderly but also women and children and even the poor. It was also good politics: as Irving Kristol, one of the movement's founding figures, would later advise other conservatives, "the welfare state is with us, for better or worse."[1] Efforts to eliminate it were quixotic and could lead to "political impotence and a bankrupt social policy."[2]

Not that neoconservatives were soft on reform or eager to see the state mount a wholesale attack on the profits and prerogatives of corporate capital. But they were critics, not reactionaries; they worried most about the inefficiencies and overreach of social policy, not the very idea of state intervention into the market. According to Nathan Glazer, another founding neoconservative and a self-described former liberal, he and his colleagues in government had been far too optimistic in the early and mid-1960s about the possibilities, and too inattentive to the "unintended consequences," of liberal reform. They had failed to see that government action almost always led to unanticipated costs that often exceeded the benefits.

But even as neoconservatives challenged the hubris of the Great Society, they accepted, even celebrated, the political accommodation between capital and labor forged in the New Deal. Those policies, especially old-age pensions but also the Medicare program adopted in 1965 to flesh out the social insurance system, should and would remain the foundation of American public policy. And that became the "responsible" conservative position on the welfare state in the early 1970s. Even Richard Nixon endorsed it. As Roy Ash, Nixon's budget director, put it, Americans wanted benefits that only "the mechanisms of government" could provide. "Voluntarism," he advised corporate America, "no matter how virtuous, will not do the job."[3]

Today, each of these assumptions has been roundly rejected by the political Right. Nearly all card-carrying conservatives believe that with regard to human needs, the market nearly always knows best. In a little more than two decades—between the early 1970s and the mid-1990s—the original neoconservative effort to reform activist government by paying closer attention to its unintended consequences was replaced by a far more extreme denunciation of the very idea of a progressive social policy. Neoconservatives like Kristol and Glazer gave way to New Right champions like conservative activist Grover Norquist, whose goal—to get government down to a size such that he could "drag it into the bathroom and drown it in the bathtub"—became the right-wing mantra.[4] In 2005, George W. Bush attempted to return responsibility for old-age security to the private sector. In proposing to expand health savings accounts in his 2006 State of the Union Address, he suggested a similar solution to the crisis in American health care. In the strict sense of the term, "neoconservatism" in domestic policy is now dead, replaced by a New Right movement that, as Thomas Frank has put it, "worships" markets.[5]

The Neoconservative Critique

Neoconservatives, however, did not only want a smaller, smarter, more efficient liberal state—they were not, in effect, proto-neoliberals. The neoconservative critique went deeper than that.

The neoconservative case against the welfare state rested on four interrelated assumptions and arguments. The first was a rather simple and irrefutable sociological observation: values and institutions matter. They knit society together and socialize individuals to important behavioral norms. Traditional institutions like marriage and work play important roles. Reformers who challenge the well-established values and institutions that society had crafted over centuries, if not millennia, are obligated to think hard about the impact of undoing these arrangements, and what might replace them.

According to Glazer, liberals had failed to acknowledge how important families, churches, ethnic groups, and neighborhoods had been in motivating and controlling individuals. The "core problem" was that liberal social policies weakened "the position of these traditional agents" and undermined these "traditional restraints."[6] According to Kristol, social policies that "rewarded" single women for having children were especially problematic. He drew a sharp distinction between aiding "married women with children who have been divorced, or widowed, or abandoned by their husbands" and "welfare mothers" who "permit themselves to get pregnant, and to bear a child." Kristol sought to revive this hoary Victorian distinction, maintaining that while impoverished, the former held middle-class values and acted in middle-class ways, whereas the latter flaunted these indispensable norms. Social policies that failed to distinguish between the two types of mothers guaranteed growing social dysfunction.[7]

Similarly, Great Society liberals had been inattentive to the importance of economic incentives, especially the work ethic. New Deal social policies had rewarded work: old-age pensions supported adults who had spent their lives working; wage and hour standards protected employees *at work* from predatory employers. These social policies honored and rewarded the "productive" working class. Other New Deal social policies provided assistance to people not expected to work: widowed mothers, the disabled, and children. But the New Deal had offered very little to able-bodied men who simply "chose" not to work. In contrast, in the name of ending poverty and promoting equality, the Great Society had blurred the distinction between the "deserving" and the "undeserving" poor. In offering help to everyone in need, liberals had undermined work incentives and allowed and encouraged too many people to drop out of the labor market.

Neoconservatives also believed that there are strict limits to what government can and should do about economic and social inequality. Even though there might be political imperatives and ethical justifications for state intervention to reduce inequality, government is not likely to solve it once and for all. To the contrary, only some kinds of inequality are even amenable to public policy. Moreover, because inequality is relative, even small differences in condition or opportunity can loom large, particularly once larger, even more egregious and obviously unfair, gaps are closed. Absent perfect equality—inherently unachievable—there will always be differences in income, wealth, and status to rankle those who have less of one or another. Worse, by attempting to address these inequalities, liberals had fed a rising tide of expectations that simply could not be satisfied. Even as the Great Society reduced inequality and increased opportunity, the poor grew angrier and more demanding, eventually rioting. According to Glazer, in this way, social policy had "created new and unmanageable demands," unintended consequences resulting from counterproductive policies.[8]

Finally, neoconservatives thought that liberals had misjudged the impact of grass-roots participation on government and society. Based on the experience of the civil rights and student movements, it had become axiomatic on the Left that it was always better to encourage participation. Workers should have more control over the workplace; neighborhoods should have more say over local economic development; poor people should have more control over the implementation and even the design of antipoverty programs. These measures would, it was believed, reduce alienation and increase social cohesion. The War on Poverty's Community Action Program built this assumption into federal policy. Neoconservatives strongly disagreed. Having witnessed campus revolts, inner-city riots, and the rise of the student, Black Power, and radical feminist movements, neoconservatives worried that demands for increased political participation would, like demands for greater equality, prove unquenchable; the political process could easily spin out of control. In combination, demands for greater participation and greater equality would put capitalism and democracy themselves at risk.

In the academy, the neoconservative complaint was backed by a number of interesting and provocative studies of policy failure. Journals such as the *Public Interest* and *Commentary* devoted considerable space to detailing the hidden and not-so-hidden "costs" of good intentions. Though liberals could and did respond to each of these complaints, what is most striking from today's perspective is just how reasonable were the neoconservatives' criticisms. Government intervention *does* have a variety of second-order effects that, depending on the circumstances, can be quite undesirable and even counterproductive. In a capitalist society, where individuals and organizations respond to market forces, incentives *are* an issue. State bureaucracies *can* be unresponsive. Bureaucrats *can* be hostile and indifferent. Markets *do* meet some needs well. Even the neoconservatives' more radical claims follow from two plausible, even if debatable, assumptions: that human nature is far more sinister than liberals believe and that collective action, particularly state action, is far less reliable.

Reagan and the New Right

It was left to the New Right to call government itself into question. Influenced by the free-market theories of Milton Friedman, Ludwig von Mises, and Friedrich Hayek, and inspired by Margaret Thatcher's success in Great Britain, a new generation of American conservatives targeted the interventionist state itself, or at least the social welfare and regulatory state that had been constructed by liberal reformers in the twentieth century. Deregulation, "supply-side" tax cuts, privatization of social services—these policies were carefully crafted simultaneously to take down liberal institutions while resonating with Americans who, in the aftermath of the Great Society and the economic crises of the 1970s, had grown suspicious of "big government." Ronald Reagan summed up this ground shift in conservative thought in his first inaugural address: "In this present crisis, government is not the solution to our problem; government is the problem."[9]

The New Right did share several of the neoconservatives' concerns, especially the disincentives in liberal social policy to work and to form stable families. But New Right theorists were far more apocalyptic about the impact of liberal policies on American families and far less sympathetic to the very idea that government should take responsibility for assuring economic security. Whereas neoconservatives worried about the unintended effects of liberal social policies, the New Right was certain that liberalism was responsible for almost everything wrong with America.

Published in the same year as Reagan took office, George Gilder's *Wealth and Poverty* epitomized the New Right's dual preoccupations: the decline of the American family and the liberal assault on the free market.[10] According to Gilder, America would thrive only as long as it respected patriarchy and market capitalism. These were laws of nature. Capitalism worked by rewarding success with great wealth and punishing indolence with poverty. Policies that contradicted this incentive system were not only doomed to failure; they would inevitably undermine the economy and the social structure and hurt the supposed beneficiaries.

Gilder was convinced that America was already in decline. Aid to Families with Dependent Children (AFDC) had led families to dissolve. Disability insurance had led workers to shirk employment. Public jobs were little more than make-work. Worse, the taxes needed to pay for these programs fell most heavily on the "productive" members of society (they were the only ones with the ability to pay for them), reducing *their* incentives to work, save, and invest. The end was near.

Only a restoration of market values, traditional family structures, and religious observance could save America from further decline. With regard to welfare itself, Gilder argued that "the crucial goal should be to restrict the system as much as possible, by making it unattractive and even a bit demeaning."[11] Channeling the spirit of the Poor Laws enacted in mid-nineteenth-century Britain, Gilder claimed that "the poor need most of all the spur of their poverty."[12] To ensure that incentive meant "gradually lowering the real worth of benefits" until even the lowest paid work is preferable to welfare.[13]

Although a popular read in the Reagan White House, Gilder's messianic call to family, faith, and capitalism was relatively easy to dismiss. Charles Murray's provocative attack on the welfare state, published in 1984, proved a more formidable challenge to the liberal policy establishment.[14]

Murray was no less radical than Gilder. Rather than reform and reorient social policy, as neoconservatives wanted, Murray proposed "scrapping the entire federal welfare and income-support structure for working-aged persons, including AFDC, Medicaid, Food Stamps, Unemployment Insurance, Worker's Compensation, subsidized housing, disability insurance, and the rest."[15] This was far more than an attack on the Great Society. In targeting unemployment and disability insurance, Murray set his sights on the New Deal itself. And in taking on unemployment insurance, he in fact reached back even further, challenging one of the most important legacies of the Progressive era. Murray's solution to the welfare "crisis" was simple. Government aid would be available only to the very young and the very old. Social Security and direct aid to children would be left intact. But working-age individuals would have "no recourse whatsoever except the job market, family members, friends and public or private locally funded services."[16]

Though Murray's thesis—that the Great Society had actually increased poverty in America by encouraging the poor not to work—was roundly challenged,[17] the publication of *Losing Ground* was a watershed in the debate on the welfare state. Murray had succeeded in recasting what had been easily dismissed as an ideological fantasy into a social scientific critique. Whether or not other social policy experts bought Murray's argument—few apart from committed conservatives did—the New Right treated *Losing Ground* as gospel. They now had their proof that Reagan was right—government *was* the problem.

In practice, of course, Reagan was still not willing, or able, to propose razing the liberal state. Harboring both neoconservatives and New Rightists, and faced with considerable opposition in Congress after 1981 to the wholesale gutting of the social safety net, the Reagan administration moved more cautiously than fundamentalists like Murray and Gilder were advocating. Rather than deep, across-the-board cuts, Reagan proposed a combination of targeted program cuts and administrative reforms.

In fact, following the neoconservatives, Reagan distinguished between New Deal programs that benefited working Americans and Great Society programs that squandered taxpayer money on the shiftless—"welfare queens" in Reagan's political iconography. But the New Right did not come up entirely empty-handed. As Murray wanted, Reagan tried to cut assistance programs that helped the able-bodied, including cash and in-kind assistance to the working poor, and eliminate the work incentives that liberals had included in AFDC to allow welfare clients to combine work and public aid. And although Reagan did not suggest eliminating Social Security or Medicare, he did propose cutting federal spending on those programs.

Still, despite the New Right's subsequent idolization of Ronald Reagan as a founding father, the Reagan years turned out to be deeply disappointing to conservative activists who had wanted to see more done to bring down big government.[18] All the principal income-maintenance and health-security programs that conservatives railed against remained intact. In the end, the Reagan administration eliminated only two major programs: general revenue sharing and public service employment. Means-tested programs that helped the needy did suffer disproportionately, but even in these cases, instead of the deep program cuts that they had wanted, the radical Right had to settle for slowing the increase in the rate of spending. Moreover, most of the damage was done in Reagan's first year, and all the proposed cutbacks were found in the first two Reagan budgets. By 1983, the idea of making further major reductions to antipoverty programs was off the table.

Even worse, because they were so shallow, the Reagan cuts proved easy to undo. When the Republicans lost control of Congress in 1986, the Democrats set out to restore eligibility and benefits in many of the hardest hit income-transfer programs. Eligibility for AFDC and Medicaid was liberalized, and aid recipients were once again allowed to combine work and welfare. At least in social policy, it appeared that the Reagan Revolution, only just begun, had already run out of steam. In fact, Reagan's vice president and successor, George H. W. Bush, showed little enthusiasm for contentious debates over social policy, and the issue all but dropped off the national agenda during his term.

But the New Right had not forgotten. Disappointed by Reagan's spinelessness and enraged by Bush's decision in 1990 to strike a budget deal with the Democrats—reneging on his "no new taxes" pledge—House Republicans, led by Minority Leader Newt Gingrich, abandoned the first Bush and set out to push their own New Right agenda.[19]

The Conservative Opportunity Society

Seeking to make political capital out of Congress's failure to reform public assistance in the Reagan and Bush years, the New Right intensified its attack on the very idea of public provision in the 1990s. Echoing Gilder and Murray, the 1994 Contract with America targeted the welfare state, and House Republicans proposed a welfare reform bill based on the Contract's "Personal Responsibility Act." Pledging to "discourage illegitimacy and teen pregnancy," the Contract promised to prohibit all welfare aid to minor mothers and to deny AFDC benefits to any child born to a mother already on welfare. The Contract also called for sharp cuts in social spending for all welfare programs, as well as a tough, nonnegotiable two-year limit on welfare eligibility.[20]

To Gingrich, the Contract's principal architect and the New Right's leader in Congress, welfare reform was one part of a larger effort to refashion the welfare state into an "Opportunity Society." Gingrich had been working to refashion traditional conservatism since the early 1980s, when he had formed the Conservative Opportunity Society. Gingrich's eventual goal was the repeal of the New Deal itself, in part to end programs that he thought inadvisable and in part to eliminate the institutions that helped sustain political support for liberals and Democrats.[21]

In *To Renew America*, his 1995 call to arms, Gingrich repeated now-familiar neoconservative themes. The welfare state, he argued, "reduces the poor from citizens to clients. It breaks up families, minimizes work incentives, blocks people from saving and acquiring property."[22] America needed, he maintained, to clearly distinguish between the "deserving" and the "undeserving" poor, crafting policies to reward the first while punishing the second.

But the New Right radical was also apparent in *To Renew America*. Citing the work of Marvin Olasky, a University of Texas journalism professor who had become the darling of the New Right for advocating greater reliance on religious institutions in public life, Gingrich wanted to shift responsibility for caretaking to charitable, including religious, institutions. Even more extreme, Gingrich urged those institutions to deny benefits to poor people whose conduct they found unacceptable. In this way, not only would an important welfare-state function be privatized, it would be sanctified.[23]

Privatization was in fact Gingrich's preferred solution to almost every problem. Private "enterprise zones" would replace government-sponsored economic development programs. Public housing would be turned over to the tenants who could afford to buy it. Vouchers would be used to reform education and undermine the pubic school "monopoly."[24]

In 1996, the New Right finally won the struggle over welfare reform. Taking advantage of Bill Clinton's political weakness, and the Democratic Party's own divisions over social policy, Republicans passed and Clinton signed the Personal Responsibility and Work Opportunity Reconciliation Act. The changes were historic. AFDC was converted to a block grant, ending its entitlement status. A tough work requirement was imposed: the law required states to place at least 25 percent of cash-welfare recipients into jobs or work programs by 1997, and 50 percent by 2002. Adults who failed to find work within two years were to be denied all federal funds. No one could receive federal cash assistance for more than five years. States could deny welfare benefits to women who had additional children while on welfare and to unmarried persons under eighteen. Federal funds were denied to unmarried parents under eighteen who did not live with an adult and attend school. Legal immigrants' access to any form of public assistance was radically limited. In one fell swoop, the nation had given up its commitment to income maintenance as a "right."[25]

But even before reformers had time to assess the damage done to the welfare state, the New Right set another, even more ambitious target: old-age pensions and medical care. As this new generation of radical conservatives had warned from the beginning, their goal was not only the elimination of the Great Society's antipoverty programs, or even the reformation of the New Deal. They wanted to take government out of the business of public provision entirely. Soon, congressional Republicans and their allies in the business community and academia were warning that Social Security and Medicare could not be sustained. Both would have to be privatized. Individuals would have to take greater responsibility for their own pension and health security. Risk would not be shared in the conservative opportunity society.

By the nomination of George W. Bush in 2000, it had become clear that there was little room in the Republican Party for a view of the welfare state that made concessions to organized labor and embraced active government. For all of Bush's talk of "compassionate conservatism," it was clear to most observers that the party's core constituents, as well as its activists, were far closer to the radicalism of the New Right than to Glazer's and Kristol's more humane neoconservatism.

Explaining the New Right

By 2005, the New Right's radical rejection of the principle that government should help the working and middle classes had entirely supplanted neoconservatism as *the* reigning conservative idea. It had become so hegemonic on the Right that Bush used the State of the Union address to recommend that Americans give up their publicly guaranteed pensions in return for the right to bet on the stock market. How could an administration guided by Karl Rove (by all accounts the most savvy Republican strategist of his generation) imagine that the average American was ready to overthrow the most successful social program in seventy years?

Conservatives argue that the triumph of New Right ideas (and the inevitable triumph of New Right policies) reflects a large shift to the right in American public opinion. Americans, they believe, have finally come to their senses, recognizing the limits of government and the virtues of laissez faire.

But the evidence belies that claim. Certainly, if we equate liberalism with "big government" and conservatism with "limited government" and ask Americans whether government should be "big" or "small," most Americans are conservatives. But this is a very crude and misleading measure.

For one thing, although there are more "conservatives" than "liberals" (using self-identification as the measure, 32 percent versus 23 percent), 40 percent of self-identified conservatives say they are only "slightly" conservative.[26] But any sorting by ideological labels should be suspect. Americans are notoriously confused about the meaning of these political labels and the relationship between abstract political principles and specific policies. For example, taking support for government intervention on *issues* of concern as their measure, Erikson, MacKuen, and Stimson have found that there has been majority support for *programmatic* liberalism in the United States since 1960.[27] In other words, while Americans like the *idea* of free markets and support the *principle* of limited government, they strongly support public provision and welcome active government. A clear majority of Americans supports using government to address economic issues like joblessness, education, health care, and old-age pensions. In fact, large majorities want the government to spend money (even more than it does now if necessary) on things like education, Social Security, Medicare, and environmental protection.[28] New Right ideas may be hegemonic among conservatives and Republican Party activists, but in practice, most Americans turn out to be quite liberal, even if they reject the label. Perhaps most damning for the New Right, Americans are less conservative today than they were twenty years ago.[29]

Rather than trends in public opinion, other, more complicated political changes explain the triumph of the New Right's radical vision and the eclipse of the neoconservatives' more modest critique. Two changes altered the political environment itself. The first was the emergence of a radical brand of Protestant fundamentalism that proselytized not only for a particular brand of rebirth and redemption but also for market capitalism. The theological condemnation of liberal public policy and the demonization of the liberal state as secular and therefore sinful influenced the thinking of millions of Americans who might otherwise have looked to government for aid. In this way, religious revivalism helped the New Right appeal to downscale voters despite the fact that New Right politicians were advocating cutting many of the social and economic programs that helped those voters.

The New Right also benefited from a concerted corporate campaign to weaken the labor movement, deregulate industry, and roll back the share of the national income going to labor. Reacting to the gains made by labor unions and the new social movements in the 1960s and early 1970s, as well as the impact of heightened international competition on market shares and profit rates, corporate America went searching in the late 1970s for politicians who would carry their message about the threat of "big government."

Both of these changes helped create an electoral and financial base for the new generation of Sunbelt conservative activists who had been plotting to capture the commanding heights of the Republican Party since Barry Goldwater's failed presidential campaign in 1964. With little if any connection to the Washington establishment, and an almost inbred antipathy to the federal government, these right-wing shock troops finally succeeded in carrying their laissez-faire message into the heart of government itself in the 1980s.

Still, if all that mattered were the electoral connection, New Right activists might have failed. Given the gap between their personal ideological obsessions and majority opinion, the Republican Party's campaign strategists might have thought long and hard about embracing a brand of conservatism that flew in the face of the average voter's policy preferences.

But by the 1990s, Republican strategists such as Rove and Norquist had settled on an even more ambitious strategy: build a permanent Republican Party majority—in effect, a one-party state. To make this happen, Republicans had to do several things. First, they needed to weaken if not eliminate the organizations and institutions that routinely favored Democrats over Republicans. Most important, Republicans needed to accelerate the decline of organized labor as a political force. To this end, they sought to stack the National Labor Relations Board with antiunion members, to block every Democratic attempt to reform the National Labor Relations Act to make it more union-friendly, and to encourage corporate America in its efforts to resist further unionization.

To block Democratic Party efforts to raise corporate money (worried about the impact of organized labor's decline on the party's coffers, Democrats had turned to capital in the 1980s and 1990s), Republicans under Gingrich and House Majority Leader Tom DeLay of Texas initiated what came to be known as the "K Street" project. This meant making sure that the most important lobbying organizations in Washington chose Republicans rather than Democrats to represent them and that these organizations favored Republicans candidates and elected officials. In return, the Republicans promised and, as the 2006 scandal surrounding Jack Abramoff revealed, delivered very special favors: those corporations and industries that signed on were not only given special "access" to Republicans legislators; they were allowed to write legislation that directly affected them.

Finally, Republican hegemony required a direct attack on the welfare state itself. If successful, this assault would accomplish several things simultaneously: it would allow the Republicans to cut taxes on the well-to-do (a very important part of their coalition); it would eliminate public-sector jobs (weakening the public-sector unions that were the beating heart of the labor movement); and because social programs would radically shrink, it would convince Americans that they had no choice but to rely on themselves. Once Americans knew that, they would no longer see the point of paying taxes or voting for Democrats. In this way, Republican political dominance would be assured.

It was precisely this sort of Machiavellian thinking that animated Republican strategist William Kristol's (son of Irving Kristol) famous advice to the party to vote against Bill Clinton's health-care proposal "sight unseen."[30] Any new entitlement program, he argued, would further convince middle-class Americans that the welfare state and, by extension, the Democratic Party served their interests. Better to kill any health-care reform, however needed, so that Americans might be convinced to give up entirely on Democrats, liberalism, and the state.

Reform and Reaction

As American liberalism was peaking in the early 1970s, neoconservatives challenged the American Right to finally embrace the modern world—to accept the reality and necessity of active government even while remaining skeptical of it. Or, as Aaron Wildavsky, a neoconservative political scientist who made a career out of doubting liberalism, put it, conservatives should rein in the hubris of big government by "speaking truth to power."[31] But as American politics shifted sharply to the right, the political space that neoconservatives had hoped to occupy shrank and then, as America entered the twenty-first century, disappeared.

Sparked by a new generation of conservative activists who had come of age politically in the Barry Goldwater campaign and emboldened by their movement's electoral successes in a transformed and increasingly Republican South, the New Right took American conservatism in a more extreme direction: toward a rendezvous with the nineteenth century. In so doing, the New Right not only transformed American conservatism; it fundamentally changed American politics. Glazer and Kristol, however much revered by conservatives, looked increasingly like apologists for what Gingrich et al. dismissed as a doomed political regime.

The elder Kristol's warning that efforts to abolish the welfare state were both politically quixotic and bad policy proved only partly true. However bad these ideas were as *policy*, they served an important political purpose. Despite the large gap between what the New Right believed and what Americans wanted, the New Right's condemnation of the welfare state proved enormously successful among the political class. In the face of a hard-fought campaign by liberal social scientists to publicize the theoretical and evidentiary problems in the New Right's view of state and society, New Right ideas took root. Conservative think tanks like the Heritage Foundation, the Cato Institute, and the American Enterprise Institute pumped out one brief after another for the market and against government. Whatever the issue, from education to worker health and safety, conservatives touted market-based solutions as the only sensible, realistic, adult approach to hard choices. Steadily, the debate shifted rightward, until even advocating more government was seen as a sign of naiveté or worse.

Of course, the New Right cannot claim all the credit (or blame). Economic problems—"stagflation" in the 1970s, slow growth in the 1980s—made economics more important, and American economists proved themselves equally in love with markets. The corporate campaign to discredit the consumer, environmental, and health and safety regulations of the 1960s and 1970s also played a large part in changing the intellectual climate: Americans were inundated with probusiness propaganda consciously designed to challenge the social and political values that had inspired so many political activists in the 1960s.

But whatever the precise mix of factors, the effect is clear. An unusually —indeed a radically—conservative movement of political activists remade the social policy debate, changing the way that many in power, including a fair number of Democrats, thought about the state itself. The New Deal's attempt to limit the sway of too-often destructive market forces was now seen by many *in* government as what Margaret Thatcher condemned as a "nanny state"—an overly protective and intrusive obstacle to freedom rather than an indispensable public agent organized to accomplish necessary social goals. The New Right managed to redefine "progress" itself. Even as these New Right conservatives sought to limit the scope of American democracy so that it might better accommodate corporate power, limit grass-roots participation, and accustom Americans to working harder for less, they claimed the mantle of reform.

NOTES

1. Irving Kristol, "A Conservative Welfare State," in Irwin Stelzer, ed., *The Neocon Reader,* 143–148 (New York: Grove, 2004), 145.

2. Ibid.

3. Roy Ash, "Rhetoric vs. Reality: The Dilemma of Social Cost," *Conference Board Record* 8 (July 1971): 39.

4. Thom Hartmann, "Healthcare Reveals Real 'Conservative' Agenda—Drown Democracy in a Bathtub," Common Dreams News Center, February 25, 2003. The Norquist quotation is from an NPR *Morning Edition* interview with Mara Liasson on May 25, 2001, http://www.commondreams.org/views03/0225-10.htm.

5. Thomas Frank, *One Market under God* (New York: Doubleday, 2005).

6. Nathan Glazer, *The Limits of Social Policy* (Cambridge, MA: Harvard University Press, 1988), 3, 8, 13.

7. Kristol, "Conservative Welfare State," 147.

8. Glazer, *Limits of Social Policy,* 4–5.

9. President Ronald Reagan, "First Inaugural Address," January 20, 1981.

10. George Gilder, *Wealth and Poverty* (New York: Bantam, 1981).

11. Ibid., 143.

12. Ibid., 144.

13. Ibid., 148–149.

14. Charles Murray, *Losing Ground: American Social Policy, 1950–1980* (New York: Basic Books, 1984).

15. Ibid., 227–228.

16. Ibid., 228.

17. See David Ellwood, "Welfare and Work: A Symposium," *New Republic* (October 1986): 18–23; William Julius Wilson, *The Truly Disadvantaged: The Inner City, the Underclass, and Public Policy* (Chicago: University of Chicago Press, 1986); Sar A. Levitan, *Programs in Aid of the Poor* (Baltimore: Johns Hopkins University Press, 1990), 55; David Ellwood, *Poor Support* (New York: Basic Books, 1988), 57–65; Christopher Jencks, *Rethinking Social Policy* (Cambridge, MA: Harvard University Press, 1992); Christopher Jencks, "Is the American Underclass Growing?" in Christopher Jencks and Paul Peterson, eds., *The Urban Underclass* (Washington, DC: Brookings Institution Press, 1991).

18. Dan Balz and Ronald Brownstein, *Storming the Gates* (Boston: Little, Brown, 1996), 131.

19. Ibid., 135, 140.

20. http://www.house.gov/house/Contract/CONTRACT.html.

21. Elizabeth Drew, *Showdown: The Struggle between the Gingrich Congress and the Clinton White House* (New York: Simon and Schuster, 1996), 26.

22. Newt Gingrich, *To Renew America* (New York: HarperCollins, 1995), 76.

23. Ibid., 79–80.

24. Ibid., 86–90.

25. Charles Noble, *Welfare as We Knew It* (New York: Oxford University Press, 1997), 128.

26. The ANES Guide to Public Opinion and Electoral Behavior, http://www.umich.edu/~nes/nesguide/toptable/tab3_1.htm.

27. Robert S. Erikson, Michael B. MacKuen, and James A. Stimson, *The Macro Polity* (New York: Cambridge University Press, 2002), 193–205.

28. Ibid., 228–230.

29. Ibid., 193–205.

30. http://www.sourcewatch.org/index.php?title=Harry_and_Louise_ads_defeat_health_care_reform.

31. Aaron Wildavsky, *Speaking Truth to Power: The Art and Craft of Policy Analysis* (Boston: Little, Brown, 1979).

Chapter 6

Tearing Down the Wall
Conservative Use and Abuse of Religion in Politics

Diana M. Judd

> It is proper to take alarm at the first experiment on our liberties.
>
> —James Madison (1785)[1]

Politics is about power. Contemporary neoconservatives have, for the moment at least, considerable power over both public policy and political legislation. The 1994 congressional elections increased the Republican presence in the House of Representatives by 13 percent, resulting in a crucial 53 percent majority, while in the Senate, Republicans rose from a 43 percent minority to a 52 percent majority. With both victories came control over all congressional committees and possession of the most powerful position in Congress, the speakership of the House. Newt Gingrich ascended to this role, where he effectively controlled how, when, and what legislation was debated on the House floor. While the political platforms of the then newly ascendant Republicans centered more around fiscal responsibility and the end of big government than around moral or religious issues, it was the concomitant rise of the religious Right, exemplified by such powerful organizations as Pat Robertson's Christian Coalition, that soon changed the Republican focus. Apparent concern over America's decaying morality and the destruction of "family values" intensified among neoconservative Republicans in direct proportion to the increasing power of the religious Right. It was not long before previously marginalized religious fundamentalist concerns dominated the Republican agenda. Not all Republicans are neoconservatives, of course: the series of fractures within the Republican Party that began in 2004 and that grow sharper with each internal squabble between neoconservative, traditional, and fiscal Republicans are sufficient proof of this. But it is the dominant, neoconservative arm of the Republican Party that now takes its direction from the religious Right, to whom it seems completely beholden.

Despite the lip service neoconservatives pay to God, family values, tradition, and the sanctity of marriage, their primary concern is to hold on to and increase if possible their own status and the political power they have enjoyed since the 104th Congress convened in 1995. Their use and abuse of religion is wholly connected to achieving these ends, and it presents a clear and present danger to the fabric of the nation into which is woven the principles of classical liberalism, specifically the existence of unalienable rights, the rule of known law, and the justification of political authority. This essay is divided into three sections, each representing one prong of my overall argument: that the neoconservative tie to a previously marginal and marginalized religious Right counters the ideas and ideals of the framers of the U.S. Constitution, endangers faith and trust in political leadership, and, worst of all, damages America's self-image as a nation that values freedom, individual liberty, and the rule of law.

Countering the Ideas and Ideals of the Framers

Although the U.S. Constitution is a secular document,[2] it is true that the United States has never been a completely secular nation. As Daniel Bell noted accurately in 1955, "the enforcement of public morals has been a continuing feature of our history."[3] Religious sensibilities have influenced the direction of American culture and history since before the Revolutionary War. Now, however, we seem to have entered an era when Christian fundamentalist religious views are being promoted as both popular and standard, and when tearing down the "wall of separation" (to use Jefferson's metaphor) between church and state is passed off as fulfilling the general will. Of course, not all Christian views can be categorized as fundamentalist. By this admittedly incendiary term I mean various conservative sects of Christianity in the United States that hold the following to be true: the Bible contains the inspired word of the Judeo-Christian God and as such is both infallible and eternal; this text should thus be interpreted literally, including in some instances the notion that humans and the earth were created in six days by a divine act. In addition, most fundamentalist

Christians consider evangelism to be central to their mission: since all humans are creatures of God, it is the duty of members to expend personal effort to return the "lost," be they individuals or nations, to God's love.

Although I believe our current political situation is unique, there has always been a tension between religion and politics in America. Perhaps the most interesting example took place at the founding of the country. The ratification debates of the U.S. Constitution produced some of the richest, most interesting, and oft-quoted American political thought in our history. Yet while the arguments on the winning side of the debate —the Federalists, which included James Madison, Alexander Hamilton, and James Wilson—are famous, the arguments of the opposing side—the so-called anti-Federalists—are largely ignored. The Federalists favored a strong, national government and a secular state in which religion played no official role; the anti-Federalists, on the other hand, believed in state sovereignty and that religion, education, and local government should work together to produce a moral, virtuous citizenry. These debates are of much more than mere historical interest. Several anti-Federalist proposals and arguments offer considerable insight into contemporary political issues, including those not imagined by either the Federalists or anti-Federalists, such as the teaching of "intelligent design"—the idea that life on earth is too complex to have developed without an intelligence at the helm—alongside evolution, the ethics of human cloning, or the legality of same-sex marriage. It is worth a brief exploration of anti-Federalist thought on the topics of church and state separation in particular and the role of religion in politics in general, as it may shed light on some of the actions of today's neoconservatives.

In 1784, Patrick Henry—statesman, gifted orator, and ardent anti-Federalist—introduced a bill into the Virginia state legislature proposing a property tax to pay for the public teaching of Christianity to those students unable to afford a private education. Henry's reasoning is thoroughly in line with typical anti-Federalist thought on the importance of religion: "the general diffusion of Christian knowledge hath a natural tendency to correct the morals of men, restrain their vices, and preserve the peace of society, which cannot be effected without a competent provision for learned teachers."[4] The bill created much controversy, with the most eloquent counterargument coming from James Madison, whose *Memorial and Remonstrance against Religious Assessments* is quoted by the Supreme Court to this day.

Madison's oratory before the General Assembly of Virginia was based on the principles of classical liberalism: humans are born with natural, unalienable rights that cannot be taken away; individual liberty has pride of place over that of groups or the state; political authority must be justified and must originate from the people themselves, as opposed to being ruled by an authority based solely on force or custom; and we should be governed by known laws and not dictatorial whim. In *Memorial and Remonstrance* Madison argued that since the free exercise of religion is an unalienable right, it is both "exempt from the cognizance" of civil society and subject neither to the authority of civil society nor to the power of the legislature. To have it otherwise would be a dangerous abuse of power on the part of government, whose very existence depends on the people themselves, and not the other way around. Since the primary purpose of a "free government" is to protect the unalienable rights of its citizens, it must not "overleap the great Barrier which defends the rights of the people. The Rulers who are guilty of such an encroachment, exceed the commission from which they derive their authority, and are Tyrants. The People who submit to it are governed by laws made neither by themselves nor by an authority derived from them, and are slaves."[5] Four years earlier, Thomas Jefferson had iterated the same idea somewhat more colorfully in *Notes on the State of Virginia*: "the legitimate powers of government extend to such acts only as are injurious to others. It does me no injury for my neighbor to say that there are twenty gods, or no god. It neither picks my pocket nor breaks my leg."[6]

Thus began the debate in the United States over the proper role of religion in government. Though the Federalists consistently argued for a secular national government, it is worth noting that they were neither agnostic nor atheist, even by the rather stringent definitions of the eighteenth century, nor were they hostile to religion in general. They were, however, versed in ancient and modern history and philosophy, and since they were dedicated to forming "a new order of the ages," they were adamant about keeping the new government out of direct religious involvement.[7]

The Federalists' arguments during the Constitutional Convention in Philadelphia make clear that goal. On June 6, 1787, James Madison remarked to the convention on the topic of faction, "Respect for character is always diminished in proportion to the number among whom the blame or praise is to be divided. Conscience, the only remaining tie, is known to be inadequate in individuals: In large numbers, little is to be expected from it. Besides, Religion itself may become a motive to persecution and oppression—These observations are verified by Histories of every Country ancient and modern."[8] This sentiment was largely shared by other Federalists. Another oft-repeated theme in the Constitutional Convention debates and in the *Federalist Papers* was that a reliance on religion in particular or human virtue in general is insufficient to maintain liberty, justice, or good government. In Federalist No. 10 and No. 51, James Madison directly counters anti-Federalist arguments by stating that motives spurred by religious or moral concerns are as likely to produce faction—any group driven by self-interest against the common good—as are economic inequality or differing "passions and interests." As Madison put it in Federalist No. 10, "The latent causes of faction are thus sown in the nature of man; . . . A zeal for different opinions concerning religion, concerning government, and many other points, as well of speculation as of practice; an attachment to different leaders ambitiously contending for pre-eminence and power; . . . have, in turn, divided mankind into parties, inflamed them with mutual animosity, and rendered them much more disposed to vex and oppress each other than to co-operate for the common good."[9] Indeed, "if the impulse and the opportunity be suffered to coincide, we well know that neither moral or religious motives can be relied on as an adequate control" to prevent "schemes of oppression."[10]

Unlike the Federalists, anti-Federalists tended to be quite disparate in their views. In fact, one of the few binding elements of their thought in 1787–89 is reminiscent of the Republicans in 1994: they were defined by what they opposed. What commonality the anti-Federalists shared centered around the belief that true liberty could be realized only in a democracy exercised on a small scale and across a small territory, among a homogeneous population whose education, mores, and religious values were geared toward local attachments and thus the common good. Or as "Brutus," one of the most respected and well-known anti-Federalist writers argued, "in a republic, the manners, sentiments, and interests of the people should be similar. If this be not the case, there will be a constant clashing of opinions; and the representatives of one part will be continually striving against those of the other."[11] Some anti-Federalists believed that "the whole organization of the polity [should have] an educative function."[12] The inculcation of civic virtue, "a devotion to fellow citizens and to country so deeply instilled as to be almost as automatic and powerful as the natural devotion to self-interest," was central to this education.[13]

The reasoning behind Patrick Henry's proposed bill in 1784 was shared among many anti-Federalists. As one anonymous writer from Massachusetts explained, "there are but three ways of controlling the 'turbulent passions of mankind': by punishment; by reward; and 'by prepossessing the people in favour of the virtue by affording publick protection to religion.'" Likewise, Mercy Warren noted that "the history of republics is the history of strict regard to religion."[14] Charles Turner expressed the wish that "the first Congress under the Constitution would recommend to the states the institution of such means of education 'as shall be *adequate* to the *divine, patriotick purpose* of training up the children and youth at large, in that solid learning, and in those pious and moral principles, which are the *support,* the *life* and SOUL of republican government and liberty, of which a free Constitution is the body.'"[15] The idea that it was the rightful duty and obligation of good government to foster piety, religion, and morals toward the ultimate goal of making the "people more capable of being a Law unto themselves"[16] did not fade away in the years after the successful ratification of the Constitution. It has cropped up periodically with various shifts in power among political parties at both the state and the national level, and it remains to this day.

Before turning to contemporary neoconservative issues, one final point warrants discussion. It was the anti-Federalists who demanded that a Bill of Rights containing a provision for religious freedom along with a clear statement of states' rights be added to the Constitution. In fact, its addition was the final provision for ratification. On the surface, this demand might seem contradictory to the anti-Federalists' views. Consider, though, that as a group the anti-Federalists were alarmed at the prospect of a central, consolidated authority, one they often compared to the monarchy they had recently fought so hard against. Since the Revolutionary War, most states had drawn up bills of rights as part of their constitutions, and they did not relish the prospect of a new national authority using its power to contradict the laws, practices, or will of the states. Thus, the anti-Federalists saw no conflict whatsoever between their demand that the new national government clearly state in a Bill of Rights that it would "make no law respecting an establishment of religion or prohibiting the free exercise thereof" and their insistence that local government, education, and religion be enmeshed for the common good. What they wanted to prevent the *national* government from establishing—a particular sect's beliefs or liturgies as "official"—or from prohibiting—the *states'* free exercise of any religion—they saw fit to promote among their own populace.

This point is crucial and resonates to this day. In almost every Supreme Court case dealing with separation of church and state issues, proponents of acts such as school prayer or the federal funding of state or local religious programs pin their arguments to the "free exercise" clause of the First Amendment ("prohibiting the free exercise thereof") by claiming that the federal government is in effect discriminating against their particular religious beliefs by denying their public funding, promotion, or practice. On the other hand, those who see such acts as an encroachment of religion into the public sphere usually argue from the standpoint of the First Amendment's "establishment clause" ("Congress shall make no law respecting an establishment of religion") on the grounds that if federal, state, or local government allows such funding, promotion, or practice in the public sphere, it would be tantamount to privileging one religion or sect over others, which is the first step toward the establishment of an official state church.

Nearly half a century after the ratification of the U.S. Constitution, Alexis de Tocqueville remarked that when religion "founds its empire only upon the desire of immortality that lives in every human heart, it may aspire to universal dominion; but when it . . . form[s] an alliance with a political power, religion augments its authority over a few and forfeits the hope of reigning over all."[17] Tocqueville might have had the fate of the Catholic Church in France in mind when he wrote these words, but the message behind his warnings extends beyond the borders of nineteenth-century France. Tocqueville knew that the marriage of church and state denigrates both, for the former, as he put it, "cannot share the temporal power of the state without being the object of a portion of that animosity which the latter excites."[18] In other words, given that there will always be critics of government, incorporating religious policies into those of the state will inevitably lead to the criticism of religion in general.

There are two possibilities why today's neoconservatives are striving to entangle education, government, and religion. One, they have forgotten or never knew the lessons offered by history on the subject of uniting religion with politics, or two, they are consciously endeavoring to counter our nation's classical liberal tradition of unalienable rights, the justification of political authority, and rule of known law. Lest America be doomed either to repeat the mistakes of history or to make them anew in our own particular way, we would do well to remind ourselves that the liberal tradition was created to counter arbitrary religious and governmental authority, as we would do well to remember the arguments of the framers of the Constitution of the United States and the debates surrounding its ratification.

Endangering Trust in Political Leadership

Contemporary neoconservatives have two things in common with yester-day's anti-Federalists. First, their message appears at times disparate, and second, they are most clearly defined by what they oppose, real or per-ceived. In the mid-twentieth century, Daniel Bell noted that when it came to the roots of American religious fervor, two particularly evangelical Protestant sects, the Methodists and the Baptists, were characterized by egalitarianism and anti-intellectualism. These two characteristics accu-rately describe many anti-Federalists at the time of the founding. The ex-ample of the "yeoman farmer" was repeatedly invoked as the ideal citizen: honest, hardworking, virtuous, neither wealthy nor poor. By contrast, a mostly northern, urban "aristocracy" was attempting to appropriate the country and consolidate national power into the their own hands for per-sonal gain—or so was the perception of many anti-Federalists. Then as now, however, politics is about power. Contemporary neoconservatives tend to conceal their hopes and fears of gaining or losing political power. This was not the case for the anti-Federalists; as a group they were quite vocal in their fears of the marginalization of state power and control at the hands of a national government. As Patrick Henry told the Virginia Ratify-ing Convention in 1788, "the fate of this question and America may de-pend on this: Have they said, we the States? Have they made a proposal of a compact between States? If they had, this would be a confederation: it is otherwise most clearly a consolidated government. The question turns, Sir, on that poor little thing—the expression, We, the People, instead of the States of America."[19] Where the Federalists saw a larger, more diverse un-ion as the means of achieving political stability and preserving individual liberty, the anti-Federalists saw a conspiracy, an effort to redefine the United States of America into two significant units: the people and the na-tion, with no meaningful power left in the hands of the states. These days, it is no coincidence that many neoconservative efforts to insert religion or religious characteristics into public places and institutions take place, for the most part, at the state and local level.

Given the insight of Bell's analysis of religious fervor in the United States and its connection to neoconservatism in the mid-twentieth cen-tury, it is surprising that he did not discuss the anti-Federalists at the time of the founding. He correctly noted that "moralism and moral indignation are characteristic of religions that have largely abandoned other-worldly preoccupations and have concentrated on this-worldly concerns. . . . This is a country, and Protestantism a religion, in which piety has given way to moralism, and theology to ethics."[20] He was also correct in stating that this American brand of religious moralism has a "peculiar schizoid character: it [is] imposed with vehemence in areas of culture and conduct—in the censorship of books, the attacks on 'immoral art,' etc., and in the realm of private habits; yet it [is] heard only sporadically regarding the depredations of business or the corruption of politics."[21] There are, no doubt, faiths and religious organizations that work with the zeal of the righteous to convince wider audiences of the rectitude of their position—the American religious right is only one example among many. Yet "moral indignation" or "true-believerism" (for lack of a better term) hardly explains the behavior of those who today hew to a neoconservative line in politics, nor, for that matter, does it completely explain the motives of the anti-Federalists during the Constitutional ratification debates. At the end of the day, politics is not about piety or moral rectitude. It is about power. One need not be overly cynical to suspect that a goal other than the salvation of America's immortal soul is at stake in contemporary politics. Richard Hofstadter began to identify the crux of the matter in 1955 by explaining what he termed Americans' "peculiar scramble for status and [their] peculiar search for a secure identity."[22] Although Hofstadter's analysis was more cultural and psychological than political, he did hit on a characteristic of contemporary neoconservatives: their search for a unified identity, which has led them to ally themselves ideologically with the religious Right, and their constant attempts to increase their own status in American social and political culture by promoting certain policies that, until relatively recently, were viewed as either unpopular, backward, or just plain mean. A consequence of this promotion is something yet more crucial, something that promises long-term negative effects: the erosion of the classical liberal principles on which this country was founded. If Chief Justice John Marshall was correct in 1803 when he confirmed that "the government of the United States has been emphatically termed a government of laws, and not of men,"[23] what of the character of the United States if the rule of known law is replaced by the rule of religious dicta or of unquestioned and unquestionable political authority? Should individuals' unalienable rights be replaced by the infallibility of religious text?

It would be largely inaccurate to portray President George W. Bush as a through-and-through neoconservative. However, many of the policies carried out by his Executive branch reflect neoconservative thinking. For example, within days of Bush's inauguration in 2001, U.S. funds to all international family-planning groups offering abortion and abortion counseling were blocked. Soon after, Bush established the Office of Faith-Based and Community Initiatives, the first federal office intended to promote the integration of religious groups into federally funded social services. John DiIulio was appointed to head the office, and from the beginning he performed a treacherous tightrope walk between the first two clauses of the First Amendment. According to the Supreme Court, the establishment clause and the free-exercise clause are often in tension.[24] "Yet," writes the Court, "we have long said that 'there is room for play in the joints' between them." In other words, there are actions permitted by the first clause but not the second, and vice versa. For example, to prove religious discrimination, a petitioning party would have to show such actions as an imposition of "criminal [or] civil sanctions on any type of religious service or rite," a denial "to ministers the right to participate in the political affairs of the community," or a governmental requirement that a group or individual "choose between their religious beliefs and receiving a government benefit." For example, public money may not be used to fund religious training or instruction, as "training for religious professions and training for secular professions are not fungible." In other words, to deny public money to religious groups or individuals seeking to use that money to instruct or proselytize does not constitute religious discrimination according to U.S. constitutional law. In fact, it has been argued that to allow public money to fund religious training is tantamount to a governmental establishment of a particular religion.

To promote his newly established office, on March 7, 2001, DiIulio delivered a speech before the National Association of Evangelicals in which he quoted President Bush's vision for the government's involvement in faith-based charities, a significant aspect of the president's published platform in the 2000 campaign: "We must heed the growing consensus across America that successful government programs work in fruitful partnership with community-serving and faith-based organizations whether run by Methodists, Muslims, Mormons, or good people of no faith at all."[25] DiIulio reminded his audience that "our plan will not favor religious institutions over non-religious institutions" and that "[we] will not fund a church or a synagogue or a mosque or any religion, but instead, we will be funding programs that affect people in a positive way."[26]

Statements such as these were meant to reassure the public that Bush was not challenging the Constitution, even while he and DiIulio both utilized the rhetoric of ending governmental "discrimination" against religious groups. Despite these assurances, however, the Office of Faith-Based Initiatives at once drew fire from both the Left and the Right, with the former voicing concern over the erosion of civil liberties and the latter worrying about the ramifications of government oversight on what were considered private and/or local affairs. Of course, the second concern is hardly new: it mirrors almost perfectly the anti-Federalist fear of a national government trumping the rights and powers of the states.

The controversy came to a head in July 2001 when the Office of Faith-Based and Community Initiatives received a letter from John Conyers of the House Judiciary Committee and Jerrold Nadler of the Subcommittee on the Constitution requesting all materials regarding interactions between the administration and the Salvation Army. As Conyers and Nadler wrote, "We are deeply concerned about today's press reports that the Bush Administration may have agreed to issue an administrative legal action cutting back the employment rights of minorities, including gays and lesbians, in exchange for obtaining the Salvation Army's political support for H.R. 7."[27] More broadly than this, Conyers and Nadler expressed their misgivings over the Office of Faith-Based Initiatives itself:

> we have long been concerned that proposals such as H.R. 7 are merely tools to permit increased discrimination and which would inappropriately entangle religion in our political affairs. This is why H.R. 7 is so strongly opposed by civil rights groups such as the NAACP and the Leadership Council on Civil Rights. As Members with a long time interest in civil rights matters, we would never want to see a bill purportedly designed to strengthen religion be used as an excuse to weaken our civil rights laws. It would be more objectionable yet if as part of the process of pushing this legislation, additional civil rights safeguards were forfeited in a "back room deal" outside of public scrutiny.[28]

One month later, DiIulio resigned.

The promotion of the Office of Faith-Based Initiatives was virtually nonexistent in Bush's 2004 reelection campaign. Although the office still exists today, the religious component of its agenda has been toned down considerably, and it has received relatively little national media attention. Today, efforts to instill and institutionalize religious views into politics and the public sphere still exist; the difference is that these efforts happen, more often than not, on the level of state and local politics. For example, in early 2006 the *New York Times* reported that "Missouri's legislature is considering a bill requiring 'critical analysis' in teaching evolution" and that a member of the Indiana state legislature "called evolution a type of religion and proposed a bill banning textbooks that contain fraudulent information."[29] Other examples abound. The effects of this unfortunate trend have even been felt at the National Aeronautics and Space Administration (NASA). In early 2006, a twenty-four-year-old presidential appointee in NASA's press office sent a message to the agency's Web designers, who were working on a set of presentations on Einstein for middle-school students. "The message said the word 'theory' needed to be added after every mention of the Big Bang," on the grounds that it is not a proven fact and that it was thus not "NASA's place, nor should it be to make a declaration such as this about the existence of the universe that discounts intelligent design by a creator."[30] The message at once drew sharp criticism from NASA's administrator, Michael D. Griffin, who in an email addressed to all of the agency's nineteen thousand employees stated that "it is not the job of the public-affairs officers . . . to alter, filter or adjust engineering or scientific material produced by NASA's technical staff."[31]

Although the appointee resigned from his position almost immediately, the entire affair is telling. The fact that the memo was intended to alter a presentation meant for schoolchildren is significant, making it similar in purpose if not in form to efforts by local and state legislators to instill the teaching of "intelligent design" and/or "creationism" into public school biology classes. The goals of NASA as a whole—the exploration of space and the solar system, along with the development of related technologies—are ostensibly not political. NASA is a scientific, nonpartisan agency whose technical staff are well aware of the difference between science and religion. *Science* denotes an activity wherein data are gathered, hypotheses are formed, repeatable experiments are conducted, results are observed, and theories are constructed to explain the results. Theories are tested until proven; if one theory is disproven, a new theory is formed to account for the new results. *Religion,* on the other hand, is a belief based on unprovable, untestable, and unfalsifiable assumptions. Christianity in particular, according to its own tenets, requires a "leap of faith." When it comes to attempts to equate religion and science, contemporary neoconservatives either have very little idea of what science actually is or are aware of what it is and are consciously trying to confuse and obfuscate its significance by claiming discrimination or hostility against religion. The scientific method, unlike religion, requires observation and demonstrability.

The method itself affords an external criteria by which we can judge the truth content of a particular claim about the nature of the universe. In other words, anyone, regardless of religious beliefs or political partisanship, is welcome to witness a one-pound weight falling to the ground at the same speed in Washington, D.C., as it does in Shanghai, China, or the combining of the correct proportions of oxygen and hydrogen to produce water. Both of these phenomena are able to be observed and repeated. Religion, on the other hand, depends on the word of authority. Among fundamentalists of any religion, the truth content of religious tenets is unquestionable, and evidence or demonstration contrary to those tenets are impossible, even irrelevant. What does the equation of religion and science mean politically? If neoconservatives are successful in demolishing the idea of external verification of truth content, the idea of evidence itself becomes moot. Unquestioned and unquestionable authority becomes the only means of promoting or countering statements in the scientific or the political realm.

NASA is hardly alone in grappling with these issues. In February 2006 a bill was introduced into the Utah state legislature that would "require science teachers to offer a disclaimer when introducing lessons on evolution—namely, that not all scientists agree on the origins of life."[32] Utah is a relatively conservative state, with 90 percent of the elected officials in Salt Lake City belonging to the Church of Jesus Christ of Latter-Day Saints. Despite their relatively homogeneous religious adherence, even some Republicans in the state legislature opposed the bill's adoption on the grounds that it "threatens religious belief by blurring the lines between faith and science."[33] Despite the reservations of some Utah lawmakers, the bill passed the Senate. Three weeks later it was defeated in the House by a vote of 46–28. Some legislators voted against the bill on the grounds of maintaining the separation of church and state, and others reported that they opposed the bill because "intelligent design was not in keeping with traditional Mormon belief."[34]

Although the attempt to legislate the teaching of religious beliefs in public institutions failed in Utah, it has succeeded elsewhere. Once a bill becomes a law, the only way to strike it down short of a referendum is for one or more citizens to appeal to the courts. This is precisely what has happened in other states in recent years. Appeals to state and federal courts, or even to the U.S. Supreme Court, to determine the constitutionality of laws surrounding the teaching of Darwinian evolution versus religious explanations are becoming increasingly commonplace. With apologies to Clausewitz, it seems that the law is becoming the mere continuation of politics by other means.[35]

Damaging Freedom and Individual Liberty

Engel et al. v. Vitale et al. is a case in point. Though decided by the Supreme Court in 1962, the nature of the case and the grounds for the decision rendered by the justices shed considerable light on the nature of many such cases being brought today. The Board of Education of New Hyde Park, New York, claimed that it acted in its official capacity under state law to require the recitation of the following prayer in front of a teacher at the start of each school day: "Almighty God, we acknowledge our dependence upon Thee, and we beg Thy blessings upon us, our parents, our teachers and our Country."[36] The prayer was recommended by the State Board of Regents, the members of whom claimed that it was a part of their "Statement on Moral and Spiritual Training in the Schools" and that they believed "that this Statement will be subscribed to by all men and women of good will, and we call upon all of them to aid in giving life to our program."[37] This statement virtually mirrors the original arguments of many anti-Federalists in their insistence that religion, education, and local government should work together to produce a virtuous citizenry. It also reflects modern-day attempts to instill a kind of "civic virtue" in a generation to create a similarity of religious and cultural beliefs as well as a disposition to elect politicians who share them.

The plaintiffs in *Engel v. Vitale* were the parents of ten pupils who argued that

> the use of this official prayer in the public schools was contrary to the beliefs, religions, or religious practices of both themselves and their children. Among other things, these parents challenged the constitutionality of both the state law authorizing the School District to direct the use of prayer in public schools and the School District's regulation ordering the recitation of this particular prayer on the ground that these actions of official governmental agencies violate that part of the First Amendment of the Federal Constitution which commands that "Congress shall make no law respecting an establishment of religion"—a command which was made applicable to the State of New York by the Fourteenth Amendment of the said Constitution.[38]

The respondents in this case argued that since the prayer was non-denominational and since students unwilling to recite the prayer had the option of remaining silent or of leaving the room, it did not violate the establishment clause. The majority of the Court disagreed. In their opinion, delivered by Justice Black, the prayer did violate the establishment clause even though it did not violate the free exercise clause. "Although," he wrote, "these two clauses may in certain instances overlap, they forbid two quite different kinds of governmental encroachment upon religious freedom." Furthermore, "when the power, prestige and financial support of government is placed behind a particular religious belief, the indirect coercive pressure upon religious minorities to conform to the prevailing officially approved religion is plain. . . . [The] first and most immediate purpose [of the establishment clause] rested on the belief that a union of government and religion tends to destroy government and to degrade religion."[39]

To support the Court's decision, Justice Black chose to quote the following from James Madison's *Memorial and Remonstrance against Religious Assessments*:

> It is proper to take alarm at the first experiment on our liberties. . . . Who does not see that the same authority which can establish Christianity, in exclusion of all other Religions, may establish with the same ease any particular sect of Christians, in exclusion of all other Sects? That the same authority which can force a citizen to contribute three pence only of his property for the support of any one establishment, may force him to conform to any other establishment in all cases whatsoever?[40]

Other judges have used more direct language. On December 20, 2005, a federal judge in Pennsylvania ruled that "to present intelligent design as an alternative to evolution in high school biology courses" is unconstitutional, as "it is a religious viewpoint that advances 'a particular version of Christianity.'"[41] The case was brought before the federal court by eleven parents who sued the Dover school board for causing teachers to recite a statement to students in their ninth-grade biology classes. "The statement said that there were 'gaps in the theory' of evolution and that intelligent design was another explanation they should examine."[42]

After six weeks of arguments, Judge Jones (a Republican appointed by President George W. Bush) concluded that "intelligent design was not science, and that in order to claim that it is, its proponents admit they must

change the very definition of science to include supernatural explanations."[43] Just as Justice Black did in *Engel v. Vitale,* Jones concluded that the
teaching of intelligent design violated the establishment clause of the First
Amendment. Unlike Justice Black, however, Jones "issued a broad, stinging
rebuke to its advocates and provided strong support for scientists who
have fought to bar intelligent design from the science curriculum." Moreover, he accused the members of the school board of lying "to cover up
their religious motives, [making] a decision of 'breathtaking inanity' and
[dragging] their community into 'this legal maelstrom with its resulting
utter waste of monetary and personal resources.'"[44]

Thus far, the rulings of federal district courts and the Supreme Court
have upheld the "wall of separation" between church and state, but such
cases will most likely increase, not decrease, in frequency. With two ostensibly conservative justices—Roberts and Alito—appointed to the Supreme Court by President Bush in 2006, the tide may yet turn and the
"wall of separation" could be torn down, brick by brick. As for the continuing political efforts by neoconservatives at the state and local level, they
will increase until the political tide turns, as history tells us it will. This
does not mean that those who cherish individual liberty and freedom of
conscience should sit back and "wait for the inevitable." The use and abuse
of religion for the political end of achieving power will accomplish very
little but the debasement of religion and the degradation of government,
as Tocqueville well knew. Along with the erosion of classical liberal principles, it would not be alarmist to state that all these elements constitute a
clear and present danger to the cultural and political fabric of the nation.
Neoconservative political ties to a previously marginal and marginalized
religious Right counter the ideas and ideals of the framers of the U.S.
Constitution, endanger faith and trust in political leadership, and damage
America's self-image as a nation characterized by individual liberty, unalienable rights, the rule of known law, and the justification of political
authority. In order to maintain our freedoms and liberties, We the People
would do well to remember the words Thomas Jefferson wrote in 1781 on
their inherent fragility:

> I doubt whether the people of this country would suffer an execution for
> heresy, or a three years imprisonment for not comprehending the mysteries
> of the Trinity. But is the spirit of the people an infallible, a permanent re-
> liance? Is it government? Is this the kind of protection we receive in return

for the rights we give up? Besides, the spirit of the times may alter, will alter. Our rulers will become corrupt, our people careless. . . . It can never be too often repeated, that the time for fixing every essential right on a legal basis is while our rulers are honest, and ourselves united. . . . It will not then be necessary to resort every moment to the people for support. They will be forgotten, therefore, and their rights disregarded. They will forget themselves, but in the sole faculty of making money, and will never think of uniting to effect a due respect for their rights. The shackles, therefore, . . . will remain on us long, will be made heavier and heavier, till our rights shall revive or expire in a convulsion.[45]

NOTES

1. James Madison, *A Memorial and Remonstrance on the Religious Rights of Man* (1784), in *A Wall of Separation*, ed. Mary Segers and Ted Jelen (New York: Rowman and Littlefield, 1998), 133.

2. God is never mentioned in the Constitution, and in the body of the document religion appears only once. Article VI states that "no religious test shall ever be required as a qualification to any office or public trust under the United States." The First Amendment, added in 1789, contains the only other mention of the topic: "Congress shall make no law respecting the establishment of religion, or prohibiting the free exercise thereof."

3. Daniel Bell, ed., *The Radical Right* (Garden City, NY: Doubleday, 1963), 50.

4. Patrick Henry, "A Bill Establishing a Provision for Teachers of the Christian Religion," *Journal of the Virginia House of Delegates*, entry dated December 24, 1784.

5. Madison, *Memorial and Remonstrance*, 133.

6. Thomas Jefferson, *Notes on the State of Virginia*, in *Thomas Jefferson: Writings*, ed. Merrill D. Peterson (New York: Library of America, 1984), 286.

7. "A new order of the ages," or *novus ordo seclorum*, is found on the reverse side of the Great Seal of the United States and is printed on the back of the one-dollar bill.

8. "The Federal Convention of 1787: Electing Representatives (June 6)," in *The Anti-Federalist Papers and the Constitutional Convention Debates*, ed. Ralph Ketcham (New York: Penguin, 1986), 52.

9. Alexander Hamilton, James Madison, and John Jay, *The Federalist Papers*, ed. Clinton Rossiter (New York: Penguin, 2003), 73.

10. Ibid., 75.

11. "Brutus," "Essays I, VI, X–XII, and XV," in Ketcham, *Anti-Federalist Papers*, 277.

12. Herbert J. Storing, *What the Anti-Federalists Were For* (Chicago: University of Chicago Press, 1981), 21.

13. Ibid., 20.

14. Ibid., 22.

15. Ibid., 23 (emphasis in original).

16. Ibid.

17. Ibid.

18. Ibid.

19. "Speeches of Patrick Henry," in Ketcham, *Anti-Federalist Papers,* 199.

20. Bell, *Radical Right,* 50.

21. Ibid., 51.

22. Richard Hofstadter, "The Pseudo-Conservative Revolt—1955," in Bell, *Radical Right,* 69.

23. *William Marbury v. James Madison, Secretary of State of the United States,* 5 U.S. 137 (1803). Justice Marshall delivered the opinion of the court.

24. This discussion is taken from *Locke, Governor of Washington, et al. v. Davey,* U.S. Supreme Court, case no. 02-1315 (February 25, 2004). Chief Justice Rehnquist delivered the opinion of the Court, with Justices Scalia and Thomas dissenting.

25. John J. DiIulio Jr., "Compassion in Truth and Action: How Sacred and Secular Places Serve Civic Purposes, and What Washington Should and Should Not Do to Help," speech delivered before the National Association of Evangelicals in Dallas, Texas, U.S. Newswire, March 7, 2001.

26. Ibid.

27. Conyers/Nadler Letter to Dr. John DiIulio, Director of White House Office of Faith-Based and Community Initiatives, July 10, 2001, House Judiciary Committee Archives of the 107th Congress.

28. Ibid.

29. Kirk Johnson, "Evolution Measure Splits State Legislature in Utah," *New York Times,* February 2, 2006.

30. Andrew Revkin, "NASA Chief Backs Agency Openness," *New York Times,* February 4, 2006.

31. Ibid.

32. Johnson, "Evolution Measure."

33. Ibid.

34. Kirk Johnson, "Anti-Darwin Bill Fails in Utah," *New York Times,* February 28, 2006.

35. Clausewitz's original statement is "War is a mere continuation of politics by other means." Carl von Clausewitz, *On War* (1832; repr., New York: Penguin, 1982), 119. When he wrote these words in 1832, Clausewitz did not mean to diminish either the importance or horrors of war. Quite the opposite. His main argument is that war is not a game; it should never be entered into lightly. Every war waged should accomplish a clear political goal by all military means at a comman-

der's disposal. The book is perhaps the quintessential expression of *realpolitik* in the nineteenth century and is still widely read.

36. *Engel et al. v. Vitale et al.,* 370 U.S. 421 (1962).

37. Ibid.

38. Ibid.

39. Ibid.

40. Madison, *Memorial and Remonstrance,* 133.

41. Laurie Goodstein, "Issuing Rebuke, Judge Rejects Teaching of Intelligent Design," *New York Times,* December 21, 2005, A34.

42. Ibid.

43. Ibid.

44. Ibid.

45. Jefferson, *Notes on the State of Virginia,* 288.

Chapter 7

Paradox or Contradiction
The Marriage Mythos in Neoconservative Ideology

R. Claire Snyder

We believe our families to be the first, the best and the original department of health, education and welfare.
—William Bennett[1]

Marriage is the best welfare program.
—Independent Women's Forum report[2]

Feminists have created a malodor around the institution [of marriage] (patriarchal, repressive, blah, blah, blah).
—Rich Lowry[3]

The American Right is not a monolith but a coalition of three different strands of conservatism, historically defined as libertarianism, traditionalism, and anticommunist militarism.[4] In today's incarnation, these strands appear as the market fundamentalism of neoliberals and libertarians, the antifeminist and antigay moralism of the Christian Right, and the imperialist militarism of neoconservatives. At first glance, the battle against gay marriage would seem to fit into the Christian Right strand, while contradicting many of the liberal principles of the first strand and having little to do with the third. As it turns out, however, the fight to preserve male-dominated, heterosexual-only marriage also holds a central place within neoconservatism. Not only does traditional marriage play a role in the normative vision of American greatness that neocons espouse, but it does important ideological work holding the three potentially contradictory strands together. The claim that democracy requires patriarchy aims to reverse the progress of feminism and lesbian/gay rights, and keeping the focus on the family undermines support for social welfare programs, increases the problems of collective action, and weakens the power of the state. Thus, the mythology of family values helps neoconservatives to form and maintain coalitions with Christian conservatives and market fundamentalists.

What Does Neoconservatism Have to Do with Marriage?

Neoconservatism is a powerful ideological project that seeks to neutralize progressive politics and push public opinion and policy toward the right. Traditionally, conservatism has been resistant to change; it has sought to *conserve* tradition.[5] But as the traditions of WASP supremacy, male dominance, and heterosexism have been eroded by the liberal commitment to universal principles that proclaim liberty and equality for all and that preclude quasi-theocratic government and legal discrimination, many conservatives—*neo*conservatives—now advocate radical changes in current mores. They seek to reverse the progress of feminism and reinstall the patriarchal family to its previously dominant place in American society and to restore or even increase legal discrimination against lesbian and gay citizens. As Stephen Bronner notes, "Neo-conservatives lack the complacent 'disposition,' the elitist *longeur*, the respect for established hierarchies, the fear of change, and the staid preoccupation with stability of more traditional conservatives. . . . They are revolutionaries or, better, 'counter-revolutionaries' intent upon remaking America."[6] They seek to construct an ideology to fill the void left by the collapse of the Left, to undo progressive gains over the past forty years, and to prevent any future demands for economic justice.

Neoconservatism is an ideology that supports the interests of economic elites by disseminating values that hinder progressive politics and advancing public policies that benefit their material interests. Although many neocons are "not particularly elite" themselves, "they became beneficiaries of economic and political elites: funded by big business, influential within corporate-backed think tanks, and appointed to government agencies under the Reagan-Bush (and Clinton) administrations," and they became extremely powerful during the tenure of George W. Bush.[7] Neocons have been able to cast their arguments in a way that resonates with the commonsense beliefs or wishful thinking of ordinary Americans.[8]

Neoconservatism can be seen as putting a civilized intellectual patina on right-wing power politics, but this does not mean that neocon intellectuals do not genuinely believe their own arguments. Whether they do or not, however, is beside the point. What matters are the political consequences of their arguments.

Although often "associated with a core group of standard bearers"— such as its founders, Irving Kristol (and Gertrude Himmelfarb), Norman Podhoretz (and Midge Dector), Nathan Glazer, Daniel Bell, and Seymour Martin Lipset—neoconservatism is best understood as "a commitment to a set of policy preferences" rather than a list of particular people.[9] Neoconservatives today are best known for the key role they play in the Bush administration's foreign policy. For example, in "Neocon 101," the *Christian Science Monitor* describes them as follows:

> "Neocons" believe that the United States should not be ashamed to use its unrivaled power—forcefully if necessary—to promote its values around the world. Some even speak of the need to cultivate a US empire. Neoconservatives believe modern threats facing the US can no longer be reliably contained and therefore must be prevented, sometimes through preemptive military action.[10]

The Wikipedia, a commonly used source of information on the Internet that many people look to for information, states,

> *Neoconservatism* refers to the political movement, ideology, and public policy goals of "new conservatives" in the United States, who are mainly characterized by their relatively interventionist and hawkish views on foreign policy, and their lack of support for the "small government" principles and restrictions on social spending, when compared with other American conservatives such as traditional or paleoconservatives.[11]

The Wikipedia definition highlights the tensions within the Right. Both definitions overlook the role that the traditional family plays in neoconservative ideology and the ways in which commonly held myths about the family function to maintain a coalition among different strands within the Right that might not always stand together.

Contrary to popular opinion, defending the patriarchal family has long been part of the neoconservative agenda. In 1965, Senator Daniel Patrick Moynihan laid out the neocon position in his report on the African American family, in which "he linked the absence of a strong father figure in many black homes to a 'tangle of pathology,' beginning with high rates of juvenile delinquency, teen pregnancy, and 'illegitimate' births, and leading to persistent poverty and welfare dependency."[12] In an oft-quoted paragraph Moynihan says,

> a community that allows a large number of young men to grow up in broken families, dominated by women, never acquiring any stable relationship to male authority, never acquiring any set of rational expectations about the future—that community asks for and gets chaos. Crime, violence, unrest, unrestrained lashing out at the whole social structure—that is not only to be expected; it is very near inevitable.[13]

Moynihan's argument laid the groundwork for both attacks on the welfare state and support for reestablishing patriarchy, which allows neocons to make common cause with both fiscal and social conservatives—an in some ways precarious coalition that underwrote the election of the Reagan administration and has maintained power ever since.

Prior to the 1980s, neoconservatives were not firmly in the Republican camp. In the 1960s, they "were vehemently anti-communist and strong on defense" but accepted the civil rights movement and the need for some New Deal–style social welfare programs. This makes sense because a commitment to liberal principles underlies both the justification for American superiority and the rationale for ending racism and combating poverty. As the civil rights movement yielded calls for economic justice and gender equality, however, neocons began to fear the radical effects of the logical extension of liberal principles.

The Paradox of Neoconservatism

Neoconservatives embrace the liberal principles that justify the free market, but they seek to prevent the logical extension of those very same principles so that they cannot be used to eliminate male dominance, economic injustice, and heterosexual privilege. Their veneration of America and Western civilization leads them to rhetorically embrace universalism, democracy, and human rights, while their defense of patriarchy, the market, and elite interests requires them to oppose the political project of the Left that utilizes these same principles. Achieving this hypocritical goal poses a serious political challenge, but neoconservatives have made necessity a virtue by portraying this contradiction as an intellectual paradox and making it a central feature of their ideology.

Embracing the concept of paradox, Gertrude Himmelfarb notes that in 1976 Daniel Bell identified "the contradictions inherent in an economy that requires, for its effective functioning, such moral restraints as self-discipline and deferred gratification, but at the same time stimulates a hedonism and self-indulgence impatient of all restraints."[14] In 1985, in the fortieth-anniversary edition of *Commentary*, Irving Kristol argued that "secular, 'progressive' liberalism—in its modern versions, anyway—exacerbates our social problems, while creating a spiritual and moral void in which they proliferate as so many cancers." As examples, he pointed to the very social problems that many neocons focus on today: "crime, drug addiction, family disintegration, sexual promiscuity and illegitimacy among teen-agers, rampant homosexuality, and widespread pornography."[15]

Peter Berkowitz, a fellow at the Hoover Institute, further develops the theme laid out by Bell and Kristol, arguing that the extension of liberal principles—self-interest, anti-authoritarianism, and choice—has undermined the conditions necessary for the flourishing of liberal society[16] and created a "paradox of freedom." "Freedom depends," he tells us, "upon a variety of beliefs, practices, and institutions that are weakened by the increasingly forceful reverberations of freedom throughout all facets of moral and political life," including education, work, romantic love, family, and faith.[17] Berkowitz explains that conservatives believe that "the birth control pill, cohabitation before marriage, no-fault divorce, laxness concerning adultery, and the movement of women out of the home and into the workplace" have helped "undermine marriage," yet he insists that any solutions must be compatible with the liberal principles of a free society, which neocons also embrace.[18] So what is to be done?

Patriarchy as Feminism

The paradox outlined by Berkowitz and others can be resolved if women *choose* to embrace patriarchy, and one important argument that neocons make is that patriarchy actually serves the interests of women and so is, in a sense, feminism. This move hinges on the idea that patriarchal marriage protects women by domesticating men who would otherwise pose a threat and by forcing them to take responsibility for the children they father. In return, of course, the father must be recognized as head of the household —a position explicitly endorsed by the Christian Right.[19]

This neoconservative view of marriage currently finds support from a wide array of constituencies under the rubric of the "crisis of fatherhood." Neoconservatives believe that the best way to ensure that men will consistently provide for and nurture young children is to have a social structure in which men can be assured of paternity (i.e., the traditional nuclear family). Without the social institution of marriage, men are likely to impregnate as many women as possible, without behaving responsibly toward their offspring. If men can be induced to take care of young children, their unique, masculine contribution significantly improves developmental outcomes for children. This is especially true for boys, who need a male role model to achieve a psychologically healthy masculine gender identity.[20]

This argument justifies attacks on feminism, which has contested male dominance in the family, and leads to arguments for traditional gender roles.[21] Although the contention that children do best when they have married, heterosexual parents accords with the commonsense beliefs of many Americans, social science researchers Louise B. Silverstein and Carl F. Auerbach demonstrate that this assumption is not supported by empirical data. Their studies reveal that "neither a mother nor a father is essential" to the production of healthy children and that "a wide variety of family structures can support positive child outcomes." They conclude that although two-parent families are preferable, children do well as long as they have "at least one responsible, caretaking adult who has a positive emotional connection to them and with whom they have a consistent relationship. . . . Neither the sex of the adult(s) nor the biological relationship to the child has emerged as a significant variable in predicting positive development. One, none, or both of those adults could be a father (or mother)."[22]

The arguments made by neoconservative social scientists directly connect to their political agenda because they argue "that responsible fathering is most likely to occur within the context of heterosexual marriage. This perspective," Silverstein and Auerbach note, "is generating a range of governmental initiatives designed to provide social support preferences to fathers over mothers and to heterosexual married couples over alternative family forms." They explain, however, that "the neoconservative position is an incorrect or oversimplified interpretation of empirical research. Using a wide range of cross-species, cross-cultural, and social science research, the authors argue that neither mothers nor fathers are essential to child development and that responsible fathering can occur within a variety of family structures."[23] There is no valid empirical evidence to confirm the commonsense assumption that heterosexual married couples do a better job of raising children than same-sex couples.[24]

The neoconservative argument parallels arguments made by the Christian Right, except that the latter grounds its vision in God-given gender differences rather than simply nature. For example, James Dobson, founder and president of Focus on the Family, argues that feminists have undermined the traditional family by refusing to accept innate gender differences, rejecting the rightful, God-given authority of the husband/father as the head of the household, attempting to change the sexual division of labor, and propagating the idea that a woman can fulfill the role traditionally played by a man. Consequently, men have lost interest in fulfilling their traditional family responsibilities, and boys have no one to teach them how to become responsible men. Detached from the civilizing influence of the traditional patriarchal family, males increasingly cause a wide array of social problems, and everybody suffers. In short, feminism hurts women, whereas patriarchy helps them.[25]

The neoconservative argument about the family also dovetails with sociobiological arguments, often embraced by market fundamentalists.[26] For example, according to Lionel Tiger, effective contraception, increased job opportunities for women, and other social changes inaugurated by feminism have made it increasingly possible for women to bear and raise children without the support of men. While women have become less dependent on and more equal to men, "a large and increasing number of men have become redundant and peripheral"[27] and consequently less interested in participating in family life. In other words, the erosion of "male dominance in marriage" has resulted in a "massive migration of men from domestic responsibility."[28] Absent the civilizing discipline of marriage and family life, men revert to their essential nature as predators.[29] Thus, by attacking the traditional gender hierarchy, feminism has undermined the very system that constrained male aggression for the benefit of women and children.

As Tiger tells it, "the bellicosity of males, particularly young ones, is a burden to many communities. From adolescence on, males are overwhelmingly responsible for one of the most predictable and chronic social problems—violent crimes. . . . Males remain the sex most likely to engage in genocide, rape, gang warfare, plunder, terrorism, prisoner abuse, and an extensive array of other violations of military and civil decency. . . . It is plain that men in groups can turn dangerous, reckless, and antisocial."[30] Socializing males away from their natural tendencies constitutes the central task of civilization, and the patriarchal family historically played a key role in this process.

Stanley Kurtz makes a similar argument to justify continuing discrimination against lesbians and gay men. He takes on the conservative argument for gay marriage, advanced by Andrew Sullivan and Jonathan Rauch, that same-sex marriage could play an important role in domesticating gay men, who are supposedly promiscuous. In a pair of articles in the *National Review*, Kurtz maintains,

> It is the unique sexual dynamic between men and women that domesticates men. Marriage ratifies and reinforces the basic effect, but cannot create it out of whole cloth. The ethos of marriage builds upon a series of shared and pre-existing expectations about the way a man ought to treat a woman —because of her sexual vulnerability, and because of her need for support as a mother. So . . . simply redefining the union of two men as a "marriage" will not bring those social expectations into play.[31]

In typical neoconservative style, Kurtz portrays his ideological argument with sad resignation:

> As I have said publicly, I personally do not see homosexuality as sinful, and do not wish to see a return to the fifties. This battle has an element of tragedy about it, for while I do not believe gay marriage will succeed in domesticating gay men, or even in entirely removing the stigma of homosexuality, I do believe that gay marriage would be received by a stigmatized group as a welcome sign of social approval. But I also believe that the price of that sign is too high—that gay marriage will be a major step in the further unstringing of our most fundamental—and most fundamentally threatened—social institution. And in the end, because we are all children first, gay marriage will hurt all of us far more than it will help. All reasonable people must agree: We cannot extend liberal principles like legal equality to lesbians and gay men without undermining our entire society.[32]

Interestingly, some neoconservatives also imply that the legalization of gay marriage is un-American and might undermine American culture in particular, a claim that links their domestic and foreign policy agendas.

For example, Maggie Gallagher summons the specter of Islamism when she argues for the legal imposition of Christian ideals of monogamous marriage[33] on American society via the Federal Marriage Amendment:

> Our basic ideas about marriage are rooted in specific religiously inspired ideas. Not just the idea that it takes a husband and a wife to make a marriage (which is a human universal), but also other ideas, such as: Men have an obligation to be sexually faithful to their wives (not a human universal), and you can't marry two women at the same time. If the first idea is illegitimate because it is rooted in religious ideas, what happens to the other two? . . . After all, if Unitarian ministers in New Paltz have a constitutional right to create legal marriages of any kind they choose, then so do Muslim clergy in Brooklyn.[34]

Here Gallagher links the defense of monogamous, heterosexual marriage to the survival of Western civilization, formerly called Western Christendom.[35]

Seedbeds of Patriarchy

The other way in which neoconservatives claim to solve the "paradox of freedom" is by arguing that the traditional family—particularly heterosexual marriage and fatherhood—forms the "seedbed of virtue" that undergirds democratic self-government. This in itself is paradoxical: how can patriarchal marriage, which reinforces male dominance, provide the foundation for democracy since democracy requires equality for all citizens, including women? The neoconservative position directly contests the feminist argument that the patriarchal family undermines rather than undergirds democracy by directly contributing to the inequality of women, which by definition erodes democracy as we know it today, which is premised on the principle of equality for all citizens.[36]

In her book *Gender, Justice, and the Family* (1989), Susan Okin explains the ways in which the traditional family reinforces gender inequality and negatively influences the political socialization of children. In short, in a society in which safe, affordable childcare is rare and employers generally do not enact family-friendly policies, the expectation of marriage and motherhood, and the need to balance work and family, contributes to women's educational and job "choices" and the consequent wage differential between male and female workers. Once they marry, women often find that their lower earning power gives them less leverage in their marriages vis-à-vis their husbands, that economic dependence renders them more vulnerable to physical and sexual abuse, and that their lack of job skills makes them less able to support themselves after divorce. The counterargument that the traditional family actually undergirds rather than undermines democracy is not strongly argued by neocons. Instead, their position seems to rely on commonly held attachments about the ideal of the family—on ideology, mythology, and nostalgia rather than empirical evidence or reasoned argument—and its advocates seem to let their scholarly credentials stand in place of actual argumentation.[37]

Peter Berkowitz advances the neoconservative position that roots the alleged demise of American democracy in divorce, unwed motherhood, and fatherless families and that portrays the traditional family and organized religion as "seedbeds of virtue" necessary to the proper functioning of a free society. For Berkowitz, "intact, two-parent families" are a vitally important source of the moral virtue on which liberal democracy depends.[38] But "with more than half of all new marriages expected to end in divorce," he argues, "with unwed mothers accounting for 30 percent of all births, and with single-parent families becoming increasingly common, the family . . . cannot readily serve . . . as a steady reservoir of the necessary virtues."[39] Berkowitz lauds the "formation of character" through "the family and the discipline of religion" in early America.[40]

In making the case for the importance of virtue in liberal society, however, Berkowitz, like others, inserts a conservative political agenda into his argument, an agenda that he neither explains nor supports with evidence. First, he shifts from a discussion of the virtues needed by a democratic society to an argument for *moral* virtue, a term that implies a connection with a larger metaphysical belief system, usually religion. Arguing "that the public good in a liberal state depends upon moral virtue," he suddenly announces "that *the sources of moral virtue in such a state are intact, two-parent families,* a vibrant civil society, and active citizen participation."[41] Berkowitz does not actually demonstrate that "intact, two-parent families," as opposed to other types of functional families, are the source of moral virtue but, rather, simply asserts it.

Gertrude Himmelfarb agrees that the family constitutes a necessary "seedbed of virtue" but insists that only bloodlines and state authority can determine who constitutes a family. She ridicules the proposal of Jeffrey Weeks that "commends the new family as the 'family of choice.'" In her view, the "family of choice" is not really a family because it "is defined not by ties of blood, marriage, or adoption, but by varieties of relationships and habituations among 'autonomous,' 'consensual' adults and their off-spring." For Himmelfarb, this is just a way of condoning "divorce, serial marriages, cohabitation, single-parentage, and 'alternative lifestyles.'"[42]

Jean Elshtain makes a similar argument, claiming that "now more than ever," the traditional family, defined as "mothers, fathers, and children," is a necessary prerequisite for "democratic civil society . . . to function."[43] Elshtain chairs the Council on Civil Society, which issued the report *A Call to Civil Society: Why Democracy Needs Moral Truth* (1998), which makes the neoconservative argument that to strengthen democracy we need to support families with two married parents and increase the "influence of religion in public life."[44] The report does not call for strengthening all families, only those headed by married heterosexuals. The report advances a neoconservative argument, even though it is endorsed by thinkers from a number of different political positions.[45]

Although the report remains silent on the issue of gay marriage, Elsh-tain opposes allowing lesbian and gay couples access to civil marriage.[46] Mary Ann Glendon, another member of the council, also opposes same-sex marriage. In fact, Glendon so strongly opposes same-sex marriage that she has taken an active role in drafting both the Federal Marriage Amend-ment and the Massachusetts amendment designed to re-outlaw same-sex marriage in that state. Moreover, according to a spokesman from the Coa-lition for Marriage, Glendon serves as "an on-call [person], someone to give us legal opinions on various language proposals, and she has been helping us to understand various proposals offered by legislators." This has been particularly helpful, the spokesman notes, because "when some-one like Professor Glendon speaks, she speaks with authority and is well-respected." In fact, Glendon is currently considered "the leading legal ex-pert for gay-marriage opponents on Beacon Hill." Furthermore, because of her conservative views on homosexuality and abortion, in 2004 Pope John Paul II appointed Glendon "to lead the Pontifical Academy of Social Sciences, which produces research to help the church establish its social policy."[47]

Neoconservative theorists of virtue provide the theoretical underpin-nings for the Republican Party's platform position: "We rely on the home, as did the founders of the American Republic, to instill the virtues that sustain democracy itself. That belief led Congress to enact the Defense of Marriage Act, which a Republican Department of Justice will energetically defend in the courts. For the same reason, we do not believe sexual preference should be given special legal protection or standing in law."[48] In the platform, the emphasis on the home as the primary "seedbed of virtue" gets associated with an antigay political agenda, although it is not clear why it has to be. For example, Okin agrees with neoconservatives that the family plays a key role in the socialization of children for democratic citizenship, but she argues that only a family founded on principles of justice can teach children the "sense of justice they will require as citizens of a just society,"[49] a point neocons generally dismiss rather than address. As the editor of the *National Review* puts it, "Feminists have created a malodor around the institution [of marriage] (patriarchal, repressive, blah, blah, blah)."[50]

Marketing Marriage

The Bush administration has accepted and actively espouses the position on traditional marriage and fatherhood laid out by neoconservatives. His Healthy Marriage Initiative (HMI)—administered by the U.S. Department of Health and Human Services (HHS)—uses government money to publicize the importance of marriage to a wide array of people, including not only the poor (through the Temporary Aid to Needy Families pro gram) but also high school students and the general public. Bush says his initiative will "help couples develop the skills and knowledge to form and sustain healthy marriages," a term that remains undefined. HHS also sponsors a Fatherhood Initiative because "the President is determined to make committed, responsible fatherhood a national priority."[51] This approach illustrates the neoconservative commitment to social engineering. HMI "parallel[s] the position taken by the foreign policy neocons: government [is] no longer the enemy of the people, but an instrument that could be a force for good if properly wielded." Neocons want to tailor government-provided "benefits in a way that rewards, rather than punishes, so cially desirable behavior."[52] Statecraft has once again become soulcraft.

To help advance its ideology, the Bush administration secretly hired antigay activist Maggie Gallagher, the president of the Institute for Mar riage and Public Policy, to push the neoconservative agenda in the mass media and on the Web.[53] Like most advocates for heterosexual marriage, Gallagher idealizes the institution, portraying it as a virtual panacea for a host of societal and human shortcomings.[54] Gallagher sees marriage as the (obvious) solution to the problem of unwed motherhood and advocates inserting a promarriage message into teen sex-education programs.[55] She advocates government-funded marriage counseling for the poor that explicitly advocates against divorce. She believes that people who want to get divorced should be subjected to mandatory divorce-education programs before they are allowed to end their marriages.[56]

Even though *single mothers* are most likely to be impoverished, Gallagher explicitly advocates government-funded economic assistance for *married fathers*. She recommends the following:

> *Target job training and earnings supplements for low-income married fathers.* There is considerable evidence that male wages and job stability play a significant role in the formation and maintenance of stable marriages. While economic factors alone cannot explain all or even most of the decline of marriage, men and women are more likely to get and stay married when men are able to get and keep jobs. Male unemployment, low earnings, and job instability are cross-culturally associated both with lower marriage rates and with marital disruption.[57]

Advancing the interests of men is the best way to help women.

The neoconservative argument that heterosexual marriage is the best solution to the poverty of women and children justifies cutting government social welfare programs. Critics point out, however, that this strategy will not go very far in remedying the problem of poverty. Fathers should certainly take economic responsibility for their children, but it is important to remember that the fathers of poor children are generally quite poor themselves and so cannot adequately support a family. Consequently, insisting that *only* they, and not the government, have a responsibility to support their children will not actually ameliorate the problem of childhood poverty. Consequently, this policy "solution" suggests that neoconservatives are more concerned about cutting the welfare state and reconsolidating patriarchy than they are in actually solving social problems.

In response to this criticism, neoconservatives point out that the men who father children with unmarried poor women earn "on average $17,000 a year." Since HHS sets the poverty line at $16,600 for a family of three, these men are not poor, assuming they have only one child.[58] In fact, they are "quite 'marriageable.' Very few have drug, alcohol, or physical abuse problems."[59] Although $17,000 a year is a very low income, the Heritage Foundation claims that if unmarried parents were to marry, "marriage would increase median family income of mothers . . . by between $10,200 and $11,400 per year. (The increase in median family income is less than the median annual earnings of the fathers—$17,500—because marriage entails an offsetting loss of welfare benefits for the mother.)" The report concludes, "If they were to marry the mothers of their children, 75 percent of the mothers would be lifted out of poverty. In roughly two-thirds of the cases, the mothers would be lifted out of poverty without even having to work themselves."[60]

Neoconservatives do not consider pay equity, guaranteed maternity leave, government-sponsored family support, or living-wage laws as options for addressing the feminization of poverty. The Heritage Foundation report notes that "the median wage rate of fathers is $8.55 per hour, compared to $7.00 per hour for the mothers." It even comments that "the wage rates for the mothers are inferred, based on the last job they held, given that most of these women would be on maternity leave or another work break at the time of the survey."[61] Yet the authors suggest no policies to increase women's pay or implement paid maternity leave. Instead, they blame welfare for creating poverty: "The 1960s War on Poverty was intended to eliminate child poverty nationwide through a variety of income transfers and human development programs. However, during the first three decades of the War on Poverty, there was little net decline in the child poverty rate."[62] Apparently, it is just another sad paradox that providing money and programs to help poor people just makes them poorer.

Marketing Neoconservatism

The mythology of traditional marriage and fatherhood does important ideological work for neoconservatives, not only undergirding its contradictory agenda but also holding the three strands of the Right together. First, it helps consolidate the neoconservative alliance with the Christian Right, which explicitly espouses male dominance and female submission and actively works to reverse the progress of feminism.[63] Arguments for male responsibility in the family play to the fears and anxieties of women who live in the wake of a partially completed feminist transformation. Feelings of resentment and economic vulnerability can be assuaged by the idea that individual fathers are expected to take responsibility for the children they father. Taxpayers should not be forced to pay for other people's children, and irresponsible behavior should be punished with poverty and suffering. This approach resonates particularly with the theology of conservative Protestants.[64]

Continuing to portray feminists and gays as the enemy helps the Right maintain its base. The New Right was able to gain enough support to elect Ronald Reagan and stymie the progress of feminism in the 1970s by mobilizing conservatives in opposition to the Equal Rights Amendment and *Roe v. Wade*.[65] Today conservatives of all stripes hope to maintain Republican dominance and continue the rightward slide of American politics by mobilizing against same-sex marriage and demonizing lesbians and gays. This effort has been quite successful so far. Getting an antigay marriage amendment on the ballot is a sure way to turn out conservative voters, as evidenced by the 2004 elections. With no Left agenda coming from the Democratic Party, people who should be "voting blue" on the basis of economic issues are "voting red" because of their attachment to family-values mythology.[66]

Second, the mythology of the traditional family also helps maintain the alliance of neoconservatives and market fundamentalists. The ideology of the self-sufficient family unit provides a justification for cutting back the social services side of government. Cutting programs allows for tax cuts that disproportionately benefit corporations and economic elites. Moreover, "starving the beast," as they call it, weakens the power of the state so that it is less able to regulate corporations or support policies that benefit working people. Continuing poverty essentially maintains a large pool of desperate and disempowered individuals, which advantages business by creating downward pressure on wages. Fear of competition from low-paid foreign workers undercuts support for a Left agenda.

Finally, keeping the "focus on the family" undermines the ability of people to work together for progressive change. Not providing health insurance or safe, affordable childcare and cutting the meager antipoverty programs that previously existed functions to increase the burdens of working people and the unemployed, thus creating conditions that make it harder for people to make it through the day, much less take action to create a better world. The rhetoric of "family values" increases collective-action problems by encouraging individuals to identify as family members rather than as workers, as participants in a feminist movement, or even as citizens. This makes it more difficult for social justice movements to develop.

Neoconservatives portray their ideology as a solution to the paradoxes of liberal society. They argue that the extension of freedom threatens to destroy a free society; that political equality requires legal discrimination; that democracy, the rule of equals, requires inequality to function; that patriarchy advantages women more than men. But these apparent contradictions are not really paradoxes; they are merely contradictions. Liberal principles still include liberty, equality, the rule of law, secular government, and a respect for human dignity. Neoconservatives hope to prevent the logical extension of liberal principles, perhaps through their mean-spirited policies of immiseration, but they will help create the conditions for their own demise.

NOTES

1. William Bennett, remarks introducing Dan Quayle as vice presidential candidate, August 19, 1992, available online at http://www.forerunner.com/forerunner/X0407_Remarks_by_William_B.html (accessed 14 December 2005).

2. April Lassiter, "Rebuilding Civil Society: Issue 1: Marriage" (Washington, DC: Independent Women's Forum, 2005), available online at http://www.iwf.org/pdf/civ_soc_marriage1.pdf (accessed 14 December 2005).

3. Rich Lowry, "Married to the Solution: The Greatest Anti-Child-Welfare Program Predates America," *National Review,* January 16, 2004, available online at http://www.nationalreview.com/script/printpage.p?ref=/lowry/lowry200401160653.asp (accessed 2 March 2006).

4. Sara Diamond, *Roads to Dominion: Right-Wing Movements and Political Power in the United States* (New York: Guilford, 1995), 7.

5. Stephen Eric Bronner, "Constructing Neo-Conservatism," *Logos* 3.2 (spring 2004): 11–22, 9.

6. Ibid., 11.

7. Diamond, *Roads to Dominion,* 179.

8. See Stephanie Coontz, *The Way We Never Were: American Families and the Nostalgia Trap,* 2nd ed. (New York: Basic Books, 2000).

9. Diamond, *Roads to Dominion,* 181, 180.

10. "Neocon 101," *Christian Science Monitor,* available online at http://www.csmonitor.com/specials/neocon/neocon101.html (accessed 14 December 2005).

11. Wikipedia, "Neoconservatism in the United States," http://en.wikipedia.org/wiki/Neoconservatives (accessed 13 January 2006).

12. Diamond, *Roads to Dominion,* 186.

13. Daniel Patrick Moynihan, *The Negro Family: The Case for National Action* (Washington, DC: U.S. Department of Labor, 1965). Cited in Judith Stacey, *In the Name of the Family: Rethinking Family Values in the Postmodern Age* (Boston: Beacon, 1996).

14. Gertrude Himmelfarb, *One Nation, Two Cultures: A Searching Examination of American Society in the Aftermath of Our Cultural Revolution* (New York: Vintage, 2001), 15.

15. Quoted in Diamond, *Roads to Dominion*, 280.

16. Peter Berkowitz, *Virtue and the Making of Modern Liberalism* (Princeton, NJ: Princeton University Press, 1999), 174–75.

17. Peter Berkowitz, "The Liberal Spirit in America," *Policy Review* (August 2003), available online at http://www.policyreview.org/aug03/berkowitz.html (accessed January 12, 2006)

18. Peter Berkowitz, "The Court, the Constitution, and the Culture of Freedom," *Policy Review* (August 2005), available online at http://www.policyreview.org/aug05/berkowitz.html (accessed January 12, 2006).

19. For example, see Beverly LaHaye, *The Desires of a Woman's Heart: Encouragement for Women When Traditional Values Are Challenged* (Wheaten, IL: Tyndale House, 1993), and Tim LaHaye, *Understanding the Male Temperament* (Colorado Springs, CO: Fleming H. Revell, 1996). For examples from the Promise Keepers, see Russ Bellant, "Promise Keepers: Christian Soldiers for Theocracy," in *Eyes Right! Challenging the Right Wing Backlash,* ed. Chip Berlet, 81–85 (Boston: South End Press, 1995). For a critical discussion, see R. Claire Snyder, "The Allure of Authoritarianism: Bush Administration Ideology and the Reconsolidation of Patriarchy," in *W Stands for Women: Feminism, Gender, and Security in the Presidency of George W. Bush,* ed. Michaele Ferguson and Lori Marso (Durham, NC: Duke University Press, forthcoming).

20. Louise B. Silverstein and Carl F. Auerbach, "Deconstructing the Essential Father," *American Psychologist* 54:6 (June 1, 1999): 398.

21. For example, see David Blankenhorn, *Fatherless America: Confronting Our Most Urgent Social Problem* (New York: Basic Books, 1995), and James Dobson, *Bringing Up Boys: Practical Advice and Encouragement for Those Shaping the Next Generation of Men* (Wheaton, IL: Tyndale House, 2000).

22. Silverstein and Auerbach, "Deconstructing the Essential Father," 397–98.

23. Silverstein and Auerbach, "Deconstructing the Essential Father," 397.

24. See also Judith Stacey, *In the Name of the Family: Rethinking Family Values in the Postmodern Age* (Boston: Beacon, 1996), 128–39.

25. Dobson, *Bringing Up Boys.*

26. For a discussion of how these two discourses work together, see Linda Kintz, *Between Jesus and the Market: The Emotions That Matter in Right-Wing America* (Durham, NC: Duke University Press, 1997).

27. Lionel Tiger, *The Decline of Males: The First Look at an Unexpected New World for Men and Women* (New York: St. Martin's Griffin, 1999), 27.

28. Ibid., 130, 135.

29. Ibid., 74.

30. Ibid.

31. Stanley Kurtz, "Love and Marriage: A Combination Necessarily Exclusive to a Man and a Woman," *National Review,* July 30, 2001, available online at http://www .nationalreview.com/contributors/kurtzprint073001.html (accessed 7 July 2001).

32. Stanley Kurtz, "Point of No Return: Marriage Needs a Man and a Woman. And, an Amendment." *National Review,* posted August 3, 2001, available at http:// www.nationalreview.com/contributors/kurtz080301.shtml (accessed 3 August 2001).

33. For a full explanation of how monogamous marriage is actually an ideal rooted in Christianity, see R. Claire Snyder, *Gay Marriage and Democracy: Equality for All* (Lanham, MD: Rowman and Littlefield, 2006).

34. Maggie Gallagher, "The Road to Polygamy," *Town Hall,* March 16, 2004, available online at http://www.townhall.com/columnists/maggiegallagher/mg2004 0316.shtml (accessed 2 April 2004).

35. Samuel P. Huntington, *The Clash of Civilizations and the Remaking of the World Order* (New York: Touchstone, 1996), 46.

36. See Snyder, "Allure of Authoritarianism."

37. For my full response to Okin, see Snyder, "Allure of Authoritarianism."

38. Berkowitz, *Virtue,* 26.

39. Ibid., 173–74

40. Ibid., 188.

41. Ibid., 26 (emphasis added).

42. Himmelfarb, *One Nation,* 51.

43. Jean Bethke Elshtain, "The Family and Civic Life," in *Rebuilding the Nest: A New Commitment to the American Family,* ed. David Blankenhorn, Steven Bayme, and Jean Bethke Elshtain (Milwaukee, WI: Family Service America, 1990), 122.

44. Council on Civil Society, *A Call to Civil Society: Why Democracy Needs Moral Truth: A Report to the Nation from the Council on Civil Society* (1998), 18, 26. Available online at http://www.americanvalues.org/html/r-call_to_civil_society .html (accessed 24 June 2004).

45. The report's signatories include prominent neocons such as Francis Fukuyama, Glenn C. Loury, Margaret Steinfels (of *Commonweal* magazine), and James Q. Wilson. The council is cosponsored by the Institute for American Values, headed by David Blankenhorn, a leader of the Fatherhood Movement. Antigay activists Maggie Gallagher and William Mattox are affiliate scholars of the institute, and antifeminist writer Christina Hoff Sommers, the author of *The War against Boys,* serves as an adviser.

46. Jean Bethke Elshtain, "Against Gay Marriage II: Accepting Limits," *Commonweal* 118:22 (1991): 685—86.

47. Scott S. Greenberger, "Harvard Law Professor Named to Vatican Post," *Boston Globe,* March 10, 2004.

48. Republican National Committee, "Party Platform," available online at http://www.rnc.org/About/PartyPlatform/default.aspx?Section=4 (accessed 5 August 2004). The Defense of Marriage Act seeks to trump the Constitution's "full

faith and credit" clause by proclaiming that no state can be required to recognize same-sex marriages certified in other states and denies any such marriages access to federal benefits.

49. Susan Moller Okin, *Justice, Gender, and the Family* (New York: Basic Books, 1989), 17.

50. Lowry, "Married to the Solution."

51. See U.S. Health and Human Services, Administration for Children and Families Web site, home page for Healthy Marriage Initiative, http://www.acf.hhs .gov/healthymarriage/about/mission.html (accessed 10 August 2005).

52. Irwin Stelzer, "Neoconservatives and Their Critics," in *The Neocon Reader,* ed. Irwin Stelzer, 3–28 (New York: Grove, 2004), 19–20.

53. In 2005 it was revealed that Gallagher's activism was secretly underwritten by HHS and Justice Department contracts. When her funding sources were exposed, Gallagher "apologized . . . for failing to reveal her contract to assist HHS while writing about the marriage initiative in articles and columns, one of which referred to Bush's 'genius.'" In her words, "It was a mistake on my part not to have disclosed any government contract. It will not happen again." This exposure of undisclosed funding to Gallagher and others prompted the president to denounce his administration's practice of secretly paying pundits to support his agenda. Howard Kurtz, "Bush Urges End to Contracts with Commentators," *Washington Post,* January 27, 2005, A4.

54. Linda J. Waite and Maggie Gallagher, *The Case for Marriage* (New York: Broadway Books, 2000).

55. Maggie Gallagher, "Can Government Strengthen Marriage? Evidence from the Social Sciences," National Fatherhood Initiative Institute for Marriage and Public Policy Institute for American Values, 2004, 11, 13, available online at http:// www.marriagedebate.com/pdf/Can%20Government%20Strengthen%20Marriage .pdf (accessed 27 July 2005).

56. Ibid., 20–21.

57. Ibid., 25

58. "The 2006 HHS Poverty Guidelines," HHS Web site, http://aspe.hhs.gov/ poverty/06poverty.shtml (accessed 3 March 2006).

59. Lowry, "Married to the Solution." Lowry's information comes from Robert E. Rector, Kirk A. Johnson, Patrick F. Fagan, and Lauren R. Noyes, "Increasing Marriage Will Dramatically Reduce Child Poverty" (Washington, DC: Heritage Center for Data Analysis, 2003).

60. Ibid., 9.

61. Ibid., 2.

62. Robert Rector, Kirk A. Johnson, and Patrick F. Fagan, "The Effect of Marriage on Child Poverty," Heritage Foundation Web site, April 15, 2002, http:// www.heritage.org/Research/Family/CDA02–04.cfm (accessed 3 March 2006).

63. Snyder, "Allure of Authoritarianism."

64. Christel Manning, *God Gave Us the Right: Conservative Catholic, Evangelical Protestant, and Orthodox Jewish Women Grapple with Feminism* (New Brunswick, NJ: Rutgers University Press, 1999).

65. Jane Mansbridge, *Why We Lost the ERA* (Chicago: University of Chicago Press, 1986).

66. Thomas Frank, *What's the Matter with Kansas? How Conservatives Won the Heart of America* (New York: Holt, 2005).

Chapter 8

The Neoconservative Assault on the Courts
How Worried Should We Be?

Thomas M. Keck

When Ronald Reagan was elected president in 1980, the principal conservative position on the federal courts was a call for judicial restraint. The term was not always used with precision, but the general point, as Reagan-appointed federal judge Richard Posner put it some years later, was that "the power of [the] court system relative to other branches of government should be reduced."[1] Since the rights revolution of the Warren Court era, conservatives had complained that the unelected judiciary was improperly interfering with democratic governance. Reagan's proposed solution was to appoint judges who would exercise their authority with self-restraint and, in the meantime, to shame the sitting members of the federal bench into exercising greater restraint by denouncing their usurpations of legislative prerogative at every turn.

Like balanced budgets and realist foreign policy, however, this long-standing commitment to judicial restraint was largely abandoned once conservatives found themselves in control of the national government. It is no surprise that minority parties in the legislature find it easy to criticize deficit spending but much harder to abandon the practice once they come to power. Similarly, conservatives had long criticized the "democracy-building" efforts of Democratic presidents, but with neoconservatives at the helm during the George W. Bush administration, it seemed far more tempting to use the Pentagon and foreign-policy apparatus to promote conservative ends on a global scale. So too with judicial politics. It was easy enough to criticize the judicial activism of liberal judges in the 1960s and 1970s, but conservatives proved less willing to relinquish judicial power once it was in their own hands.

In this chapter, I consider two of the most significant constitutional conflicts of the George W. Bush era: one that was purportedly responsible for his 2004 reelection and another that is likely to be his most transformative legacy (and that probably played a bigger role in his reelection than the first one). On the issues of both same-sex marriage and executive power during wartime, conservatives are rhetorically committed to a posture of sweeping judicial deference that, if enacted by the federal courts, would undermine important values of left-liberals. In each case, however, conservatives have themselves proved willing to call for active intervention by the federal courts to promote conservative visions of the law.

This tension—between conservatives' continuing demand for judicial restraint and their ever-increasing willingness to deploy judicial power themselves—has been the subject of increasing notice in recent years, but its implications for left-liberal political goals have not been fully elaborated.[2] The tension has produced important internal divisions among judicial conservatives, and the outcome of those intramural battles has significant implications for rights-based movements on the Left. In particular, for the sweeping conservative vision of judicial restraint to become entrenched in the law would be bad for left-liberals, but not catastrophic. After all, left-liberal movements would still be in a position to fight all their battles in other arenas, as the whole point of judicial restraint is to allow greater freedom for the democratically accountable institutions of government to make policy. Far worse for left-liberal movements would be the entrenchment of an activist judicial conservatism, with life-tenured federal judges invalidating whatever policy gains left-liberals manage to eke out in the other branches.

Consider the most persistently salient constitutional conflict of the past thirty years. Since *Roe v. Wade* (1973), the primary conservative position on abortion rights has been that the courts should defer to state and federal legislative institutions. The argument is straightforward: *Roe* illegitimately invented a constitutional right to abortion and, hence, should be overturned. The people and their elected representatives would then be free to regulate abortion in any manner they please.[3] But some pro-life conservatives have advanced a far different argument: fetuses are constitutional "persons" who have judicially enforceable rights to life and liberty and to equal protection of the laws.[4] If the former argument wins out, that would be a significant setback for reproductive rights, but pro-choice advocates would still be free to lobby, vote, and protest for legislative defense of those rights. Many women in the South and Midwest would be seriously harmed, but in much of the country, the pro-choice efforts would be successful, and the judicial reversal of *Roe* would (in those regions) have little practical effect. If the right-to-life argument wins out, however, the legislative battle would be foreclosed, with the courts requiring every state in the Union to protect fetal life. This outcome is unlikely in the extreme, but other recent constitutional conflicts have witnessed more success—or a greater likelihood of future success—for conservative calls for judicial activism.

The Rhetoric of Restraint

The critique of federal judicial power as antidemocratic has been around for a long time, and it has not always been a conservative sentiment. From the founding to the New Deal, it was most often voiced by left-liberal movements concerned that the federal courts would become—and later, had become—unaccountable allies and defenders of property. In the mid-twentieth century, leading New Deal liberals like Felix Frankfurter developed a comprehensive account of the limited reach of federal judicial power that they hoped to entrench on the Court. Other judicial liberals chose a different path, however, and as the postwar Court set out to actively defend civil liberties and minority rights against majoritarian infringement, judicial conservatives adopted the mantle of restraint.

Conservative critics of the Warren Court advanced two principal arguments for restraining judicial power: that the active assertion of judicial authority is presumptively illegitimate in a democratic polity and that courts lack the institutional capacity to craft rational and effective social policy. The first argument was developed most fully by law-school-based constitutional scholars following the path marked out by Frankfurter's former clerk, Alexander Bickel. In a widely influential 1962 book, *The Least Dangerous Branch*, Bickel characterized judicial review as "a deviant institution in the American democracy" and launched a generation of constitutional scholars on a quest to resolve this "counter-majoritarian difficulty."[5] For the next thirty years, the central preoccupation of academic constitutional theory was to figure out the conditions, if any, under which judicial authority could be asserted in a manner that was consistent with democratic governance. Most scholars articulated some such conditions but found that the justices stubbornly refused to adhere to these limits; some influential scholars concluded that judicial review should more or less be abandoned.[6]

Less widely noted but equally significant, Court critics argued that the activist decisions of the 1960s and 1970s had far exceeded the institutional capacity of the courts. The normative constitutional theorists sometimes made this point in passing, but it was most fully developed by the leading neoconservative intellectuals of the 1970s. These scholars and policy analysts often joined their allies in the legal academy in criticizing judicial authority on the grounds of democratic legitimacy—note Nathan Glazer's influential 1975 critique of the "imperial judiciary"—but they supplemented this argument with a distinct complaint about judicial capacity. As part of their broader critique of Great Society social policy, Glazer and his fellow neocons insisted that judicial policymaking was likely to be particularly ineffective. If the federal legislature and bureaucracy could not manage to rationally administer complex programs of "social engineering," the neocons insisted the federal courts certainly were not going to be up to the task. Writing in the *Public Interest* in 1975, for example, Glazer complained that the courts "now reach into the lives of the people, against the will of the people, deeper than they ever have in American history." Noting that the justification usually offered for judicial activism was that the other branches had failed to act, Glazer claimed that the political branches often refused to address particular social problems because they had correctly concluded that there was no clear knowledge of how government should go about doing so. In expanding the reach of government, then, the courts were ignoring the fact that it was "already grossly expanded beyond its capacity to perform." Glazer argued that legislatures and executives had more resources than courts to determine how best to respond to public problems and that when they refused to respond, it was "because no one knows how to, or [because] there is not enough money to cover everything, or because the people simply don't want it. These strike me as valid considerations in a democracy, but they are not considered valid considerations when issues of social policy come up as court cases for judgment."[7]

This neoconservative critique of judicial policymaking dovetailed nicely with the contemporaneous partisan attacks on the courts because it emphasized both the undemocratic character of "government by judiciary" and the wrongheadedness of the liberal social engineering in which the courts were engaged. Glazer's most frequent target was the Burger Court's school busing decisions, which, from his perspective, were simply the worst example of a more general pattern in which the federal courts were undertaking ever-broader efforts to reform governmental institutions.[8] When Donald Horowitz published a book-length treatment of *The Courts and Social Policy* in 1977, he provided four case studies of allegedly ineffective judicial policymaking, and all four were exemplars of post-1960s liberal egalitarianism.[9]

By this point, Court bashing had been a staple of conservative election-year rhetoric for more than a decade. From Barry Goldwater to Ronald Reagan, Republican presidential candidates had criticized the liberal decisions of the Warren and Burger Courts on the campaign trail and had pledged to appoint justices who would avoid "legislating from the bench."[10] Republican presidents made ten consecutive appointments to the high Court from 1969 to 1991, but once Bill Clinton recaptured the presidency for the Democrats, it fell to Republicans in the Senate to hold the line as best they could. Shortly after Clinton's reelection in 1996, Senate Judiciary Committee Chairman Orrin Hatch declared that "those nominees who are or will be judicial activists should not be nominated by the president or confirmed by the Senate, and I personally will do my best to see to it that they are not."[11] Despite what most scholars considered to be a relatively moderate Clinton record on federal judicial appointments, the Republicans continued to appeal to their conservative base by highlighting this issue.[12]

George W. Bush echoed the theme during his two successful national campaigns, repeatedly noting that his favorite justices were Antonin Scalia and Clarence Thomas and that if elected, he would appoint more like them. In a nationally televised debate with Al Gore, for example, Bush declared in October of 2000 that

> voters will know I'll put competent judges on the bench. People who will strictly interpret the Constitution and not use the bench for writing social policy. That is going to be a big difference between my opponent and me. I believe that the judges ought not to take the place of the legislative branch of government. That they're appointed for life and that they ought to look at the Constitution as sacred. They shouldn't misuse their bench. I don't believe in liberal activist judges. I believe in strict constructionists. Those are the kind of judges I will appoint.

A few moments later, Bush sharpened the contrast with his opponent, insisting that Gore would appoint "liberal activist justices who will use their bench to subvert the legislature."[13]

Similarly, the Republican Party's 2000 national platform complained about "scores of judges with activist backgrounds in the hard-left," judges who "make up laws, invent new rights, free vicious criminals, and pamper felons in prison" and who "have arbitrarily overturned state laws enacted by citizen referenda, utterly disregarding the right of the people and the democratic process." Objecting that "[t]he sound principle of judicial review has turned into an intolerable presumption of judicial supremacy," the platform endorsed a variety of Court-curbing proposals but noted that "the most important factor is the appointing power of the presidency."[14] The GOP platform reiterated these themes four years later, repeating much of the language from 2000 and endorsing President Bush's "solid record of nominating only judges who have demonstrated respect for the Constitution and the democratic processes of our republic."[15]

Bush had not yet had the opportunity to nominate a Supreme Court justice, but his purported favorites often echoed this rhetoric of judicial restraint. Justice Thomas has been particularly influential in writing the neoconservative critique of judicial policymaking into the Court's opinions. Concurring in *Missouri v. Jenkins* (1995), in which the Court put a halt to an extensive, eighteen-year effort by a federal district court to integrate the Kansas City schools, Thomas cited Horowitz's *The Courts and Social Policy* and complained that too many judges had "directed or managed the reconstruction of entire institutions and bureaucracies, with little regard for the inherent limitations on their authority."[16] The following year, when the Court rejected a class-action challenge alleging that the Arizona Department of Corrections was providing inadequate legal research facilities and thereby depriving inmates of their right of access to the courts, Thomas again wrote separately to articulate his own sweeping denunciation of the remedial authority of the federal courts. He complained that the remedial decree under review was a "textbook example" of "gross overreaching by . . . federal district court[s]," who have too often been willing to "effect wholesale takeovers of state correctional facilities and run them by judicial decree." And he insisted that "[p]rinciples of federalism and separation of powers" preclude the federal courts from taking "control of core state institutions like prisons, schools, and hospitals, and [from] assum[ing] responsibility for making the difficult policy judgments that state officials are both constitutionally entitled and uniquely qualified to make. . . . The federal judiciary is ill equipped to make these types of judgments," Thomas concluded, and "[t]he Constitution is not a license for federal judges to further social policy goals that prison administrators, in their discretion, have declined to advance."[17]

Justice Scalia has also criticized judicial overreaching on a regular basis, complaining that "this Court seems incapable of admitting that some matters—*any* matters—are none of its business."[18] His judicial opinions are well known for this sort of mocking and dismissive tone, a style that some scholars have found more appropriate to a political tract than a federal judicial opinion.[19] Even more unusual, however, has been his habit of expressing these intemperate views in public speeches as well. Although it is not unheard of for sitting justices to publicly discuss their views of the broad constitutional issues of the day, Scalia's pointed criticism of particular decisions has been noteworthy. For example, when he used a 2003 Religious Freedom Day event in Fredericksburg, Virginia, to criticize a recent Ninth Circuit decision that the modern version of the Pledge of Allegiance ("one Nation, under God") represented an unconstitutional government endorsement of religion, he needlessly forced his own recusal when this case arrived at the high Court.[20] Later that year, he made headlines with another public speech to a conservative gathering, in which he reportedly "adopted a mocking tone to read from the court's" opinion striking down a criminal sodomy statute in *Lawrence v. Texas*.[21] Three years later, he instigated another request for his recusal by publicly mocking the civil liberties claims of enemy combatants in U.S. custody at Guantánamo Bay, claims his Court was scheduled to hear in the case of *Hamdan v. Rumsfeld* just one month later.[22]

The Rhetoric and the Reality

The long-standing conservative denunciation of judicial activism in defense of civil rights and civil liberties has produced a clear expectation that a vote for Republican presidents (and senators) is a vote for restrained judges. Confounding this explanation, judicial conservatives have proven quite willing to call for the active exercise of judicial authority, even in those legal contexts where they have preached judicial restraint most loudly. In a wide variety of legal contexts, conservatives have called for judicial deference to other institutions when they themselves have been winning in those other institutions, but they have called for active judicial intervention when they have been losing. Like any rational political actor, conservatives recognize that when they are losing in a particular arena, it makes sense to shift the battle someplace else. Again and again, they have been willing to do so even if that means calling on the unelected federal courts to overturn decisions issued by political institutions with much greater democratic accountability. The tension is clearest when conservatives call for federal judicial enforcement of constitutional limits on Congress, but it potentially comes into play whenever they call for a court to overturn a left-liberal victory in another institution of government—even another court.

Consider the constitutional controversies arising out of the 2000 presidential election and the Terri Schiavo case. In each case, conservatives called on federal courts to reverse state court decisions that had gone against their interests. In each case, conservatives had majority support in Congress, which might provide some democratic legitimacy for their actions, but each time, they called for federal courts to make an essentially unprecedented intervention into a dispute over the meaning of state law.[23] At least when the stakes are this high—defending human life, winning a presidential election—conservative political actors have been happy to call on the assistance of the federal courts.

Same-Sex Marriage

For religious conservatives, preserving the traditional institution of marriage is a goal of similar importance. Thus, although their opposition to same-sex marriage (SSM) has been couched as a complaint about "activist judges," they themselves have turned to the courts whenever SSM advocates have made headway elsewhere. Put another way, the predominant institutional dynamic in the SSM conflict has been a struggle between the litigation efforts of advocates for lesbian, gay, bisexual, and transgender (LGBT) rights and the electoral efforts of their conservative opponents, but there have been repeated instances in which those roles were reversed.

Every time a court has taken a step toward recognizing same-sex marriages—a series of state appellate courts in Hawaii, Alaska, and Vermont did so during the Clinton years, and the Massachusetts Supreme Court joined the conflict with its 2003 decision in *Goodridge v. Department of Public Health*—conservatives have charged the judges with illegitimate activism and sought to overturn their decision in the political arena. In his 2004 State of the Union address, delivered just two months after the *Goodridge* decision, President Bush complained that the "activist judges" of the Massachusetts court had "redefine[d] marriage by court order, without regard for the will of the people and their elected representatives. On an issue of such great consequence, the people's voice must be heard. If judges insist on forcing their arbitrary will upon the people, the only alternative left to the people would be the constitutional process."[24] One month later, Bush called more explicitly for a constitutional amendment, reiterating that "[a]ctivist courts have left the people with one recourse. If we are to prevent the meaning of marriage from being changed forever, our nation must enact a constitutional amendment to protect marriage in America."[25]

Meanwhile, Republican members of Congress were voicing a similar take on gay rights and the courts. In March 2004, Representative Steve Chabot, chairman of the House Judiciary Subcommittee on the Constitution, insisted that the proposed Federal Marriage Amendment was a necessary response to "rogue judges legislating from the bench." Representative Marilyn Musgrave, author of the proposed amendment, complained that "certain judges do not seem to care about the text and structure of the Constitution or the unbroken history and traditions of our nation. Instead, they seek to use their power to interpret the Constitution as a means of advancing a social revolution unsought and unwanted by the American people." In Musgrave's view, the Constitution was clearly "on the verge of being amended, and the only choice we have in the matter is whether it will be amended . . . through the democratic process . . . or . . . by court ruling."[26] Similar rhetoric emerged from the Senate, where John Cornyn, Republican chairman of the Senate Subcommittee on the Constitution, Civil Rights, and Property Rights, sponsored hearings on the topic of "Judicial Activism v. Democracy." Cornyn himself complained that "activist judges [were] abolishing American traditions by judicial fiat," and Senator Hatch, chairman of the full Judiciary Committee, noted that the *Goodridge* decision has made "clearer . . . than ever that courts are usurping the role of legislatures by imposing their own definitions of marriage on the people and that we must do something about this."[27] When the Federal Marriage Amendment reached the Senate floor, the conservative denunciations of activist judges continued, with Republican Senator Sam Brownback offering this representative complaint: "Most Americans believe homosexuals have a right to live as they choose. They do not believe a small group of activists or a tiny judicial elite have a right to redefine marriage and impose a radical social experiment on our entire society."[28]

Republicans made heavy use of this rhetoric throughout the campaign season, with Bush himself reiterating the complaint about activist judges on at least two nationally televised occasions.[29] The 2004 GOP platform objected that "[a]fter more than two centuries of American jurisprudence, and millennia of human experience, a few judges and local authorities are presuming to change the most fundamental institution of civilization." Quoting President Bush, the platform declared that "[w]e will not stand for judges who undermine democracy by legislating from the bench and try[ing] to remake America by court order." It then proceeded to endorse both the Federal Marriage Amendment and a jurisdiction-stripping bill that would preclude federal judges from forcing other states to recognize Massachusetts marriages.[30]

These national legislative efforts went nowhere, but SSM opponents had much greater success at the state level.[31] In 2004 alone, the voters of thirteen states amended their constitutions via initiative or referendum to outlaw SSM. These ballot measures were a direct response to *Goodridge,* and all thirteen were enacted by wide margins, topping out at 86 percent of the vote in Mississippi. These electoral successes reinforced the impression that SSM advocates were relying on the support of activist judges, whereas their opponents were interested only in vindicating the popular will. The widespread sense that Bush had been reelected in part because of the popular reaction against the Massachusetts judges reinforced this narrative as well.[32]

Even in this context, however—where the conservative rhetoric of judicial restraint has been so widespread—SSM opponents have been quick to turn to the courts when they lose in the elected institutions. No matter how loudly they have complained about activist judges, they have been equally opposed to same-sex marriage rights that have been extended by democratically accountable institutions, and in these instances, the SSM opponents themselves have called on the courts to intervene. Just since the *Goodridge* decision in November 2003, for example, state or federal appellate courts have heard challenges to the legality of marriage, civil-union, or domestic-partnership policies adopted by local elected officials in Ann Arbor, Michigan; Multnomah County, Oregon; New Orleans, Louisiana; New Paltz, New York; Philadelphia, Pennsylvania; Portland, Maine; San Jose and San Francisco, California; and Seattle, Washington.[33]

Some of these have been local conflicts initiated by disgruntled taxpayers, but many of them have been organized and supported by one (or more) of the national organizations dedicated to using the courts to promote conservative visions of law and policy. The Virginia-based Liberty Counsel (LC) has played a particularly active role. Founded in Florida in 1989 by Mat Staver, and later affiliating with Jerry Falwell Ministries in Virginia, LC is a "nonprofit litigation, education and policy organization dedicated to advancing religious freedom, the sanctity of human life and the traditional family." LC originally focused on defending the freedom of speech for activists and organizations on the religious Right, but it has since expanded its efforts to many other areas, including the defense of traditional conceptions of marriage.[34]

In San Francisco, when city officials acting on Mayor Gavin Newsom's orders issued marriage licenses to more than four thousand same-sex couples in early 2004, LC joined state Attorney General Bill Lockyer and several other conservative organizations in challenging Mayor Newsom's actions in state court. Newsom argued that the state's marriage law was in conflict with both the state and federal constitutions and hence that he was duty-bound not to enforce it, but LC's lawyers replied that the courts, and the courts alone, had the authority to make such a determination. This appeal to judicial supremacy was successful, as the California Supreme Court ruled in *Lockyer v. San Francisco* that Mayor Newsom's actions were illegal and that the four thousand marriages were "void and of no legal effect."[35] When the mayor of New Paltz followed Newsom's lead, LC launched a similar litigation effort, which has yielded similar results.[36]

Similarly, when state legislatures have extended marriage rights of varying degrees to same-sex couples, conservative organizations have invariably challenged these statutes in court. In California, the legislature adopted a domestic-partnership statute in 1999 (without judicial prodding) and subsequently amended it on several occasions to expand the protections offered. Most recently, the California Domestic Partner Rights and Responsibilities Act of 2003 provided that "[r]egistered domestic partners shall have the same rights, protections, and benefits, and shall be subject to the same responsibilities, obligations, and duties" that state law provides to spouses. Opponents of SSM, led by the Campaign for California Families, responded with a series of state lawsuits challenging the legality of the legislature's actions.[37]

These litigation efforts have been unsuccessful so far, as have LC's similar efforts in Massachusetts. The institutional dynamics (and the legal arguments) were somewhat different in Massachusetts, as it was a judicial rather than elected institution that first authorized same-sex marriages, but here too, opponents of SSM called on the courts to intervene. On May 10, 2004, just a week before same-sex marriages were set to begin, LC's lawyers filed a federal lawsuit on behalf of eleven state legislators and Robert Largess, vice president of the Catholic Action League in Boston, in a last-ditch effort to prevent the state high court decision from taking effect. Advancing the very sort of overreaching constitutional argument that conservatives so often condemn, LC insisted that the constitutional declaration that "[t]he United States shall guarantee to every State in this Union a Republican Form of Government" authorizes the federal courts to intervene when a state court usurps the power of a state legislature. Three days later, Representative Chabot picked up on this argument in yet another round of congressional hearings on the marriage issue, arguing that the guarantee clause required that our laws be "passed by the duly elected representatives of the people, not by judges who are not charged with reflecting the people's will."[38]

It is one thing to invoke the guarantee clause as a justification for congressional action, but to succeed in court, this argument would have to overcome a 150-year-old constitutional tradition holding this clause nonjusticiable.[39] For this reason, LC's lawyers suffered a complete and utter defeat here, as first a federal district judge and then a unanimous three-judge appellate panel held that the state high court had not denied Massachusetts citizens a republican form of government. The Supreme Court refused to hear LC's appeal, leaving the First Circuit decision as the final word.[40] LC and its allies are not likely to give up, however, and because SSM advocates have recently won legislative victories in other states as well, the stakes here remain quite high.[41]

Executive Power and Civil Liberties

Although the critique of activist judges in the SSM context has been particularly popular among Republican candidates on the hustings, it is an altogether different constitutional conflict that is most important to contemporary Republican elites. In the wake of 9/11, the Bush administration has initiated a wide variety of sweeping changes in federal law-enforcement and intelligence policy, and the stated justifications of these changes have made increasingly clear that the administration's primary constitutional goal is the expansion of executive power. As with the constitutional battles of the culture wars, these arguments for reallocation of institutional authority are rooted in long-standing conservative claims.

The modern Republican Party has supported an expansive notion of executive power for a variety of reasons. Beginning with Richard Nixon's 1968 campaign, the Republican electoral coalition was quite successful in presidential contests, but Nixon, Reagan, and the first Bush all faced what seemed to be a permanently Democratic House of Representatives. In this context, any shift of power from Congress to the presidency would advance conservative goals. Beyond this political calculation, moreover, conservative legal and political elites have generally been committed to a strong executive on principle. In the foreign-policy context, as they have seen it, only a vigorous executive could wage a successful war on communism. In the law-enforcement context, the same was true for the war on drugs. In budgetary conflicts, conservatives trusted the president to protect the public fisc against the demands of rent-seeking legislators. For these reasons, the post-1994 Republican Congress was willing to expand executive authority even with a Democrat in the White House.[42]

In a variety of contexts, President Nixon's efforts to expand White House authority went too far, and the Democratic Congresses of the 1970s reasserted their own authority. In the areas of war powers and intelligence, for example, Congress imposed important limits on executive action in the 1971 Non-Detention Act, the 1973 War Powers Resolution, and the 1978 Foreign Intelligence Surveillance Act (FISA).[43] Ever since, Republican elites have sought to reclaim what they saw as the president's rightful authority, and they have advanced the constitutional theory of a "unitary executive" to justify this effort. The idea had been around for a long time, but Justice Department lawyers in the Reagan administration elaborated the claim that the Constitution vests all executive power in the president and, hence, that his exercise of that power is uncheckable by Congress.[44]

The George W. Bush administration was likely to pursue this theory regardless of circumstances, but it did so in earnest after 9/11. Two weeks after the terrorist attacks, John Yoo, deputy assistant attorney general in the Office of Legal Counsel, prepared a memo for the White House asserting that "[t]he centralization of authority in the president alone is particularly crucial in matters of national defense, war, and foreign policy, where a unitary executive can evaluate threats, consider policy choices, and mobilize national resources with a speed and energy that is far superior to any other branch."[45] In a series of subsequent internal memos, Yoo and other administration lawyers extended this theory to the war on terrorism in all its guises, including the use of military commissions to try enemy combatants, coercive detention and interrogation policies, and electronic eavesdropping without judicial approval.[46]

The most widely known of these internal documents is the infamous August 1, 2002, "torture memo." Signed by Assistant Attorney General Jay

Bybee but written by Yoo, this memo advanced a sweeping vision of the president's wartime authority, insisting that "the President enjoys complete discretion in the exercise of his Commander-in-Chief authority and in conducting operations against hostile forces." I return to this argument below, but the memo was also noteworthy for its examination of the legality of various interrogation methods then being employed or considered by American military forces or intelligence operatives. After a careful parsing of the legislative and judicial history of the relevant legal texts—principally the UN Convention against Torture, ratified by the Senate in 1990, and the antitorture statute adopted by Congress four years later—the Bybee memo concluded that "certain acts may be cruel, inhuman, or degrading, but still not produce pain and suffering of the requisite intensity to fall within" the statutory proscription.[47]

Once these memos came to light, the administration backed away from some of the more controversial assertions but continued to move forward on other fronts. On the issue of warrantless wiretapping, for example, the administration held firm even in the face of widespread criticism. In a December 2005 letter to the leaders of the House and Senate Intelligence Committees, Assistant Attorney General William Moschella argued that Congress had already authorized the National Security Agency to engage in the warrantless "intercept[ion of] certain international communications into and out of the United States of people linked to al Qaeda or an affiliated terrorist organization." Moschella found this policy change in Congress's September 18, 2001, authorization of the president "to use all necessary and appropriate force against those nations, organizations, or persons he determines planned, authorized, committed, or aided the terrorist attacks that occurred on September 11, 2001." Nothing on the face of this congressional Authorization for Use of Military Force (AUMF) purported to alter the detailed warrant requirements of the Foreign Intelligence Surveillance Act, but Moschella argued that that alteration was implicit. More significant, he argued that even if the AUMF had not authorized warrantless wiretapping, the president had independent constitutional authority to adopt the policy on his own.[48] After the Justice Department elaborated these claims in a subsequent white paper, the press reported that the asserted arguments appeared to apply to communications solely within the United States and even to physical searches as well. Administration officials have repeatedly refused to disavow these broader implications.[49]

As applied to the courts, these arguments usually amount to a call for broad judicial deference to the executive. President Bush circumvented a detailed statutory scheme requiring judicial approval of electronic surveillance because the federal courts, in his view, have no authority to interfere with the president's exercise of his authority as commander in chief. In the post-9/11 world, whenever the courts have tried to interfere in such contexts, Justice Department lawyers have loudly objected. In March 2004, for example, with the Supreme Court having agreed to consider several legal challenges to the president's policies regarding the detention of enemy combatants, Solicitor General Ted Olson filed three remarkable briefs instructing the Court to stay its hand. In *Hamdi v. Rumsfeld,* Olson argued that "the scope of judicial review that is available concerning the military's determination that an individual is an enemy combatant is necessarily limited by the fundamental separation-of-powers concerns raised by a court's review or second-guessing of such a core military judgment in wartime." Insisting that "[t]he customary deference that courts afford the Executive in matters of military affairs is especially warranted in this context," Olson noted that "[a] commander's wartime determination that an individual is an enemy combatant is a quintessentially military judgment, representing a core exercise of the Commander-in-Chief authority" and hence is entitled to the "utmost deference" from the federal courts. In the administration's view, any more skeptical judicial "review of executive branch decisions [in this context] carries the inordinate risk of a constitutionally problematic intrusion into the most basic responsibilities of a coordinate branch."[50]

Olson's arguments in the other two cases were similar but even more sweeping, each in its own way. His substantive arguments in *Rumsfeld v. Padilla* were essentially the same as in the *Hamdi* case, but whereas Yaser Hamdi had been captured on the battlefield in Afghanistan, Jose Padilla—like Hamdi, an American citizen—had been arrested by FBI agents in Chicago. In either case, Olson asserted, the president could authorize indefinite detention, without trial or counsel.[51] The plaintiffs in the third case, *Rasul v. Bush,* were not American citizens and were being detained abroad (at the U.S. naval base at Guantánamo Bay, Cuba), so Olson argued here that the federal courts lacked jurisdiction over their legal challenges altogether. For the federal courts to assert such jurisdiction, he insisted, would place them "in the unprecedented position of micro-managing the Executive's handling of captured enemy combatants from a distant combat zone where American troops are still fighting [and] would directly interfere with the Executive's conduct of the military campaign against al Qaeda and its supporters. The detention of captured combatants in order to prevent them from rejoining the enemy during hostilities is a classic and time-honored military practice, and one that falls squarely within the President's authority as Commander in Chief."[52]

As in the same-sex-marriage context, the administration's rhetoric of judicial restraint has been echoed by some conservative judges. In *Hamdi*, for example, Justice Thomas insisted that the president's detention order "falls squarely within the Federal Government's war powers, and we lack the expertise and capacity to second-guess that decision." Relying on *The Federalist*, Thomas argued that "[t]he Founders intended that the President have primary responsibility—along with the necessary power—to protect the national security and to conduct the Nation's foreign relations. They did so principally because the structural advantages of a unitary Executive are essential in these domains." In Thomas's view—as in the Bush administration's—"judicial interference in these domains destroys the purpose of vesting primary responsibility in a unitary Executive." After all, "with respect to certain decisions relating to national security and foreign affairs, the courts simply lack the relevant information and expertise to second-guess determinations made by the President based on information properly withheld."[53]

Thomas's *Hamdi* opinion might be in the running for the leading judicial endorsement of the unitary executive, but that honor probably remains with Scalia's 1988 dissenting opinion arguing that the independent-counsel statute was unconstitutional.[54] On the war-powers issue, Scalia departed from Thomas in *Hamdi* on the grounds that the constitutional text authorizes Congress, and not the president, to suspend the writ of habeas corpus. In *Rasul*, however, he proved just as critical as Thomas of judicial efforts to hamstring the commander in chief. Complaining that the Court was "boldly extend[ing] the scope of the habeas statute to the four corners of the earth," Scalia observed that

[t]he consequence of this holding, as applied to aliens outside the country, is breathtaking. It permits an alien captured in a foreign theater of active combat to bring a [habeas] petition against the Secretary of Defense. Over the course of the last century, the United States has held millions of alien prisoners abroad. A great many of these prisoners would no doubt have

complained about the circumstances of their capture and the terms of their confinement. The military is currently detaining over 600 prisoners at Guantanamo Bay alone; each detainee undoubtedly has complaints—real or contrived—about those terms and circumstances.

As a result of "[t]he Court's unheralded expansion of federal-court jurisdiction . . . federal courts will entertain petitions from these prisoners, and others like them around the world, challenging actions and events far away, and forcing the courts to oversee one aspect of the Executive's conduct of a foreign war." This "monstrous scheme," Scalia concluded, represented "judicial adventurism of the worst sort."[55]

It is clear, then, that the Bush administration's bold assertion of executive power could produce a judicial abandonment of an important set of civil liberties. Thomas and Scalia were writing in dissent in these cases, but they may well be joined by Bush appointees John Roberts and Samuel Alito in the years to come. Shortly before his nomination to the Supreme Court in July 2005, Roberts had joined a very deferential D.C. Circuit opinion in *Hamdan v. Rumsfeld,* and Alito's views on executive power are even clearer. In a 2000 speech that came to light after his own nomination to the high Court, Alito recalled that during his days in the Department of Justice's Office of Legal Counsel (OLC) in the 1980s, "we were strong proponents of the theory of the unitary executive, that all federal executive power is vested by the Constitution in the president. And I thought then, and I still think, that this theory best captures the meaning of the Constitution's text and structure" because "[t]he president has not just some executive powers, but the executive power—the whole thing."[56]

During his days at OLC, Alito played an important role in developing an additional vehicle for advancing the theory of the unitary executive: the so-called presidential signing statement. When signing a bill into law, presidents have often issued a brief statement declaring their reasons for doing so, but Alito and his fellow Justice Department lawyers in the Reagan administration suggested using such statements to assert the president's own independent interpretation of the new law. These statements were intended, in the first instance, as messages to the courts, who should consider them as part of the "legislative history" often used to discern the meaning of federal statutes. As Alito put the matter in a February 1986 Justice Department memo, "Since the president's approval is just as important as that of the House or Senate, it seems to follow that the president's understanding of the bill should be just as important as that of Congress."

He acknowledged that "[t]he novelty of the procedure and the potential increase of presidential power" were likely to provoke congressional opposition to the practice, but he insisted that "our primary objective is to ensure that Presidential signing statements assume their rightful place in the interpretation of legislation."[57]

President Bush has made unusually frequent and aggressive use of such signing statements, repeatedly announcing that the executive branch would construe a particular statute to ignore any implications or applications with which the president disagreed. The leading scholarly study counted 108 signing statements in President Bush's first term, more than any previous president. These 108 statements advanced 505 separate constitutional objections to the statutes at issue, 82 of which referenced the president's "power to supervise the unitary executive." In addition, 77 referenced the president's "exclusive power over foreign affairs," and 48 pointed to his "authority to . . . withhold information" from Congress or the public.[58]

For example, upon signing the statute creating the independent commission to investigate the 9/11 attacks, Bush noted that although the statute imposed "new requirements for the executive branch to disclose sensitive information," he would withhold such information when necessary for national security reasons.[59] Similarly, when Congress reauthorized the USA Patriot Act in March 2006, it required the Justice Department to inform Congress at regular intervals of the nature and frequency of the FBI's exercise of its expanded search and seizure authority. In his signing statement, President Bush declared his intention to construe these provisions "in a manner consistent with the President's constitutional authority to supervise the unitary executive branch and to withhold information the disclosure of which could impair foreign relations, national security, the deliberative processes of the Executive, or the performance of the Executive's constitutional duties."[60]

As with the internal memos, the most notorious of President Bush's signing statements is the one that appeared to authorize torture. On December 30, 2005, Bush announced that he was signing a supplemental appropriations bill for the Department of Defense, but he raised nine different constitutional objections to various provisions of the act, noting his determination to ignore some of these provisions and to construe others as "advisory." One of those provisions was the Detainee Treatment Act of 2005, a measure sponsored by Senator John McCain that provided that "[n]o individual in the custody or under the physical control of the United States Government, regardless of nationality or physical location, shall be subject to cruel, inhuman, or degrading treatment or punishment." In his now-familiar phrase, President Bush proposed to "construe [this provision] in a manner consistent with the constitutional authority of the President to supervise the unitary executive branch and as Commander in Chief and consistent with the constitutional limitations on the judicial power, which will assist in achieving the shared objective of the Congress and the President . . . of protecting the American people from further terrorist attacks." The clear import of this statement was that regardless of the rules laid down by Congress or the courts, the president reserves the right to order cruel, inhuman, or degrading treatment of detainees if and when he finds such treatment necessary to protect the American people from terrorist attacks. This implication was amplified by his response to another provision of the appropriations bill, the Graham-Levin Amendment, which stripped the federal courts of jurisdiction to receive habeas corpus petitions from alien detainees at Guantánamo Bay. On this point, Bush declared that the withdrawal of jurisdiction would apply retroactively, thus "preclud[ing] the Federal courts from exercising subject matter jurisdiction over any existing or future action" initiated by a Guantánamo detainee.[61]

Like the internal policy memos and the briefs filed in the course of litigation, these signing statements have emphasized the limits of judicial authority to review presidential actions. Two weeks after the president read the Graham-Levin Amendment to apply retroactively, for example, Solicitor General Clement argued that the Supreme Court lacked jurisdiction to hear Salim Hamdan's pending legal challenge to the president's executive order establishing military tribunals for the trial of alien enemy combatants.[62] Were the Court to accept this argument, the scope of judicial review of the president's wartime authority would be substantially narrowed.

In all these contexts, however, Bush administration officials have also advanced an argument that, under certain conditions, calls for the active judicial supervision of federal lawmaking. Again and again, the president has asserted his authority to ignore federal statutes on the grounds that those statutes represent unconstitutional infringements on executive authority. When this argument is pressed to its utmost, which administration officials have increasingly been willing to do, it leads to a call for judicial invalidation of congressional efforts to hamstring the president. The key theme of President Bush's signing statements has been a sweeping vision of the scope of the commander-in-chief power that cannot constitutionally be limited by Congress. Every statute that purports to impose such a limit is, on this account, unconstitutional and should, on this account, be invalidated by the courts.

The Bush administration, in short, is calling not just for judicial deference to the executive but for active judicial intervention against Congress. As Justice Jackson pointed out in the leading modern judicial opinion on the separation of powers, "When the President takes measures incompatible with the expressed or implied will of Congress, his power is at its lowest ebb, for then he can rely only upon his own constitutional powers minus any constitutional powers of Congress over the matter. Courts can sustain exclusive presidential control in such a case only by disabling the Congress from acting upon the subject."[63] The administration has repeatedly argued that this is in fact what courts should do. In the August 2002 "torture memo," Assistant Attorney General Bybee insisted that "Congress may no more regulate the President's ability to detain and interrogate enemy combatants than it may regulate his ability to direct troop movements on the battlefield." On this analysis, "Any effort to apply [the 1994 antitorture statute] in a manner that interferes with the President's direction of such core war matters as the detention and interrogation of enemy combatants . . . would be unconstitutional." Following the logic of the unitary executive, "Any effort by Congress to regulate the interrogation of battlefield combatants would violate the Constitution's sole vesting of the Commander-in-Chief authority in the President. . . . Just as statutes that order the President to conduct warfare in a certain manner or for specific goals would be unconstitutional, so too are laws that seek to prevent the President from gaining the intelligence he believes necessary to prevent attacks upon the United States."[64]

In addition to the 1994 antitorture statute, Bush administration officials have questioned the constitutionality of FISA, the Non-Detention Act, and apparently the prohibitions on assault, threats, cruelty, and maltreatment in the Uniform Code of Military Justice (UCMJ).[65] In each of these contexts, the administration has tried to avoid a direct constitutional clash by advancing narrower statutory grounds on which their claims might be supported. In each case, however, the administration has insisted that if Congress has indeed tried to infringe on the president's military authority, the courts should side with the president by invalidating the statute. The Non-Detention Act provides that "No citizen shall be imprisoned or otherwise detained by the U.S. except pursuant to an act of Congress," but Solicitor General Olson has urged the Court to interpret it narrowly so as to avoid a clash with "the well-established authority of the Commander in Chief to detain enemy combatants in wartime."[66] Similarly, administration lawyers have urged the courts to interpret the September 2001 AUMF as implicitly authorizing the president to engage in warrantless wiretapping of members and associates of al Qaeda. In the absence of such an interpretation, FISA's purported prohibition of such surveillance would be unconstitutional. As phrased in the January 2006 Justice Department white paper, "were FISA [and related statutory provisions] interpreted to impede the President's ability to use the traditional tool of electronic surveillance to detect and prevent future attacks by a declared enemy that has already struck at the homeland and is engaged in ongoing operations against the United States, the constitutionality of FISA, as applied to that situation, would be called into very serious doubt."

If the courts are willing to interpret away all congressionally imposed limits on the president, then the Bush administration is happy to avoid the constitutional clash. If not, then administration lawyers will push the unitary-executive theory as far as they can. On the Justice Department's analysis, the wiretapping conflict raises the broad constitutional question of "whether the signals intelligence collection the President determined was necessary to undertake is such a core exercise of Commander in Chief control over the Armed Forces during armed conflict that Congress cannot interfere with it at all."[67] Endorsing this argument, Senator Pat Roberts, chairman of the Senate Intelligence Committee, observed in a February 3, 2006, letter to the Senate Judiciary Committee that "[i]t is quite clear to me that Congress could not, through passage of FISA, extinguish the President's constitutional authority to conduct the terrorist surveillance program at issue."[68]

It remains too soon to tell whether this argument will carry a judicial majority, though Senator Roberts expressly predicted that it would. If his prediction proves accurate, then left-liberal advocates of civil liberties— and their allies on the right—will be foreclosed from seeking congressionally imposed restrictions on the president's wartime authority. Such efforts are difficult enough as it is; since so many of these wartime policies are authorized and conducted in secret, it is not easy for Congress (and the American public) to provide effective oversight. But if the Court starts actively striking down congressional statutes for infringing on presidential authority—as it has actively struck down congressional statutes for infringing on state authority over the past ten years—this task would become immensely more difficult.[69]

Whither Judicial Conservatism?

For some time now, the standard conservative position on the federal courts has been a complaint that unelected judges are imposing their will on the nation. This critique of "government by judiciary" has carried significant weight with the American people over the past four decades, as they have repeatedly elected Republican presidents who have promised to appoint judges committed to exercising their own power with greater restraint. Carried too far, this vision of judicial restraint is dangerous for two Madisonian reasons. Madison created a system of separate institutions checking one another to ensure that minority rights would not be left to the whim of popular majorities and that the rights of the people as a whole would not be left to the whim of unaccountable government officials. As the contemporary controversies over same-sex marriage and executive power make clear, Madison's concerns remain relevant today.

Still, the call for judicial restraint is a perfectly reasonable conception of judicial power; it has a long pedigree, and it would even have some advantages from a left-liberal point of view. Consistent adherence to such a deferential approach would mean that Congress could enact regulatory statutes without worrying about states' rights; that state legislatures could enact antidiscrimination statutes without worrying about the "free association" rights of religious organizations or the Boy Scouts; that city councils could enact zoning ordinances without worrying about property rights; and the like. The real problem for left-liberals is that some conservatives want the courts to exercise deference and restraint when conservatives are winning in the other institutions of government but to actively intervene when conservatives are losing.

Where conservatives have strong policy commitments—regarding the use of state power to defend "moral values," to unseat rogue regimes, or anything else—they will continue to call on the courts whenever their assistance seems useful. Left-liberal advocates of same-sex marriage and civil liberties during wartime face an uphill political battle, but they have each won occasional legislative victories. State legislatures in California, Connecticut, and New Jersey have recently adopted domestic-partnership or civil-union policies that extend many concrete legal rights to same-sex couples, and Congress has imposed some marginal restraints on the president's national security authority. In each case, however, these legislative victories could be undone if the federal judiciary heeds conservative calls for the active defense of traditional marriage and executive power.

In pursuit of these goals, some conservative litigators have been willing to advance relatively novel constitutional arguments, on the theory that weak arguments, over time, can become strong. Liberty Counsel's guarantee-clause challenge to the Massachusetts marriage decision was unlikely to succeed and was in fact quickly rejected by each court that heard it. Still, these lawyers and their supporters seemed convinced that, as in the Florida election controversy four years earlier, unusual intervention by the federal courts was justified here as necessary to thwart the activist pretensions of a politically motivated state supreme court. The guarantee clause may be the best constitutional hook on which to hang this argument, and if conservative litigators continue to press such claims, conservative judges may eventually be persuaded.

The conservative position on the guarantee clause was once that of Justice Frankfurter. Dissenting in *Baker v. Carr* (1962)—the first of the Warren Court's landmark reapportionment decisions—Frankfurter reiterated his long-standing objection that legislative districting was precisely the sort of "political thicket" that the courts should not enter. The plaintiffs in *Baker* had relied on the equal protection clause to challenge Tennessee's dramatically malapportioned state legislative districts, but Frankfurter complained that their argument was "in effect, a Guarantee Clause claim masquerading under a different label," and he insisted that such claims were unfit for judicial action.[70]

Frankfurter's position on the judicial role in policing the federal government's military and intelligence practices was the same. Concurring in the Court's 1952 "steel seizure" case, Frankfurter began by observing that "[t]he Framers . . . did not make the judiciary the overseer of our government." Appealing to what Bickel would later call the "passive virtues," he insisted on "[r]igorous adherence to the narrow scope of the judicial function" and avoidance of sweeping constitutional decisions whenever possible. Although the courts may sometimes "have to intervene in determining where authority lies as between the democratic forces in our scheme of government," they should be ever "wary and humble" in doing so.[71] In a separate opinion in the same case—one from which I have already quoted—Frankfurter's colleague and jurisprudential ally, Robert Jackson, observed that

the very nature of executive decisions as to foreign policy is political, not judicial. Such decisions are wholly confided by our Constitution to the political departments of the government, Executive and Legislative. They are delicate, complex, and involve large elements of prophecy. They are and should be undertaken only by those directly responsible to the people whose welfare they advance or imperil. They are decisions of a kind for which the Judiciary has neither aptitude, facilities nor responsibility and which has long been held to belong in the domain of political power not subject to judicial intrusion or inquiry.[72]

When the Senate Judiciary Committee questioned John Roberts about his understanding of the judicial role, he appealed to this legacy of judicial restraint, quoting Frankfurter's observation that "[c]ourts are not representative bodies. They are not designed to be a good reflex of a democratic society." As such, Roberts insisted that "[t]he proper exercise of the judicial role requires a degree of institutional and personal modesty and humility." Judges should remember that "[t]hey do not have a commission to solve society's problems, as they see them, but simply to decide cases before them according to the rule of law." When questioned regarding the limits on executive power, Roberts praised Jackson's steel-seizure opinion in particular.[73]

Chief Justice Roberts may well follow this path of deference and restraint, but it is far from clear how many judicial conservatives will join him. Some prominent observers were troubled by Alito's refusal, during his own confirmation hearings a few months later, to issue a direct answer when Senator Leahy asked, "Wouldn't it be constitutional for the Congress to outlaw Americans from using torture?"[74] Conservative calls for active judicial intervention in defense of conservative constitutional ends are now well within the mainstream of constitutional discourse. As far back as 1992, on a Court consisting of eight Republican appointees and one conservative Democrat, Justice O'Connor wrote for a six-justice majority in raising the possibility that the guarantee clause may be justiciable after all.[75] So although Liberty Counsel's arguments in the Massachusetts marriage case had no realistic chance of success, they were not as far beyond the pale as they once were. I do not mean to suggest that a federal judicial prohibition on state recognition of same-sex marriages is on the horizon —and neither is a sweeping judicial invalidation of congressionally imposed limits on executive action—but judicial conservatives have developed activist doctrines in other contexts with some success, and we should be wary here as well.

NOTES

1. Richard A. Posner, *The Federal Courts: Challenge and Reform* (Cambridge, MA: Harvard University Press, 1996), 314.

2. I have traced the rise of conservative judicial activism in *The Most Activist Supreme Court in History: The Road to Modern Judicial Conservatism* (Chicago: University of Chicago Press, 2004). The most influential critique of this new conservative activism has probably been Cass Sunstein's *Radicals in Robes: Why Extreme Right-Wing Courts Are Wrong for America* (New York: Basic Books, 2005).

3. See, for example, Justice Scalia's dissenting opinion in *Planned Parenthood v. Casey*, 505 U.S. 833 (1992).

4. See, for example, Robert P. George, *In Defense of Natural Law* (Oxford: Oxford University Press, 2001).

5. Alexander Bickel, *The Least Dangerous Branch: The Supreme Court at the Bar of Politics*, 2nd ed. (New Haven, CT: Yale University Press, 1986), 18.

6. For a leading example of the former, narrower claim, see John Hart Ely, *Democracy and Distrust: A Theory of Judicial Review* (Cambridge, MA: Harvard University Press, 1980). For a leading example of the latter, broader claim, see Robert H. Bork, *Slouching toward Gomorrah: Modern Liberalism and American Decline* (New York: Regan Books).

7. Nathan Glazer, "Towards an Imperial Judiciary?" *Public Interest* 41 (fall 1975): 106, 118–19.

8. Nathan Glazer, *Affirmative Discrimination: Ethnic Inequality and Public Policy* (New York: Basic Books, 1975).

9. For an extended account of these neoconservative treatments of judicial power, see Keck, *The Most Activist Supreme Court*, 134–43.

10. The stories of the Republican effort to build a conservative judiciary is well known. See, for example, David A. Yalof, *Pursuit of Justices: Presidential Politics and the Selection of Supreme Court Nominees* (Chicago: University of Chicago Press, 1999).

11. Orrin Hatch, "Remarks before the Federalist Society's 10th Anniversary Lawyer's Convention," November 15, 1996, Washington, D.C.

12. On Clinton's judicial appointments, see Sheldon Goldman, Elliot Slotnick, Gerard Gryski, and Gary Zuk, "Clinton's Judges: Summing Up the Legacy," *Judicature* 84 (2000–2001): 228–54.

13. The first Gore-Bush presidential debate, October 3, 2000, available online at http://www.debates.org/pages/trans2000a.html.

14. "Republican Party Platform of 2000," available online at http://www.presidency.ucsb.edu/showplatforms.php?platindex=R2000.

15. "2004 Republican Party Platform: A Safer World and a More Hopeful America," available on-line http://www.presidency.ucsb.edu/docs/platforms/R2004platform.pdf.

16. 515 U.S. 70, 126 (1995).

17. *Lewis v. Casey,* 518 U.S. 343, 364, 385–88 (1996).

18. *Sosa v. Alvarez-Machain,* 124 S.Ct. 2739, 2776 (2004).

19. See, for example, Richard A. Brisbin, *Justice Antonin Scalia and the Conservative Revival* (Baltimore: Johns Hopkins University Press, 1997), ix.

20. Tony Mauro, "Courtside: Speaking Freely," *Legal Times* October 20, 2003, available online at http://www.law.com/jsp/dc/pubarticleDC.jsp?id=1066605401528.

21. Anne Gearan, "Scalia Ridicules Court's Gay Sex Ruling," *Dayton Daily News,* October 24, 2003.

22. Michael Isikoff, "Detainees' Rights—Scalia Speaks His Mind," *Newsweek,* April 3, 2006, available online at http://www.msnbc.msn.com/id/12017271/site/newsweek/.

23. For helpful accounts of both cases along these lines, see Jeffrey Rosen, *The Most Democratic Branch?* (New York: Oxford University Press, 2006). On *Bush v. Gore,* see also Howard Gillman, *The Votes That Counted: How the Court Decided the 2000 Presidential Election* (Chicago: University of Chicago Press, 2001).

24. President George W. Bush, State of the Union Address, January 20, 2004, available online at http://www.whitehouse.gov/news/releases/2004/01/20040120-7.html.

25. Remarks by the President, Roosevelt Room, the White House, February 24, 2004, available online at http://www.whitehouse.gov/news/releases/2004/02/2004 0224-2.html.

26. Representatives Chabot and Musgrave were quoted in Carl Hulse, "House Panel Is Told '96 Law Protects States on Marriage," *New York Times,* March 31, 2004, A14.

27. U.S. Senate Committee on the Judiciary, Subcommittee on the Constitution, Civil Rights, and Property Rights, Hearing on "Judicial Activism v. Democracy: What Are the National Implications of the Massachusetts *Goodridge* Decision and the Judicial Invalidation of Traditional Marriage Laws?" March 3, 2004.

28. Comments on Senate floor, July 12, 2004, available online at http://marriage law.cua.edu/TestimonySenate/brownb071204.cfm.

29. President Bush's speech to the Republican National Convention, September 2, 2004, available online at http://www.2004nycgop.org/cgi-data/speeches/files/v46q7t4op6op0109d9b8i8373arhnnor.shtml; the third Bush-Kerry presidential debate, October 13, 2004, available online at http://www.debates.org/pages/trans 2004d.html. After his reelection, Bush alluded to the "activist judges" of the *Goodridge* court in his 2005 and 2006 State of the Union addresses as well.

30. "2004 Republican Party Platform."

31. The House passed the Marriage Protection Act, which purported to strip the federal courts of jurisdiction to review the constitutionality of the federal Defense of Marriage Act in July 2004, but neither this nor any of the other proposals had a serious chance of making it through the Senate.

32. The "moral values" interpretation of Bush's reelection victory was widespread in the media but remains the subject of significant scholarly dispute. Compare Michael J. Klarman, "*Brown* and *Lawrence* (and *Goodridge*)," *Michigan Law Review* 104 (December 2005): 459–73, who summarizes and echoes the media account, with Morris Fiorina, *Culture War? The Myth of a Polarized America* (New York: Pearson Longman, 2006), 145–64, who fully rejects it.

33. See, for example, *Devlin v. City of Philadelphia*, 580 Pa. 564 (Sup. Ct. Penn. 2004); *Ralph v. City of New Orleans*, 2005 WL 3701498 (La. Ct. of Appeal, 12/14/05).

34. The mission statement is from Liberty Counsel's Web site, http://www.lc.org/aboutus.html. In addition to LC, the key anti-SSM organizations have been the Alliance Defense Fund (ADF) and the American Center for Law and Justice (ACLJ), the latter of which is the largest, wealthiest, and most firmly established of the Christian Right litigation organizations. See generally Steven P. Brown, *Trumping Religion: The New Christian Right, the Free Speech Clause, and the Courts* (Tuscaloosa: University of Alabama Press, 2002), 36–44; Thomas Crampton, "Using the Courts to Wage a War on Gay Marriage," *New York Times*, May 9, 2004, 14.

35. *Lockyer v. City and County of San Francisco*, 95 P.3d 459, 464 (2004).

36. In October 2005, an intermediate New York appellate court held unanimously that Mayor West had acted illegally. Relying in part on the *Lockyer* decision from California, the court refused to comment on the substantive question of whether the state constitution required that marriage rights be made available to same-sex couples but held that in deciding this question on his own, the mayor had exceeded the limits of executive authority. Unlike the California court, however, it refused to invalidate the marriages that had already occurred because the couples themselves—the ones whose rights would be taken away—had not been represented in the proceeding. *Hebel v. West*, 2005 N.Y. Slip. Op. 7887 (2005).

37. *Knight v. Superior Court*, 128 Cal. App. 4th 14 (2005); *Campaign for California Families v. Schwarzenegger*, 2006 Cal. App. Unpub. LEXIS 751 (Cal. App., 3rd Dist., January 27, 2006); *Knight v. Schwarzenegger*, 2006 Cal. App. Unpub. LEXIS 2164 (Cal. App., 3rd Dist., March 16, 2006).

38. U.S. House of Representatives Committee on the Judiciary, Constitution Subcommittee Hearing on H.J. Res. 56, the "Federal Marriage Amendment," May 13, 2004.

39. The Supreme Court first held the guarantee clause nonjusticiable in *Luther v. Borden*, 48 U.S. 1 (1849).

40. *Largess v. Supreme Judicial Court of Massachusetts*, 2004 U.S. LEXIS 7727.

41. The New Jersey legislature adopted a domestic-partnership policy in 2004 that extended many of the rights and responsibilities of marriage to same-sex couples and two years later expanded the range of rights included in the policy. The Connecticut legislature adopted a civil-union policy in 2005, extending all the state-law rights and responsibilities of marriage to same-sex couples.

42. Note, for example, the Line Item Veto Act, enacted primarily with Republican support in 1996.

43. Congress also sought to reassert its authority over federal budgetary policy. See generally Keith E. Whittington, *Constitutional Construction: Divided Powers and Constitutional Meaning* (Cambridge, MA: Harvard University Press, 2001), 158–206.

44. The argument is often traced to Alexander Hamilton, whose Federalist No. 70 identified "unity" as the first of three essential ingredients for an energetic executive, and John Marshall, who argued in the House of Representatives that "[t]he President is the sole organ of the nation in its external relations, and its sole representative with foreign nations." Annals, 6th Cong., col. 613 (March 7, 1800). The leading modern judicial endorsements of this vision are Chief Justice Taft's opinion in *Myers v. United States* (1926) and Justice Sutherland's in *U.S. v. Curtiss-Wright Export Corp.* (1936).

45. Memorandum for Timothy E. Flanigan, Deputy Counsel to the President, from John C. Yoo, Deputy Assistant Attorney General, Office of Legal Counsel, Re: The President's Constitutional Authority to Conduct Military Operations against Terrorists and Nations Supporting Them (September 25, 2001).

46. See, for example, Memorandum for Alberto R. Gonzales, Counsel to the President and William J. Hanes, II, General Counsel, Department of Defense, from John C. Yoo, Deputy Assistant Attorney General and Robert J. Delahunty, Special Counsel, Office of Legal Counsel, Re: Authority for Use of Military Force to Combat Terrorist Activities within the United States (October 17, 2001); Memorandum for Alberto R. Gonzales, Counsel to the President, from Patrick F. Philbin, Deputy Assistant Attorney General, Office of Legal Counsel, Re: Legality of the Use of Military Commissions to Try Terrorists (November 6, 2001); Memorandum for Alberto R. Gonzales, Counsel to the President and William J. Haynes, II, General Counsel, Department of Defense, from Jay S. Bybee, Assistant Attorney General, Office of Legal Counsel, Re: Application of Treaties and Laws to al Qaeda and Taliban Detainees (January 22, 2002); Memorandum for William J. Haynes, II, General Counsel, Department of Defense, from Jay S. Bybee, Assistant Attorney General, Office of Legal Counsel, Re: The President's Power as Commander in Chief to Transfer Captured Terrorists to the Control and Custody of Foreign Nations (March 13, 2002). On warrantless wiretapping, the *New York Times* has reported the existence of an as-yet-unreleased memo written by Yoo in late 2001 or early 2002. See Eric Lichtblau, "Panel Rebuffed on Documents on U.S. Spying," *New York Times*, February 2, 2006, A1.

47. The 1994 statute proscribed any "act committed by a person acting under the color of law specifically intended to inflict severe physical or mental pain or suffering (other than pain or suffering incidental to lawful sanctions) upon another person within his custody or physical control." Memorandum for Alberto R. Gonzales, Counsel to the President, from Jay S. Bybee, Assistant Attorney General,

Office of Legal Counsel, Re: Standards of Conduct for Interrogation under 18 U.S.C. 2340–2340A (August 1, 2002).

48. Letter to Senator Roberts, Senator Rockefeller, Rep. Hoekstra, and Rep. Harman, from Assistant Attorney General William E. Moschella (December 22, 2005), available online at http://www.fas.org/irp/agency/doj/fisa/doj122205.pdf.

49. The Department of Justice white paper asserted that "a consistent understanding has developed that the president has inherent constitutional authority to conduct warrantless searches and surveillance within the United States for foreign intelligence purposes." See "Legal Authorities Supporting the Activities of the National Security Agency Described by the President" (January 19, 2006), available online at http://www.usdoj.gov/opa/whitepaperonnsalegalauthorities.pdf, p. 7. In congressional testimony in April 2006, Attorney General Gonzales refused to rule out the president's legal authority to authorize warrantless wiretapping that occurs entirely within the United States. In similar testimony two months earlier, he had refused to answer questions about the president's authority to order physical searches without a warrant. See Chitra Ragavan, "The Letter of the Law," *U.S. News and World Report*, March 27, 2006, available online at http://www.usnews.com/usnews/news/articles/060327/27fbi.htm; Eric Lichtblau, "Gonzales Suggests Legal Basis for Domestic Eavesdropping," *New York Times*, April 7, 2006.

50. Brief for Respondents, *Hamdi v. Rumsfeld* (March 29, 2004).

51. Brief for Petitioner, *Rumsfeld v. Padilla* (March 17, 2004).

52. Brief for Respondents, *Rasul v. Bush* (March 3, 2004).

53. 542 U.S. 507, 579–83 (2004).

54. See *Morrison v. Olson* (1988).

55. 542 U.S. 466, 498–99, 506 (2004).

56. Address to the Federalist Society, Washington, D.C. (November 2000), quoted in Charlie Savage, "Schumer Questions Nominee's Theory on Executive Role," *Boston Globe*, January 10, 2006.

57. Memo from Deputy Assistant Attorney General Samuel A. Alito, Jr., to The Litigation Strategy Working Group, Re: Using Presidential Signing Statement to Make Fuller Use of the President's Constitutionally Assigned Role in the Process of Enacting Law (February 5, 1986), available online at http://www.archives.gov/news/samuel-alito/accession-060-89-269/Acc060-89-269-box6-SG-LSWG-Alitoto LSWG-Feb1986.pdf.

58. Phillip J. Cooper, "George W. Bush, Edgar Allen Poe, and the Use and Abuse of Presidential Signing Statements," *Presidential Studies Quarterly* 35:3 (September 2005): 515–32.

59. Statement by the President (November 27, 2002), available online at http://www.whitehouse.gov/news/releases/2002/11/20021127-2.html.

60. President's Statement on H.R. 199, the "USA PATRIOT Improvement and Reauthorization Act of 2005" (March 9, 2006), available online at http://www.whitehouse.gov/news/releases/2006/03/20060309-8.html.

61. President's Statement on Signing of H.R. 2863, the "Department of Defense, Emergency Supplemental Appropriations to Address Hurricanes in the Gulf of Mexico, and Pandemic Influenza Act, 2006" (December 30, 2005), available online at http://www.whitehouse.gov/news/releases/2005/12/20051230-8.html.

62. Respondents' Motion to Dismiss for Lack of Jurisdiction, *Hamdan v. Rumsfeld* (January 12, 2006).

63. *Youngstown Sheet and Tube v. Sawyer,* 343 U.S. 579, 637–38 (1952).

64. Bybee memorandum (August 1, 2002).

65. On this last point, Senator Levin has publicly referred to a still-classified March 14, 2003, OLC memo titled "Military Interrogation of Alien Unlawful Combatants," which apparently asserted the executive's constitutional authority to ignore the prohibitions on assault, threats, cruelty, and maltreatment in the UCMJ. The argument here, as in the August 2002 torture memo, is that a federal statute cannot constitutionally limit the president's decisions on whether and how to interrogate enemy combatants. Senator Carl Levin, Senate Floor Speech on the Amendment to Establish an Independent Commission on Detainee Treatment (November 4, 2005), available online at http://www.senate.gov/~levin/newsroom/release.cfm?id=248311. In an unusual move, the OLC disavowed this analysis in December 2003, shortly after Jack Goldsmith replaced Bybee as head of OLC. See Daniel Klaidman, Stuart Taylor Jr., and Evan Thomas, "Palace Revolt," *Newsweek,* February 6, 2006.

66. Brief for Respondents, *Hamdi v. Rumsfeld* (March 29, 2004). See also Brief for Petitioner, *Rumsfeld v. Padilla* (March 17, 2004).

67. Department of Justice white paper (January 19, 2006), 3, 28–36.

68. Letter from Senator Roberts to Senators Specter and Leahy (February 3, 2006), available online at http://balkin.blogspot.com/roberts.fisa.unconstitutional.pdf.

69. For a similar argument on this point, see Noah Feldman, "Our Presidential Era: Who Can Check the President?" *New York Times,* January 8, 2006.

70. 369 U.S. 186, 297–98 (1962). Frankfurter first used the "political thicket" language in his plurality opinion in *Colegrove v. Green,* 328 U.S. 549, 556 (1946), a holding that was overturned in *Baker.*

71. 343 U.S. 579, 594–97 (1952). On the passive virtues, see Bickel, *Least Dangerous Branch.*

72. 343 U.S. 579, 582–83 (1952).

73. John Roberts, written responses to Senate Judiciary questionnaire (August 1, 2005), available online at http://www.washingtonpost.com/wp-dyn/content/article/2005/07/19/AR2005071900870.html#documents.

74. See Jeffrey Rosen, "Uncle Sam," *New Republic,* January 30, 2006.

75. *New York v. United States,* 505 U.S. 144, 183–86 (1992).

Part III

The Global Reach of the
New Conservative Ideology

Chapter 9

The Imperial Presidency
The Legacy of Reagan's Central America Policy

Greg Grandin

Diplomatic historian Andrew Bacevich has pointed out that in "neocon-servative lore, 1980 stands out not only as a year of crisis but as the year when the nation decisively turned things around."[1] When considering this turnaround, most casual observers usually point to the fall of the Soviet Union and the liberation of Eastern Europe, but neocons have a com-plicated relationship to those two events, coming about as they did not through confrontational militarism but through negotiation and patience. "Reagan never invaded Eastern Europe," was General Wesley Clark's re-sponse to being pressed by the Republican chair of the House Armed Ser-vices Committee to admit that George W. Bush's Iraq policy was similar to Ronald Reagan's in Europe.[2] In fact, Reagan, in sharp contrast to his rhe-torical escalation of the Cold War and his increase in defense spending, followed a course of moderation in most foreign-policy arenas, so much so that by 1986 his conservative base had taken to calling him the Soviet Union's "useful idiot" for pursuing arms negotiations with Mikhail Gor-bachev.

But there was one area where the administration's rhetoric did match its actions, and that was Central America, where Reagan patronized vi-ciously brutal anticommunist regimes in El Salvador and Guatemala and an anticommunist insurgency in Nicaragua. For many, the region became an obsession. Jeane Kirkpatrick, Reagan's ambassador to the United Na-tions, identified it as "the most important place in the world for the United States."[3] "Colossally important," she said. Commentators at the time were hard-pressed to account for such a high opinion of a handful of small, impoverished countries. They were equally perplexed by Rea-gan's refusal to negotiate an end to the region's wars, by his willingness to pursue his objectives to the point of provoking a constitutional crisis, and by his insistence that support for brutal allies was a matter of principle, of keeping faith with American ideals. Yet looking back through the prism of George W. Bush's post-9/11 diplomacy, the importance of Reagan's actions in the region does come into focus, not because of the region's geopolitical significance but because of its role in facilitating the consolidation of the modern American conservative movement.

Most accounts of the rise of the New Right focus on its domestic dimensions, linking it to a backlash against the crisis of authority and social liberalization of the 1960s and situating it within economic and demographic shifts related to the deindustrialization and the transfer of the nation's economic and political center of gravity from the northeast to the southwest and west that gained momentum in the 1970s. To the degree that it is understood in terms of foreign policy, it is associated with the backlash against defeat in Vietnam and the rise of third-world revolutionary nationalism, along with the loss of moral authority that attended those two phenomena. Few, if any, studies have explicitly understood the New Right to be not only an expansionist movement but a movement that draws its energy from that expansion. Yet the progress of the conservative revolution largely adhered to Kirkpatrick's famous description of the Sandinista Revolution: it could only sustain itself by continually marshaling its base in the name of an expansive foreign policy, pulling into its gravitational field a diverse constellation of nationalists, militarists, religionists, idealists, and economic elites, helping these groups to cohere through a renewed engagement with the world.

Central America was key to this engagement. Once in office, Reagan came down hard on the region's leftist movements, in effect letting his administration's most committed militarists set and execute policy. In El Salvador, over the course of a decade, they provided more then a million dollars a day to fund a lethal counterinsurgency campaign. In Nicaragua they set up an illegal, off-the-books logistical support network to maintain the Contras, a paramilitary force led by discredited remnants of the deposed dictator's national guard designed to roll back the Sandinista revolution. In Guatemala, the administration pressed to reestablish military aid to an army that was in the middle of committing genocide, defending the country's born-again president even as he was presiding over the worst slaughter in twentieth-century Latin America. All told, U.S. allies in Central America during Reagan's two terms killed over three hundred thousand people, tortured hundreds of thousands, and drove millions into exile.

Reagan could afford to execute such a calamitous policy not, pace Kirkpatrick, because of the region's importance but its unimportance, which made it a painless, for the United States at least, remedy for the Vietnam syndrome: "Mr. President," Secretary of State Alexander Haig assured Reagan, "this is one you can win." The fallout that resulted from a hard line there could be, if not managed, then easily ignored. Unlike the Middle East, Central America had no oil or other crucial resources. Nor did Washington's opponents in the small, desperately poor countries have many consequential friends. Unlike Southeast Asia, the region was in America's backyard—the USSR would not support the Sandinistas or the rebels in El Salvador and Guatemala to the degree it did its allies in Vietnam. "The eagle that kills the deer in Central America," declaimed national-security scholar Robert Tucker, "will not frighten the bear in the Middle East."[4] The region was not high on Reagan's agenda, concerned as he was with pushing through domestic initiatives, as well as tending to other more pressing problems in Poland, Iran, and Afghanistan, making it a cheap reward to the hawks who helped elect Reagan: "They can't have the Soviet Union or the Middle East or Western Europe. All are too important. So they've given them Central America," remarked a Senate staffer in Jesse Helms's office.[5] "There was just a vacuum," he said, and conservatives rushed to fill it.

As part of a nationalist backlash bent on reversing what many insisted was a dangerous decline of U.S. power and authority, yet occurring nearly simultaneously with U.S. victory in the Cold War, the "amazing success" of Reagan's Central America policy, as William Kristol and other New Right intellectuals judge it, led a generation of neoconservatives to insist that it was not "containment" but unapologetic, aggressive militarism that defeated Bolshevism. There were other more strategically important areas for the United States, but no other region provided such a prolonged opportunity to restore the power and privilege of the executive branch after setbacks in the 1960s and 1970s as did Central America, in ways that continue to resound in the initiatives taken after 9/11 by George W. Bush's administration. All of George W. Bush's abuses of power—the manipulation of intelligence and the media, the building of an interagency war party that operated autonomously from Washington's foreign-policy establishment, the illegal wiretaps, and the surveillance of antiwar activists—have their most immediate antecedents in Reagan's Central America policy, which in retrospect has to be understood as the first battle in the New Right's crusade to roll back restrictions placed on the executive in the wake of Vietnam, Watergate, COINTELPRO, and other scandals of the 1970s.

But perhaps even more important, it was in Central America that New Right activists began the ideological restoration of the imperial presidency, first combining the three elements that give today's imperialism its moral force: punitive idealism, free-market absolutism, and right-wing Christian populism. The first justified a belligerent diplomacy not just for the sake of national security but to advance "freedom." The second sanctified property rights and the unencumbered free market as the moral core of the freedom it was America's duty to export. The third backed up these ideals with social power, as the Republican Party learned how to channel the passions of its diverse constituencies into the international arena, both to counter the antimilitarism generated by Vietnam and to deflect the frustrations caused by its inability to complete the New Right's domestic agenda.

When Hobbes Met Kant in Central America

There has been much discussion about what to call the Bush administration's curious mix of realism—an unapologetic assertion that it is Washington's right to use preemptive violence to respond to perceived threats —and idealism—a belief that it is "America's duty," in Bush's words, to extend liberty throughout the world.[6] Some observers identify this position as "hard Wilsonianism," an embrace of Woodrow Wilson's democratic idealism but a rejection of his faith in international organizations and treaties.[7] Others have dubbed it "democratic realism."[8] Whatever it is called, most observers view the Bush Doctrine as a sharp break from the liberal internationalism of the Cold War period while admitting that it has deep roots in America's political culture. What is new, at least for the modern American state, is how intimately the two impulses have been bound together, for not since the days of Teddy Roosevelt has the United States so openly championed martial virtue and violence as the best way to spread universal rights. And it certainly is new for the modern Republican Party, dominated as it was until recently by pragmatists and realists, internationalists like Henry Kissinger who believed that the central task of his diplomatic career was to dampen the messianic zeal that marked the early Cold War period, zeal that marched the United States straight into the muck of Vietnam. Commentators have had difficulty accounting for this Republican turnaround. Pundits correctly identify a rhetorical shift taking place during Ronald Reagan's tenure as president, reflecting his efforts to restore America's pride and purpose after the melancholy 1970s. They make mention of Reagan's championing of Soviet and Eastern European dissidents and credit Paul Wolfowitz with pressing the White House to allow for reform in the Philippines. Yet they consistently ignore the one place where Republicans turned themselves into hard Wilsonians: Central America.

The realism that powered America's military resurgence in the 1980s was of a particular variety, deeply ideological and committed to a fulfillment of American purpose in the world. Central America was its proving ground, as a group of conservative defense intellectuals worked hard to restore America's sense of self-confidence in order to justify the carnage taking place there in the name of national defense. Jeane J. Kirkpatrick was the most prominent of this group, and it was she who provided the moral and intellectual framework to rationalize Reagan's Central America policy. In so doing, she began the synthesis of the realist and idealist traditions of American diplomacy into a powerful synthesis.

Kirkpatrick considered herself a realist when it came to foreign policy, in the tradition of Hans Morgenthau, Dean Acheson, and George Kennan. Though a lifelong Democrat, she found herself repulsed by the self-flagellation that she believed had overcome her party. Attracted as a result to Reagan's bid for the White House, Kirkpatrick met with the candidate early in 1980 and pronounced his "intuitive grasp" of foreign affairs "generally correct and very realistic" and soon accepted his invitation to join his campaign.[9] As an "action intellectual"—to borrow a phrase coined by Theodore White to describe the academics who abandoned their scholarship to join FDR's New Deal and JFK's New Frontier governments—Kirkpatrick combined practice and theory to rebut the philosophical premises that underwrote post-Vietnam antimilitarism. Appointed by Reagan to the position of ambassador to the United Nations, she served notice that condemnation of Washington, which had come too easy in the past, would now have a cost. In her speeches and writings, she repeatedly pointed out the hypocrisy of condemning Israel while praising Libya, say, or censuring apartheid in South Africa while ignoring human rights violations in Cuba.

But Kirkpatrick did more than just point out double standards. Prior to serving as ambassador to the United Nations she worked as a Georgetown political scientist who mostly researched the arcanum of the presidential nominating process. She had a broad engagement with intellectual history, however, and wrote accessible essays that updated the conservative tradition to the current moment. Drawing on Thomas Hobbes's respect for the centrality of power in human affairs and Edmund Burke's respect for the intractability of tradition to understand the limits of that power, Kirkpatrick not only pointed out what she described as the hypocrisy behind criticisms of countries such as El Salvador and South Africa but actively defended the institutions of those countries as important bulwarks of order and stability.

It was in Latin America where Kirkpatrick's ideas were most fully elaborated and applied. In a series of articles, she used the region to refute what at the time seemed like an emerging dominant consensus regarding what should be the role of America in the world. The U.S. military's defeat by a poorly armed peasant insurgency in Vietnam led many in the Democratic foreign-policy establishment to rethink the wisdom of seeing all global conflict through the bifocal lens of superpower conflict. They began to recommend an acceptance of "ideological pluralism"—the belief that not all societies will follow the same road to development. According to this new perspective, third-world nationalism, of the kind that drove the United States out of Southeast Asia, should be dealt with on its own terms and not as a cat's paw for Soviet Communism. Kirkpatrick responded point by point to this sanguine philosophy of international relations and broadly countered it with an old-fashioned conservative insistence on the dark side of human nature. Jimmy Carter either ignored or opposed much of the new liberal internationalism, yet Kirkpatrick successfully linked it to his administration to account for the fall of Nicaragua and Iran, the spread of insurgencies in El Salvador and Guatemala, the ongoing influence of Castro, and the emergence of revolutionary nationalism throughout the Middle East, Latin America, and the Caribbean.

Kirkpatrick provided the Republican administration with the argument it needed to justify ongoing support for brutal dictatorships.[10] Autocrats, no matter how premodern their hierarchies and antimodern their values, allowed, she said, for a degree of autonomous civil society. By contrast, Marxist-Leninist totalitarians such as the Sandinistas mobilized all aspects of society, which made war, as a means to maintain such mobilization, inevitable. Since political liberalization was more likely to occur under a Somoza than a Marxist regime like that of the Sandinistas, Kirkpatrick insisted that a foreign policy that forced allies to democratize was not only bad for U.S. security but detrimental for the concerned countries as well: it led in Nicaragua and Iran not to reform but to radical regimes and was threatening to do the same in Bolivia, El Salvador, Guatemala, Brazil, Argentina, Chile, Uruguay, and South Africa. But Kirkpatrick went beyond merely justifying alliances with unseemly allies. In repudiating the "rational humanism" of the liberal internationalists, she gave voice to what may be called the Hobbesian impulse in U.S. foreign policy—an insistence that brute power and not human reason establishes political legitimacy. In a 1980 essay titled "The Hobbes Problem: Order, Authority and Legitimacy in Central America," she invoked the seventeenth-century philosopher to attack Carter's conditioning of military aid to El Salvador on the implementation of social reforms, including a land reform, and on the reduction of human-rights violations.[11] Such requirements, she wrote, were wrong-headed because they ignore the fact that "competition for power" rooted "in the nature of man" is the foundation of all politics. Kirkpatrick advised the incoming Republican administration to abandon Carter's reform program and sanction the Salvadoran military's effort to impose order through repression, even if it meant the use of death squads. Such a course of action was justified, she contended, because Salvador's political culture respects a sovereign who is willing to wield violence—proof of which was that one of the death squads took the name Maximiliano Hernández Martínez, a dictator who in 1932 slaughtered as many as thirty thousand indigenous peasants in the course of a week. Kirkpatrick described Hernández Martínez as a "hero" to Salvadorans and argued that by taking his name the assassins sought to "place themselves in El Salvador's political tradition and communicate their purpose." (Perhaps a similar logic explains why a notoriously corrupt and brutal Contra unit in Nicaragua took the name the "Jeane Kirkpatrick Task Force").[12] Washington needed to think "more realistically" about the course of action it pursued in Latin America, Kirkpatrick argued elsewhere: "The choices are frequently unattractive."

Kirkpatrick also repeatedly attacked what might be called the Kantian impulse in U.S. foreign policy, the belief that human progress would result in a peacefully ordered world government. Again and again she hammered against the conceit that U.S. power should and could be used to promote universal, internationalist abstract goals such as "human rights," "development," and "fairness." She warned against trying to be the "world's midwife" to democracy. "No idea," she complained, "holds greater sway in the mind of educated Americans than the belief that it is possible to democratize governments, anytime, anywhere, under any circumstances."

It is important to emphasize that Kirkpatrick was not arguing against morality in foreign policy. Far from it, for she believed that a conviction in the righteousness of U.S. purpose and power was indispensable in the execution of effective diplomacy. But for America's foreign-policy establishment, Vietnam shook that conviction. The optimism with which liberal internationalists approached the world, she charged, was but a thin mask to hide the shame they felt over American power. The problem was not idealism as such but Carter's misplaced application of it, which not only led him and his advisers to doubt American motives but to abandon the responsibility of power for the abstractions of history. Setting the stage for today's neocons, she called for a diplomacy that once again valued human action, resolve, and will. If America acted with moral certainty to defend its national interests, the consequence would, by extension, be beneficial for the rest of the world. "Once the intellectual debris has been cleared away," she believed, "it should become possible to construct a Latin American policy that will protect U.S. security interests and make the actual lives of actual people in Latin America somewhat better and somewhat freer." American diplomacy here, even in the hands of a committed realist such as Kirkpatrick, is an article of faith, expressed in the self-confident writ of policymakers that when America acts in the world, even when it is doing so expressly to defend its own interests, the consequences of its actions will be in the general interest. It is in such assuredness that the roots of the punitive idealism that drives the new imperialism can be found, roots that first began to sprout in Reagan's Central America policy.

Just before his inauguration, Reagan described to *Time* magazine the approach he planned to take in El Salvador, sounding like he ripped a page straight out of Kirkpatrick's "The Hobbes Problem": "You do not try to fight a civil war and institute reforms at the same time," the president-elect said. "Get rid of the war. Then go forward with the reforms."[13] But once in office, Reagan picked up the torch of idealism traditionally borne by Democrats and embraced human rights and democracy as vital foreign-policy concerns. This shift is often credited to the first generation of midlevel neoconservative policymakers, such as Elliot Abrams and Paul Wolfowitz, who shared Kirkpatrick's disdain of liberal internationalism yet felt that hardheaded appeals to the moral legitimacy of national defense would not serve to excuse alliances with death squads and dictators. They pushed for a foreign policy that made an ethical distinction between the USSR and the United States. In 1981, Abrams, as Secretary of State for Human Rights, circulated a memo approved by his boss, Alexander Haig, arguing that although a military response to the Soviets remained crucial, the U.S. also needed an "ideological response." "We will never maintain wide public support for our foreign policy unless we can relate it to American ideals and to the defense of freedom," Abrams wrote. "[O]ur ability to resist the Soviets around the world depends in part on our ability to draw this distinction and to persuade others of it. . . . Our struggle," Abrams proclaimed, "is for political liberty."[14]

Reagan greatly expanded Carter's "nation-building" program and even continued his predecessor's land reform and advocacy on behalf of human rights. Not since Vietnam, according to former Rand Corporation analyst Benjamin Schwarz, had Washington ever "been so deeply and intimately involved in attempting to transform a foreign society that it had not defeated in war and hence did not control."[15] Likewise, in Nicaragua, Reagan broke with diplomatic protocol and insisted that the Sandinistas not only stop arming rebels in El Salvador and Guatemala but also hold free elections, respect human rights, and protect political pluralism.

It was in Central America, more than anywhere else, where nationalists once again cast the Cold War as a moral struggle between good and evil. In Vietnam, as the war progressed and American involvement grew both more violent and more damned, idealism slowly drained out of Washington's public pronouncements. By the war's end, Nixon rarely justified the conflict in terms of promoting democracy but rather by the need to protect national security and save face. In Central America, the opposite occurred. In the face of mounting evidence of atrocities committed by U.S. allies, Reagan, in his fights with Congress, consistently raised the ethical stakes. By the mid-1980s, the Great Communicator was peppering his speeches on Central America with references to the Great Emancipator. Continued aid to the Nicaraguan Contras, whom he raised to the "moral equivalents of America's founding fathers," would keep faith with the "revolutionary heritage" of the United States, a heritage that, borrowing from Lincoln, bestowed a "hope to the world for all future time." "Who among us," he asked Congress in 1986, "would tell these brave young men and women: 'Your dream is dead; your democratic revolution is over; you will never live in the free Nicaragua you fought so hard to build?'" ("Address to the Nation on United States Assistance for the Nicaraguan Democratic Resistance," June 24, 1986).

One reason for this elevated oratory was that the Reagan administration faced resistance to its Central America policy from a grassroots movement that, although growing out of the peace demonstrations of the 1960s and 1970s, had much more of a prominent religious component than did the mobilization protesting the Vietnam War. Quakers, Catholics, and liberal Protestants cast opposition to Reagan's wars in Nicaragua and El Salvador in the language of Christian social justice, organizing rallies, speaking to church groups, holding candlelit prayer vigils, and providing sanctuary for Central American refugees fleeing violence perpetrated by U.S.-backed regimes. The White House needed something more than cold realism to reply to this challenge.

The inclusion of democracy and human rights in Washington's diplomacy also came from intramural struggles early in the Reagan presidency, as the hawks sought to wrest foreign policy out of the hands of establishment diplomats. Reagan, as mentioned earlier, pursued a course of moderation in most foreign-policy areas. But conservative activists considered Central America theirs, hence their anger when Thomas O. Enders was appointed Assistant Secretary of State for Inter-American Affairs, a position responsible for formulating Central American policy. Enders was no dove. Educated at Exeter, Yale, Harvard, and the Sorbonne, Enders, from wealthy Republican banking family, had helped direct the aerial bombing of Cambodia from the U.S. embassy in Pnomh Penh. "He took charge of administering the Nixon Doctrine," wrote William Shawcross in *Sideshow: Kissinger, Nixon, and the Destruction of Cambodia,* "with a vigor" that others in the embassy "found distasteful."[16] But Enders was a career diplomat, not a movement conservative, and thus suspicious to Jesse Helms and other militarists. Helms, who exerted a good deal of control over foreign-policy appointments, held up Enders's confirmation for months until the nominee agreed to staff his office with New Right ideologues.

Upon taking office, Enders confirmed Helms's suspicions by his willingness to consult with Democrats to find a negotiated solution to the crises in Central America. He laid out his plans for El Salvador in a speech to the World Affairs Council in July 1981, in which he proposed to continue Jimmy Carter's policy of land distribution, human rights, and elections—the very kind of social reforms that Kirkpatrick and other hawks condemned. Enders also incensed conservative militants when he proposed giving Congress the power to review and certify progress on human-rights issues and political reform. Like Elliot Abrams, Enders believed that the language of human rights and social justice that had gained ground with the antiwar movement could be harnessed on behalf of U.S. foreign policy. Enders's strategy worked, winning over enough congressional

Democrats with his talk of promoting democracy and human rights to allow Reagan to continue funding the Salvadoran military. And so, over the objections of the militarists, Washington embarked on its most ambitious liberal democratic nation-building program since Vietnam, one that not only entailed spending billions and billions of dollars on military aid to stop a revolution but, theoretically at least, distributing land, transforming the country's legal and fiscal structure, and cultivating a culture of tolerance and respect for human rights.

In Nicaragua, though, concern for democracy and human rights came from an unexpected source—from Enders's opponents, the hawks. During the first year of Reagan's term, Enders worked to find a negotiated settlement with the new Nicaraguan leadership. In his talks with the Sandinistas, he downplayed democracy and did not push for internal reforms, instead focusing on security issues. "You can do your own thing," Enders told a high-ranking Sandinista official, "but do it within your own borders, or else we are going to hurt you." Mindful of American might, Sandinista leaders cooperated, and in August 1981 pledged not to export their revolution, to keep its military small, and to limit ties with Cuba and the Soviet Union. In exchange, Enders promised that Washington would restore economic aid and sign a nonaggression pact. But the war party—led by midlevel hawks at Defense, State, the National Security Agency (NSA), and the CIA, such as Oliver North and Fred Iklé, along with their upper-echelon patrons, such as William Casey and Kirkpatrick—had other ideas, demanding instead, in the words of a Helms staffer, that Enders take "harder action."[17] Turning Enders's diplomatic maneuver to their own ends, they insisted on holding the Sandinistas to the same human-rights standard to which he was holding the Salvadoran government. In February 1982, in a speech to the Organization of American States, Reagan insisted that the Sandinistas adopt internal reform. Two months later, Washington told Managua that "free elections" would be "essential elements of the political context of future relations between our two countries." Such demands derailed negotiations, with the Sandinistas balking at Enders's sudden stipulation that the United States have a say in Nicaragua's internal affairs. This suited the hawks just fine since they had already convinced Reagan five months earlier, in November 1981, to throw his support behind the Contras.

Hobbes had met Kant in Central America, and the Republicans were well on the way to becoming "revolutionaries."

A Foundation of Corpses

This embrace of human rights and democracy as a vital diplomatic interest on the part of the Republican Party corresponded to a change in military tactics. Just as policy intellectuals used Central America to invigorate America's moral purpose in the world, counterinsurgent strategists, many of them adrift since the United States withdrew from Southeast Asia, looked to the region as the ideal venue to rehabilitate unconventional warfare doctrine. And even as the rhetoric of diplomacy became ever more lofty, the application of U.S. foreign policy on the ground became ever more brutal.

For counterinsurgent strategists, El Salvador became a laboratory to correct for mistakes made in Southeast Asia. "El Salvador represents an experiment," wrote one military report in the mid-1980s, "an attempt to reverse the record of American failure in waging small wars, an effort to defeat an insurgency by providing training and material support without committing American troops to combat."[18] The problem in Vietnam, it was argued, was not counterinsurgency tactics as such, but the misapplication of those tactics. Central America provided the opportunity to get it right. It also allowed New Right defense activists, many of them radicalized by defeat in Southeast Asia by a peasant insurgency, to press the military high command once again to pay attention to the threat emanating from the third world.

But there were alterations to be made. The first change had to do with making violence and terror a more centrally acknowledged element in low-intensity warfare. Counterinsurgent strategists still talked about the need to win the "hearts and minds" of civilians, but now that campaign was largely understood not as gaining allegiance through political and economic reform but as limiting options through the application of necessary levels of repression—a low-tech precursor to Rumsfeld's exposition of "shock and awe." In El Salvador, U.S. allies murdered roughly sixty thousand civilians. In Guatemala, two hundred thousand were killed. In Nicaragua, the Contras, responsible for the deaths of thirty thousand civilians, slaughtered "people like hogs," according to one private mercenary who aided Reagan's freedom fighters after Congress cut off aid.[19] "The horrible lesson of the early 1980s is that terrorism works," a U.S. military expert posted in El Salvador remarked in reference to Washington's allies.[20] "The success of the U.S. policy," admitted another, "was built on a foundation of corpses."[21]

Military advisers and diplomats continued to talk about building democratic institutions and even advocated for a land reform as a way of democratizing the economy in El Salvador. But the New Right's embrace of free-market absolutism foreclosed on the kind of "modernization" initiatives designed to break up large concentrations of wealth and political power and to create employment. Winning "hearts and minds" became in effect an exercise in the effective management of violence, of calibrating the right proportions of, as one CIA Contra training manual put it, "implicit and explicit terror."[22] In other words, even as the language used to justify the Cold War was soaring to evermore lofty heights, its execution on the ground was becoming ever more brutal.

The second alteration had to do with redefining low-intensity warfare to include not just counterinsurgencies—that is, the provision of aid to an allied government to defeat a rebel movement—but insurgencies to reverse Soviet gains, or perceived gains, in the third world. Since the beginning of the Cold War, the idea of "rollback" had percolated just under the surface of the prevailing doctrine of "containment," emerging every so often in the oratory of statesmen such as John Foster Dulles and in the actions taken by the United States in Latin America, Southeast Asia, and Africa. It was Carter, after all, who initiated support for the Mujahadeen in Afghanistan. But anticommunist true believers such as Oliver North, William Casey, and John Singlaub, who launched the Contra war against Nicaragua's Sandinista government, viewed aid to anticommunist rebels not just in instrumental terms, as a way, say, to bait the Soviet Union into its own Vietnam-style quagmire, as the Carter administration understood its support of Islamic rebels in Afghanistan. They rather related to them with deep ideological sympathy, as the vanguard of a worldwide democratic revolution. Defense intellectuals and activists who circulated around the Heritage Foundation began to take seriously Reagan's rehabilitation of the idea of "revolution" for the Republican Party. Before being busted in the Iran-Contra scandal, CIA director William Casey made plans to extend the clandestine supply operation he and North set up to support the Contras into a transnational "enterprise," as a way of providing arms, money, and training to anticommunist insurgencies throughout the world, including Cambodia, Ethiopia, Angola, Yemen, Mozambique, Cuba, and Afghanistan. "The tide has changed," proclaimed the usually taciturn Casey, and "oppressed people want freedom and are fighting for it."[23]

In other words, even as the post-Vietnam military high command was reestablishing their autonomy and professionalism and formulating the

Weinberger and Powell Doctrines so as to both limit the role of the armed forces and establish a firewall between war and politics, Central America allowed militarists to push in the opposite direction. They promoted a vision of unconventional war in which there existed no border between politics and war, a vision that would use military power not for distinct, manageable objectives but to advance what they believed to be was a "global democratic revolution."

By the time Reagan left office, New Right intellectuals and military strategists had achieved a remarkable revolution in the morality and mechanics of low-intensity warfare. The White House had expanded and increased the funding of the Special Forces, set up in the Pentagon a Special Operations Unified Command to conduct low-intensity warfare, and created a new post of Assistant Secretary of Defense for Special Operations and Low-Intensity Conflict. Despite the nominal sway of the Weinberger Doctrine, the United States was on the offensive, carrying out unconventional military operations throughout the third world. Yet despite this impressive restoration of military power and global purpose, one impediment, wrote the Pentagon's legal adviser, William O'Brien, in 1984, still remained: the "unrelenting anti-militarism" of the "American home front," whose distaste for things like torture, extrajudicial assassinations, "dead or wounded children," and "starvation as a means of combat" continued to handicap American action in the world.[24]

Going on the Offensive

More than any other twentieth-century conflict, Vietnam highlighted the porous border between foreign and domestic policy. Escalating dissent, much of it linked to a reinvigorated internationalism, not only helped end the war but led to legislative measures that curbed the power of government security institutions, most notably the Central Intelligence Agency. At the same time, an embolden press and Congress began to shine a bright light on activities normally left in the shadows of presidential prerogatives. At home, a deep skepticism shattered the governing consensus that held sway for the first two decades after World War II. In what seemed like a remarkably short period of time, the institutional pillars of society—universities, churches, newspapers, movies, Congress, and the judiciary—that had previously buttressed government legitimacy now leaned against it, advancing what some conservative critics came to deride as a permanent "adversary culture."[25] It was not just loss in Vietnam that brought about such a turnaround, but also revelations of brutality committed throughout the third world in the name of national security and perfidy conducted under the cloak of government secrecy and executive privilege.

Just as New Right activists used Central America to reinvest a sense of ethical purpose into the Cold War struggle and to rehabilitate counterinsurgency doctrine, they took the opportunity provided by the conflict to rehearse techniques to contain dissent at home. In the face of persistent and growing opposition to its policies in El Salvador and Nicaragua, the Reagan White House countered with a series of actions that eroded the boundary between imperial policies and national politics. Making little distinction between foreign enemies and domestic opponents, Reagan used the Central American wars to reinvigorate the national-security state.

In order to sell its Central America policy to the American people, the White House established in 1983 the Office of Public Diplomacy. Described by a congressional inquiry as a domestic psychological-warfare operation modeled on overseas covert action, the office was headed first by Cuban exile Otto Reich and then Robert Kagan and staffed with CIA and Pentagon operatives. Its mission was to coordinate the work of contracted Madison Avenue public-relations firms, New Right grassroots organizations, and supposedly independent scholars to pressure Congress and the media to support Reagan's Central America policy. All criticisms related to Central America, no matter how slight or serious (such as substantiated reports of torture and other human-rights atrocities committed by U.S. allies), were met with a barrage of counterfacts designed to muddy the public debate. The point, according to White House communications director Patrick Buchanan, was not to create a "consensus" for Reagan's Central America policy but to master the art of spin in order to prevent an oppositional consensus, such as what happened during the Vietnam War, from forming. Repudiated in the wake of the Iran-Contra scandal, many of the techniques pioneered by the Office of Public Diplomacy continued to be used by successive administrations, especially in the marketing campaign of the current Bush administration to manipulate the press in order to sell the Iraq war to the American public.

Public diplomacy, though, was just one part of Reagan's efforts to contain dissent. The New Right came to power in 1980 committed to rolling back restrictions placed by Congress and Carter's Justice Department on the FBI and the CIA and to reverse the Warren Court's extension of civil liberties. Conservative activists and policy intellectuals laid out a program that foreshadowed many of the provisions today found in the Patriot Act and in post-9/11 initiatives to restructure the intelligence system. At the time, many of these reforms, such as interagency file sharing, proved to be too radical to implement, but organizations like the Heritage Foundation specifically called for the monitoring of solidarity organizations that opposed Reagan's Central America policy.

As they did in the 1960s under the auspices of COINTELPRO and other covert surveillance operations, intelligence agencies—both the FBI and those authorized exclusively for foreign espionage—again turned their attention to domestic dissenters, carrying out a far-reaching operation against church groups, public-policy foundations, human-rights organizations, even congressional offices. This activity went beyond surveillance to include the harassment of activists in their homes and workplaces. In one of the more outrageous examples of government schemes to circumvent the right of due process—noteworthy in light of today's revocation of the constitutional rights of designated "enemy combatants" and the Justice Department's post-9/11 lockup of thousands of foreign nationals—the National Security Council (NSC), through the office of Oliver North, drafted plans to hold antiwar activists in detention centers in the event of a U.S. invasion of Nicaragua.

But for an emerging mass movement committed to transform America's political culture, containing dissent through propaganda and intimidating surveillance was not enough. The New Right squared off directly against what it perceived to be an entrenched culture of antimilitarist humanism and skepticism.

Midlevel operatives in the Reagan White House, most famously Oliver North, mobilized their own grassroots support. They turned to anticommunist militarists from the intelligence and defense communities radicalized by defeat in Vietnam to raise money, supply arms, and provide training to the Contras. Such logistical support, which helped bypass congressional scrutiny, entailed cobbling together a transnational menagerie of Strangelovian spooks, mercenaries, Nazis, drug runners, dictators, and Moonies. More important, the White House and the Office of Public Diplomacy marshaled evangelical Christian organizations in support of Reagan's foreign policy. The Christian Broadcasting Network offered an alternative to skeptical mainstream media coverage, while religious organizations, such as the 700 Club, raised money for counterinsurgent operations in Guatemala, established missions and schools in Nicaragua, sent preachers to minister to Salvadoran troops, and shipped hundreds of tons of humanitarian aid to the Contras. This outsourcing of the "hearts and minds" component of low-intensity warfare provided the evangelical movement with its first extensive foreign-policy experience since its retreat from the public sphere following the Scopes trial decades earlier, paving the way for a broader engagement with international affairs that continues to this day. It both sharpened the religious tone of American foreign policy and furthered the transformation of the Republican Party into a mass, populist movement. The bringing together of anticommunist militarists and evangelicals in an aggressive anticommunist campaign in Central America emboldened an increasingly bellicose, imperial Christianity, as the more messianic wing of the fundamentalist movement began to get a sense of its power within the Republican Party and to interpret foreign policy in light of its own expectations of impending rapture.

But it was more than anticommunism that created such an odd coalition in Central America. The fact that both the Central American Left and their supporters in the United States drew inspiration from Christianity provided an ideological challenge to conservatives. In Central America, the socialism of the revolutionary movements was motivated by liberation theology—a current in Catholicism that challenged Latin American militarism and sought to achieve social justice through a redistribution of wealth—as much as it was by Marxism. Many high-ranking members of the Sandinista Party were practicing Catholics and even ordained priests, while at home the solidarity movement that opposed Reagan's foreign policy was largely Christian. So when Jeane Kirkpatrick remarked that the three U.S. nuns and one lay worker who were raped, mutilated, and murdered by Salvadoran security forces in 1980 were "not just nuns, they were political activists," she was being more than cruel—she was signaling her disapproval of a particular kind of peace Christianity.

A shared opposition to the socialist values of liberation theology—which Rousas John Rushdoony, the founder of Christian Reconstructionism, the influential branch of the evangelical movement that seeks to replace the Constitution with biblical law, described as the "economics of Satan"—united mainstream Protestants and pulpit-thumping fundamentalists.[26] For instance, the Institute on Religion and Democracy (IRD), organized in 1981 by intellectuals associated with the American Enterprise Institute (AEI), presented itself as a reformist, liberal organization that supported the administration's efforts at political reform in Central America. Yet IRD allied with evangelicals like Jimmy Swaggert, Jerry Falwell, and Pat Robertson and worked with Oliver North and Otto Reich to discredit not only explicitly leftist Christian groups but also established organizations, such as the National Council of Churches, critical of the administration's Central America policy.[27] With the support of public-relations firms contracted by the Office of Public Diplomacy, the IRD engaged in a mass mailing campaign to the Catholic rank and file in order to "generate some heat"—that is, drive a wedge between liberal Catholic bishops and their supposedly more conservative flock.[28]

But such divisive tactics alone would not be enough to overcome the threat of Christian humanism. The power of liberation theology, along with other variants of peace Christianity, resided not just in its political analysis of global poverty but also in its ethical imperative that to be a good Christian one had to work not to dispense charity but to transform the structural causes of inequality and violence. In Latin America, nuns, priests, and lay Christians were not only presenting democracy and capitalism as antithetical values but were also turning to revolution as a way to bring about social justice on earth. So mainstream Christian conservatives and fundamentalists had to do more than discredit liberal religious organizations. They had to go on the offensive. Well before the elevation of Islamic fundamentalism to the status of "existential enemy," liberation theology was the political religion that had to be confronted and overcome, as mainline Protestant and Catholic conservative theologians joined with fire-and-brimstone evangels to elaborate, largely in reaction to Latin American Catholic humanism, a spiritual justification for American-style imperial capitalism.

In a series of books and articles challenging the major tenets and proponents of liberation theology, theologians connected with AEI and its affiliated IRD, such as Michael Novak and Lutheran pastor (now Catholic) Richard Neuhaus, began to elaborate a set of ideals specific to capitalism that they believed complemented the Christian understanding of free will.[29] To those who said that capitalism embodied the worst of acquisitive individualism, Novak responded by elaborating his "theology of the corporation," which held up the business firm as "an expression of the social nature of humans."[30] He dedicated much of his work to refuting liberation theology's insistence that third-world poverty could be blamed on exploitation by the first world. Instead of examining economic and political relations, he contended that Latin America's failure to modernize must be blamed on indigenous cultural factors dating back to the Spanish Crown's seventeenth-century counterreformation, which placed strictures on capitalist development.[31]

As did their mainstream coreligionists, fundamentalists formulated their free-market moralism as a quarrel with liberation theology—which they described as a "theology of mass murder" and the "the single most critical problem that Christianity has faced in all of its 2000 year history."[32] They of course dismissed Novak's pluralism but also saw capitalism as an ethical system, one that corresponds to God's gift of free will. Man lives in a "fundamentally scarce world," Christian economist John Cooper argued, not an abundant one only in need of more equitable distribution, as the liberation theologians would have it.[33] The profit motive, rather than being an amoral economic mechanism, is part of a divine plan to discipline fallen man and make him produce. Where Christian humanists contended that people were fundamentally good and that "evil" was a condition of class exploitation, Christian capitalists such as Amway's Richard DeVos, head of the Christian Freedom Foundation, insisted that evil is found in the heart of man. Where liberation theology held that humans could fully realize their potential here on earth, fundamentalist economists argued that attempts to distribute wealth and regulate production were based on an incorrect understanding of society—an understanding that incited disobedience to proper authority and, by focusing on economic inequality, generated guilt, envy, and conflict. God's Kingdom, they insisted, would not be established by a war between the classes but a struggle between the wicked and the just.

As did Novak, evangelicals sought to rebut liberation theology's critique of the global political economy. Third-world poverty, according to evangelical Ronald Nash, has a "cultural, moral, and even religious dimension" that reveals itself in a "lack of respect for any private property," "lack of initiative," and "high leisure preference."[34] Some took this argument to its logical conclusion. Gary North, another influential evangelical economist, insisted that the "Third World's problems are religious: moral perversity, a long history of demonism, and outright paganism." "The citizens of the Third World," he wrote, "ought to feel guilt, to fall on their knees and repent from their Godless, rebellious, socialistic ways. They should feel guilty because they are guilty, both individually and corporately."[35]

Evangelical Christianity's elaboration of a theological justification for free-market capitalism, along with its view of an immoral third world, resonated with other ideological currents within the New Right—particularly neoconservative disaffection with the welfare state—thus laying the groundwork for today's embrace of empire as America's national purpose. In a universe of free will where good work is rewarded and bad works punished, the fact of American prosperity was a self-evident confirmation of God's blessing of U.S. power in the world. Third-world misery, in contrast, was proof of "God's curse." David Chilton, of the Institute for Christian Economics, a think tank affiliated with the Reconstructionist branch of the evangelical movement, wrote that poverty is how "God controls heathen cultures: they must spend so much time surviving that they are unable to exercise ungodly dominion over the earth."[36] Mainstream theologians like Novak would not use such stark terms, yet the sentiment is not far removed from their logic. "God has made no special covenant with America as such," conceded the IRD's mission statement, written by Richard Neuhaus. Nonetheless, the IRD anointed the United States to be the "primary bearer of the democratic possibility in the world today."[37] Such an opinion nestled comfortably with evangel notions that America is a "redeemer nation."

The apocalyptic and universalist passions of conservative Christianity melded with other, secular elements in the Reagan coalition. Many fundamentalists followed Reagan's resuscitation of America's revolutionary heritage on behalf of, as Rushdoony put it, a "conservative counter-revolution."[38] They shared with neocons and militarists a sense that America had grown dangerously weak, and they scorned the purposelessness of détente and the naiveté of rapprochement with Communist China. As it did for militarists, the "Churchill versus Chamberlain drama" loomed large in evangelical internationalism, used to frame all foreign-policy debates in terms of resolve and appeasement.[39] Whereas neocons called for renewal of political will, evangelicals believed that America's revival would come about through spiritual rebirth. Their sense of themselves as a persecuted people, engaged in a life-and-death, end-time struggle between the forces of good and evil mapped easily onto the millennialism of anticommunist militarists, particularly those involved in Central America. Many of these militarists—Singlaub, Casey, Vernon Walters, and North (whom Falwell likened to Jesus Christ himself)—were themselves members of conservative Protestant congregations or of ultramontane sects within the Catholic Church, such as Opus Dei and the Knights of Malta.

The ties between conservative groups around Central America and the White House were tight, and grew tighter still as a result of their work. The White House Outreach Working Group on Central America coordinated the work of the NSC and CIA with more than fifty private organizations, including Jerry Falwell's Moral Majority, Pat Robertson's Freedom Council, Phyllis Schlafly's Eagle Forum, and the Heritage Foundation.[40]

Singlaub, described by Mike Wallace as the "virtual director" of the Contra war, headed the 1984 Defense Department panel that recommended the increased use of unconventional warfare tactics, solicited Contra aid from Asian dictators, and served as the NSC's primary fundraiser on Nicaragua.[41] Right-wing foreign-policy lobbying groups, such as Western Goals and Citizens for America, began to work closely with the NSC and the Office of Public Diplomacy to execute foreign policy. They disseminated information, worked on political campaigns, kept tabs on dissidents, and raised money to buy arms and supplies for the Contras and other anticommunist struggles around the world. Christian economists such as Gary North, Richard DeVos, and Rousas John Rushdoony, along with Robertson, Falwell, Schlafly, and Oliver North, himself a member of the charismatic Church of the Apostles, founded the Council for National Policy in 1981, which, as the religious Right's steering committee in the 1980s, was deeply involved in North's Central American exploits. Christian businessmen funded the myriad organizations that worked closely with the NSC and the Office of Public Diplomacy to sway public opinion and congressional votes in favor of Reagan's policy in El Salvador and Nicaragua. They raised money for arms and humanitarian work and joined with Opus Dei and other conservative Catholics to form a broad front to counter peace Christianity.

The Central American crusade also helped hold together the conservative coalition that brought Reagan to power. In retrospect, observers now stress the power and ascendancy of the New Right, yet at the time the success of the movement was by no means certain. Not only did distinct constituencies—Christian evangelicals, "Old Right" economic and law-and-order conservatives, anticommunist Republicans, and disaffected Democrats—pursue potentially competing objectives, Reagan was largely unable to fulfill many of his domestic promises. He got his tax reform through, which began the process of weakening the New Deal state, yet he was unable to dismantle social entitlements. And although he appointed close to half the judges serving in the lower federal courts, as well as two Supreme Court justices (which would pay dividends in the years to come), affirmative action remained in place, abortion stayed legal, gay rights gained momentum, and prayer in school continued to be prohibited. "Has Reagan deserted the conservatives?" asked the *Conservative Digest* as early as 1982.

Foreign policy helped hold together the alliance between the administration and its potentially rancorous base. But even here, there was conciliation (Reagan's befriending of Gorbachev), humiliations (withdrawal from Lebanon), and setbacks (sanctions on South Africa). But on Central America there was no compromise. Designed and executed by the hardest of the hardliners in his administration, Reagan's policy toward the poor, powerless region gathered together the disparate passions of the conservative alliance into a single mission. It melded diverse constituencies together, organizing them into a dense, interlocking network of action groups and social movements, uniting mainstream conservatives with militants from the carnivalesque Right. Respectable intellectuals and religious leaders from the Committee for the Free World and the Institute for Religion and Democracy and capitalists from the Business Roundtable found themselves making common cause with World Anti-Communist League revanchists, evangelicals such as Falwell, Robertson, and Schlafly, end-timers like Tim LaHaye, and Moonies from the Nicaraguan Freedom Fund.

But for an emerging movement getting a sense of its own power, Central America was too small a prize. Reagan first fully enunciated that it was American policy to support "freedom fighters" throughout the world in his 1985 State of the Union speech, specifically referring to the insurgencies in Nicaragua and Afghanistan. Others in his administration such as William Casey, Jeane Kirkpatrick, and George Schultz quickly followed, giving form to what would become known as the Reagan Doctrine. "A revolution is sweeping the world today—a democratic revolution," announced the normally staid Schultz in 1985. Though the administration, concerned with maintaining regional stability and balance of power relations, largely let its oratory outstrip its actions—except for the Contras and the Mujahadeen—New Right activists took seriously the idea of world revolution, a revolution they saw themselves leading both at home and abroad. Throughout 1985 and 1986, conservatives, many of them grouped around the Heritage Foundation, pushed the White House to make good on its promise to support insurgencies from Cambodia to Laos, Libya to Angola, Ethiopia to Mozambique, Cuba to Yemen. When no action was forthcoming, they attacked the State Department and demanded Schultz's resignation.[42]

They also took matters into their own hands. From the network built to support the Nicaraguan Contras, militarists, idealists, and religionists, together with hardliners in the NSC, CIA, and Office of Public Diplomacy, moved to extend operations across three continents. As they did for Central America, evangelical activists raised money to ship clothes, bibles, medical supplies, and guns.[43] Beyond supplying aid and weapons, militants began to coordinate a "Democratic International" to fight the "Soviet Empire"—apparently modeled on the storied Third International of communism's heyday. In June 1985, Contra supporter and head of Citizens for America Lewis Lehrman, heir to the Rite-Aid pharmacy fortune, hopped on his private jet and flew to rebel-held territory in Angola to convene a "freedom fighter" summit that brought together anticommunist rebels from Nicaragua, Afghanistan, and Laos (the Cambodians were invited but did not show up) to sign a unity pact. At a mass rally in a soccer stadium, Lehrman (today a member of the Project for the New American Century) presented the rebel delegates with a copy of the Declaration of Independence and read aloud a letter from Reagan, praising the revolutionaries —including the Mujahadeen—as part of a worldwide revolution whose "goals are [America's] goals."[44]

This transformation of conservative activists into world revolutionaries entailed adopting an ethics of absolutism, sacrificing any qualms one may have about means at the altar of ends. The violence of counterinsurgent war stoked the fires of evangelical Manichaeism, leading Falwell, Robertson, and others to ally with the worst murderers and torturers in Central and Latin America. "For the Christian," believes Rus Walton, "there can be no neutrality in this battle: 'He that is not with Me is against Me' (Matthew 12:30)."[45] Robertson befriended Guatemala's Efraín Ríos Montt, responsible for genocide, and Salvador's Roberto D'Aubuisson, behind the murder of, among untold others, Archbishop Oscar Romero, celebrating both men on his Christian Broadcasting Network. And more than a dozen Christian New Right organizations, including the Moral Majority and the Pro-Life Action Committee, presented D'Aubuisson with a plaque in 1984, honoring his "continuing efforts for freedom."[46] Many of the death-squad members were themselves conservative religious ideologues, taking the fight against liberation theology to the trenches. Guatemalan security forces regularly questioned their prisoners about their "views on liberation theology," as they did when they tortured one Clemente Díaz Aguilar, who turned out to be an evangelical himself, having been mistaken by his captors for a political dissident.[47] Others report being tortured to the singing of hymns and praying.[48] Some evangelicals excused such suffering. "Killing for the joy of it was wrong," a Paralife minister from the United States comforted his flock of Salvadoran soldiers, "but killing because it was necessary to fight against an anti-Christ system, communism, was not only right but a duty of every Christian."[49] As the involvement of evangelicals in world affairs continued, they started to align their theology to reflect the embrace of militarism that today prevails among foreign-policy elites. Mimicking Jeane Kirkpatrick's hardheadedness that the war had to be won before society could be reformed, John Eidsmoe insisted that in El Salvador "the best way to promote freedom is to first of all win the war, then work for human rights."[50] "Our government," wrote Falwell in 1980 but sounding like George W. Bush in 2002, "has the right to use its armaments to bring wrath upon those who would do evil by hurting other people."[51] And not just defensively but preemptively: "we must go on the offensive," wrote Walton in 1988.[52]

Conclusion

The bringing together of anticommunist militarists and evangelicals in an aggressive anticommunist campaign in Central America emboldened an increasingly bellicose, imperial Christianity, as the more messianic wing of the fundamentalist movement began to get a sense of its power within the Republican Party and increasingly to interpret foreign policy in light of its own expectations of impending rapture. And although many of these evangelical groups would break with the first Bush administration, which they saw as too Atlanticist, they continued their increasingly confident engagement in world affairs. After 9/11, evangelical internationalists once again joined with a now fully empowered cohort of neocons to convert George W. Bush's realism into hard Wilsonianism and to "remoralize" America's role in the world.

An expansive foreign policy remains as critical today for the conservative coalition as it did during the 1980s—even more so considering the heightened sense of expectation and entitlement conservative activists have now that they control the executive and legislative branches and are driving the agenda in the judiciary. At the same time, America's privileged position within the world's global financial system—dependent as it is on the maintenance of political primacy in order to continue to prop up a deeply indebted economy—demands an aggressive foreign policy. On this fact, neither major political party disagrees. But the need for the New Right to maintain a constant level of mobilization in order to hold its coalition together—especially since the domestic goals of many of its constituencies are unattainable—could push this aggression to an even more dangerous extreme.

To focus, therefore, exclusively on neoconservative intellectuals, as much of the commentary attempting to identify the origins of the new imperialism does, deflects attention away from the long history of American expansion. The intellectual architects of Bush's preemptive-warfare doctrine are but part of a larger resurgence of nationalist militarism, serving as the ideologues of an American revanchism fired by a lethal combination of humiliation in Vietnam and vindication in the Cold War, of which Central America was the tragic endgame.

NOTES

From Greg Grandin, *Empire's Workshop: Latin America, the United States, and the Rise of the New Imperialism* (New York: Henry Holt, 2006). Copyright © 2006 by Greg Grandin. Reprinted by permission.

1. Andrew Bacevich, *The New American Militarism: How Americans Are Seduced by War* (New York: Oxford University Press, 2005), p. 78.

2. Dana Milbank, "Same Committee, Same Combatants, Different Tune," *Washington Post*, April 7, 2005.

3. Walter LaFeber, *Inevitable Revolutions: The United States in Central America* (New York: Norton, 1993), p. 271.

4. Robert Tucker, "The Purposes of American Power," *Foreign Affairs* (winter 1980–81): p. 272.

5. LaFeber, *Inevitable Revolutions*, p. 275.

6. "Remarks by the President at 2002 Graduation Exercise of the United States Military Academy, West Point, New York," available online at www.whitehouse.gov/news/releases/2002/06/20020601-3.html.

7. Max Boot, "What the Heck Is a 'Neocon'?" *Wall Street Journal*, December 30, 2002.

8. Charles Krauthammer, "A Unipolar World," speech delivered at the American Enterprise Institute annual dinner, February 10, 2004, Washington D.C., broadcast on C-Span, February 16, 2004; Paul D. Wolfowitz, speech delivered at New School University, September 21, 2003.

9. The Heritage Foundation, "Jeane J. Kirkpatrick," www.heritage.org/About/kirkpatrick.cfm.

10. Unless otherwise cited, quotations from Kirkpatrick come from the introduction to *Dictatorships and Double Standards: Rationalism and Reason in Politics* (New York: Simon and Schuster, 1982), as well as the essays first published in *Commentary*, "Dictatorships and Double Standards" and "U.S. Security and Latin America," which are reprinted in that volume.

11. The article was published a year later as "The Hobbes Problem" in the American Enterprise Institute's *Public Policy Papers* (Washington, D.C., 1981) and

reprinted in *The Central American Crisis Reader,* Robert S. Leiken and Barry Rubin, eds. (New York: Summit Books, 1987).

12. Christopher Hitchens, "Minority Report: Rebel Movements, Nicaraguan Contras," *Nation,* July 19, 1986; Holly Sklar, *Reagan, Trilateralism, and the Neoliberals: Containment and Intervention in the 1980s* (Boston: South End Press, 1986).

13. Roy Gutman, *Banana Diplomacy: The Making of American Policy in Nicaragua, 1981–1987* (New York: Simon and Schuster, 1988), p. 27.

14. "Excerpts from State Department Memo on Human Rights," *New York Times,* November 5, 1981.

15. Benjamin Schwarz, "Dirty Hands: The Success of U.S. Policy in El Salvador —Preventing a Guerrilla Victory—Was Based on 40,000 Political Murders," *Atlantic Monthly,* December 1998.

16. William Shawcross, *Sideshow: Kissinger, Nixon, and the Destruction of Cambodia* (New York: Simon and Schuster, 1979), p. 268.

17. Gutman, *Banana Diplomacy,* p. 71.

18. Andrew Bacevich, James D. Hallums, Richard H. White, and Thomas F. Young, *American Military Policy in Small Wars: The Case of El Salvador* (Cambridge, MA: Institute for Foreign Policy Analysis, 1988), pp. 1, 14.

19. Robert Parry, *Lost History: Contras, Cocaine, the Press, and "Project Truth"* (Arlington, VA: Media Consortium, 1997), p. 89.

20. Benjamin Schwarz, *American Counterinsurgency Doctrine: The Frustrations of Reform and the Illusions of Nation Building* (Santa Monica, CA: RAND, 1991), p. 80.

21. Schwarz, "Dirty Hands."

22. Tayacán [pseudonym], *Psychological Operations in Guerrilla Warfare* (New York: Vintage, 1985), p. 20.

23. Gutman, *Banana Diplomacy,* pp. 269–270.

24. "Special Operations in the 1980s: American Moral, Legal, Political, and Cultural Constraints," in *Special Operations in U.S. Strategy,* Frank Barnet, Hugh Tovar, and Richard Shultz, eds. (Washington, DC: National Defense University Press, 1984), pp. 77–78.

25. Peter Steinfels, *The Neoconservatives: The Men Who Are Changing America's Politics* (New York: Simon and Schuster, 1979).

26. Rousas John Rushdoony, *Roots of Inflations* (Vallecito, CA: Ross House Books, 1982), pp. 22, 23.

27. See Sara Diamond, *Spiritual Warfare: The Politics of the Christian Right* (Boston: South End Press, 1989), pp. 148–153; Outreach Working Group on Central America, "Meeting with Hispanic Evangelical Leaders," September 14, 1983, National Security Archive, Iran-Contra Collection.

28. "Meeting re: Central America Freedom Program," Internal NEPL Minutes of Contra Lobbying Strategy Meeting, National Security Council, February 13, 1986.

29. Michael Novak, *Will It Liberate? Questions about Liberation Theology* (New York: Paulist Press, 1986); Peter Berger and Michael Novak, *Speaking to the Third World: Essays on Democracy and Development* (Washington, DC: American Enterprise Institute, 1985); Michael Novak and Michael P. Jackson, eds., *Latin America: Dependency or Interdependence?* (Washington, DC: American Enterprise Institute, 1985); and Richard John Neuhaus, "Liberation Theology and the Cultural Captivity of the Gospel," in *Liberation Theology,* Ronald Nash, ed. (Milford, MI: Mott Media, 1984).

30. Michael Novak, *Toward a Theology of the Corporation* (Washington, DC: American Enterprise Institute, 1981), p. 1.

31. Michael Novak, *The Spirit of Democratic Capitalism* (Washington, DC: American Enterprise Institute, 1982), p. 278.

32. Rus Walton, *Biblical Solutions to Contemporary Problems* (Brentwood, TN: Wolgemuth and Hyatt, 1988), p. 177. See also David Chilton, *Productive Christians in an Age of Guilt-Manipulators* (Tyler, TX: Institute for Christian Economics, 1981), and John Eidsmoe, *God and Caesar: Biblical Faith and Political Action* (Westchester, IL: Crossway Books, 1984).

33. Quoted in Michael Lienesch, *Redeeming America: Piety and Politics in the New Christian Right* (Chapel Hill: University of North Carolina Press, 1993), p. 97.

34. Ronald Nash, *Poverty and Wealth: The Christian Debate over Capitalism* (Westchester, IL: Crossway Books, 1986), p. 194.

35. Ibid., p. 135.

36. Chilton, *Productive Christians,* p. 92.

37. Diamond, *Spiritual Warfare,* p. 151; Cynthia Brown, "The Right's Religious Red Alert," *Nation,* March 12, 1983.

38. "Symposium on Christianity and the American Revolution," *Journal of Christian Reconstruction* 3:1 (summer 1976).

39. Francis Schaeffer, "The Secular Humanist World View versus the Christian World View and Biblical Perspectives on Military Preparedness," in Francis Schaeffer, Vladimir Bukovsky, and James Hitchcock, *Who Is for Peace?* (Nashville, TN: Thomas Nelson, 1983), pp. 30–31; Eidsmoe, *God and Caesar,* p. 223.

40. Sara Diamond, *Roads to Dominion: Right-Wing Movements and Political Power in the United States* (New York: Guilford, 1995), p. 218.

41. Holly Sklar, *Washington's War on Nicaragua* (Boston: South End Press, 1988), p. 325.

42. Jack Wheeler, "Fighting the Soviet Imperialists: The New Liberation Movements," *Reason* (June-July 1985): pp. 36–44; James T. Hackett, ed., "The State Department v. Ronald Reagan: Four Ambassadors Speak Out," Heritage Lecture No. 44, Washington, DC, Heritage Foundation, 1985; Benjamin Hart, "Rhetoric vs. Reality: How the State Department Betrays the Reagan Vision," Backgrounder No. 484, Washington, DC, Heritage Foundation, 1986; David Ottawa, "Rebels' Backers on Hill Press Aid Issue; Administration Accused of Ambiguity in Military Efforts,"

Washington Post, January 16, 1986; Howard Phillips, " 'Made in Moscow' State Dept. Policy for Angola Must Be Overturned," Conservative Caucus Member's Report 9, No. 3, December 1985.

43. "A Little Help from Friends," *Newsweek,* September 7, 1984; Alfonso Chardy, "Groups Won't Cut Contra Aid," *Dallas Morning News,* June 16, 1985; Robert Greenberger, "Right-Wing Groups Join in Capitol Hill Crusade to Help Savimbi's Anti-Communists in Angola," *Wall Street Journal,* November 25, 1985; Robert Pear, with James Brooke, "Rightist in U.S. Aid Mozambique Rebels, *New York Times,* May 22, 1988.

44. Alan Cowell, "Four Rebel Units Sign Anti-Soviet Pact," *New York Times,* June 6, 1985; Michael Sullivan, "Rebels Opposing Marxist Regimes in 4 Nations Unite," *Washington Times,* June 6, 1985; and Walter Shapiro and Peter Younghusband, "Lehrman's Contra Conclave," *Newsweek,* June 17, 1986.

45. Walton, *Biblical Solutions,* p. 165.

46. Joanne Omang, "D'Aubuisson Honored by Conservatives at Capitol Hill Dinner," *Washington Post,* December 5, 1984.

47. *Covert Action Quarterly* 27 (spring 1987): p. 26.

48. *Covert Action Quarterly* 18 (winter 1983): p. 19.

49. Diamond, *Spiritual Warfare,* p. 177.

50. Eidsmoe, *God and Caesar,* p. 214.

51. Lienesch, *Redeeming America,* p. 228.

52. Walton, *Biblical Solutions,* p. 165.

Chapter 10

The Neocon Con Game
Nihilism Revisited

Nicholas Xenos

Whenever a definition of neoconservatism is needed, Irving Kristol can be relied on to deliver one, while at the same time professing insecurity as to whether or not the term has any meaning. In 2003, in an article published in the *Weekly Standard*, edited by his son William, the elder Kristol decided that neoconservatism constitutes a "persuasion" rather than a movement. This persuasion, he claimed, has as its "historical task and political purpose" to "convert the Republican party, and American conservatism in general, against their respective wills, into a new kind of conservative politics suitable to governing a modern democracy. That this new conservative politics is distinctly American is beyond doubt." Though by no means dominant within the Republican Party, it is neoconservative policies, Kristol argued, that must be credited with the popular success of Republican presidents.[1]

What is this new, peculiarly American form designed to govern a "modern democracy"? Kristol emphasizes its "hopeful," "forward-looking," and "cheerful" qualities that apparently mark it as in "the 'American grain.'" He links it to the two Roosevelts and Ronald Reagan rather than Coolidge, Hoover, Eisenhower, and Goldwater, the latter group curiously expunged from the "American grain." Neocons support tax cuts as the engine of economic growth, tolerating budget deficits when necessary, because only such growth gives "modern democracies their legitimacy and durability." "It is a basic assumption of neoconservatism," he writes, "that, as a consequence of the spread of affluence among all classes, a property-owning and tax-paying population will, in time, become less vulnerable to egalitarian illusions and demagogic appeals and more sensible about the fundamentals of economic reckoning." And although neoconservatives "do not like the concentration of services in the welfare state and are happy to study alternative ways of delivering these services," they do not oppose a strong state. Neocons are inspired by Tocqueville's "democratic wisdom" in regard to the state.

If the state is not providing "welfare services," then whither its strength? These are concentrated in two areas. The first is the area of "culture." Neocons support government action to address "the steady decline in our democratic culture" in the areas of education, "the relations of church and state, the regulation of pornography, and the like." These policies unite neocons to traditional conservatives as well as "religious traditionalists."

The second area is of course foreign policy. Mirroring his notion that neoconservatism is not a movement but a persuasion, Kristol claims that although the neocon influence on foreign policy has gotten the greatest share of media attention, it is surprising because "there is no set of neoconservative beliefs concerning foreign policy, only a set of attitudes derived from historical experience." (He then notes that, thanks to the influence of Leo Strauss and Donald Kagan, Thucydides is "the favorite neoconservative text on foreign affairs.") The "attitudes" consist of the claims that "patriotism is a natural and healthy sentiment," that world government can lead to world tyranny, that "statesmen should, above all, have the ability to distinguish friends from enemies," and, finally, for a great power "whose identity is ideological," such as the United States, that national interest is "not a geographical term" and entails "ideological interests in addition to more material concerns."

Kristol's description of neoconservatives is vacuous, but it is illuminating just the same—illuminating in its vacuity, in fact. His account itself cuts against the "American grain" that it claims to describe. Tocqueville, a problematical ally in any event, brought a European, if not distinctly French, perspective to bear on the American democracy of the 1830s. And Thucydides? But there's more. Leo Strauss, who immigrated to the United States in 1937, aged thirty-eight, brought with him from Germany a distinctly European Weltanschauung, which included the concern with world government and its resultant "tyranny," as well as perhaps less obvious notions that underlay Kristol's account. (I will say more on Strauss's influence on the neocons later.) And finally, the necessity of distinguishing friend from enemy as a fundamental attribute of the statesman is immediately recognizable as one of the core concepts—indeed, the core concept of "the political"—bequeathed by the German jurist and political theorist Carl Schmitt. Slightly older than Strauss, with whom he engaged in an intellectual exchange in the early 1930s, Schmitt became a high official in the National Socialist state. That distasteful fact may account for Kristol's reluctance to name names in Schmitt's case, but the hardly "American" intonation remains.

The nativity of Kristol's rendition of neoconservatism can be set aside for the moment; its rhetorical function will become evident. A more historical genealogy would go something like this: Neoconservatism was originally used to describe an amorphous group of political journalists, such as Irving Kristol, and social theorists, such as Daniel Bell, who had identified with the Left, often with the Trotskyist Left, in their earlier days but moved to the right due to a conflation of three factors. The first of these was their anti-Soviet Cold War stance, a position these figures then shared with the anticommunist liberals around such journals as *Encounter,* cofounded by Kristol and the English poet Stephen Spender, and Norman Podhoretz's *Commentary.* The second and third factors are more closely related and crucial to their emerging worldview. These are a reaction to the so-called cultural revolution of the 1960s and to the welfare state. Together, these phenomena were taken to constitute a crisis of values well described in the title of Bell's important book, *The Cultural Contradictions of Capitalism,* where Bell argued that the very affluence produced by capitalist economies and redistributed through welfare provisions threatened to undermine the ethic of deferred gratification that formed capitalism's disciplined core. A culture of consumption, fueled by advertising and raising pleasure to the highest rung of individual and collective pursuit, thus endangered the social system itself.

Various of the future neocons took opposing positions on the Vietnam War, and many of them identified with the Democratic Party into the 1960s, at least until the nomination of George McGovern in 1972. (Most of the neocons still in the Democratic ranks, such as Ben Wattenberg, Richard Perle, Jeane Kirkpatrick, and Elliot Abrams, were in the Henry "Scoop" Jackson camp.) It was the rise of the New Left and the cultural politics they associated with it that appalled the likes of Kristol et al. The French journalists Alain Frachon and Daniel Vernet, in a recent book on the neocons, quote an unidentified member of the persuasion as saying that they wanted "to rebel against the rebellion of the sixties."[2] Frachon and Vernet, focused on the "messianism" underlying neoconservative foreign policy, emphasize the harsh tone of the New Left's politics; its denunciation of America as a racist, imperialist, and violent country; and the reaction to it by a group consisting mostly of the sons and daughters of Jewish and Irish immigrants. They quote Wattenberg, for example, as telling them that he responded to the New Left's "declinism" with "an immigrant's optimism," and "historical optimism," they write, "is a very neoconservative quality."[3]

Irving Kristol's emphasis on the cheerful optimism of the neoconservative persuasion echoes in this reaction to "declinism." Whatever criticisms the neocons might have of domestic and foreign policies were balanced with an embrace of the possibilities of American power. But this optimism is in apparent tension with the neoconservatives' own analysis of democratic cultural decline, the beginnings of which they associate not so much with the New Left's political critique as with the cultural radicalism of the 1960s. Kristol's wife, the historian Gertrude Himmelfarb, in an article published in the *Public Interest* in 1998, referred to problems besetting "our democratic society" as "diseases" of a moral and cultural nature rather than a political one: "the collapse of ethical principles and habits, the loss of respect for authorities and institutions, the breakdown of the family, the decline of civility, the vulgarization of high culture, and the degradation of popular culture." She characterizes the "virus" that produced this disease as "the ethical and cultural relativism that reduces all values, all standards, and all authority to expressions of personal will and inclination," making it clear that "the counterculture of yesteryear is the dominant culture today." And she invokes the usual initiators of this virus by citing elites in the universities and media.[4]

To the extent that the neoconservative persuasion can be said to have managed its dialectic of cultural decline and political optimism it has done so by an elaborate rhetorical construction. The elements of that construction can be glimpsed in the recent accounting of what went wrong in the post-9/11 world presented by Francis Fukuyama, the self-styled apostate neoconservative. Fukuyama announces his departure from the fold in *America at the Crossroads: Democracy, Power, and the Neoconservative Legacy.* In a sign that Irving Kristol's insistence on an American heritage is not peculiar to him, Fukuyama also claims that "the key principles of neoconservativism as they developed from the mid-twentieth century to the present are deeply rooted in a variety of American traditions."[5] Fukuyama delineates four strands to this tradition, the first being the morphing of prewar Trotskyites into postwar anticommunists. A second, related strand he locates in the founding of the *Public Interest* in 1965, which focused on domestic policy and which quickly became a line of resistance against the welfare-statism of the New Left, on the one hand, and Lyndon Johnson's

Great Society, on the other. The legacy of Leo Strauss forms the third strand, though Fukuyama is at pains to argue that Straussianism had little influence on the mindset that led to the Iraq war. "More nonsense," he writes, "has been written about Leo Strauss and the Iraq war than on virtually any other subject."[6] Far more important with regard to specific foreign-policy ideas was the fourth strand, descending from the theorist of so-called second-strike nuclear capability, Albert Wohlstetter. Wohlstetter's advocacy of military strategy taking precision targeting of nuclear and conventional weapons into account reverberates in Defense Secretary Donald Rumsfeld's advocacy of a lighter, more mobile military, an "instrument" that makes military intervention more attractive. And Wohlstetter shared with Strauss one overlapping concern that did contribute to neoconservative foreign policy in general and to Iraq in particular. Born out of a distrust of the Soviet Union, Wohlstetter shared with the Straussians "a belief that regimes mattered to foreign policy."[7]

"Regime" is a Straussian term of art that refers to the way of life that sustains particular political institutions. It is the central term in Fukuyama's reading of Strauss and reveals more about Straussianism and its central place within neoconservatism than he realizes. Fukuyama notes in his book's preface that "I was a student of Allan Bloom, himself a student of Leo Strauss and the author of *The Closing of the American Mind*" by way of establishing his intellectual links with this strand of neoconservative thought.[8] That lineage is important, because it links three books that are central to understanding the place that Straussianism has assumed within neoconservatism: Strauss's *Natural Right and History*, Bloom's best-selling diatribe, and Fukuyama's own best-seller, *The End of History and the Last Man*.

Two surprisingly successful books appeared in 1987 that bear directly on the twinning of political optimism and cultural decline. One was Paul Kennedy's *The Rise and Decline of the Great Powers*. Kennedy argued that the history of great powers showed a pattern of overstretching military commitments that ultimately led to decline because their military requirements placed impossible burdens on their economies. America, he thought, was on the verge of a similar fate. With the book's unexpected popularity, the Reagan administration began a public campaign to rebut the notion that the United States should cut back on its military bases abroad.[9]

The second of those 1987 books was Allan Bloom's *The Closing of the American Mind: How Higher Education Has Failed Democracy and Impoverished the Souls of Today's Students*. Whereas Kennedy provided the impetus to a rebuttal, to an affirmation of America's global power, Bloom provided the rhetorical armature for the neoconservative cultural discourse that has also proved so politically effective.[10] Coming as it did toward the end of the Reagan presidency, Bloom's book should be seen as a consolidation of already prominent misgivings about the cultural landscape of post-1960s America rather than as a creator of them. Indeed, the book's fantastic success indicates that the audience was already primed for a high-minded diatribe aimed at the state of the "souls" of the nation's youth. What caught the attention of this public was perhaps less the opening salvo directed at the belief that truth is relative, the one certainty Bloom professed to discover in his students, than the attack on rock music and popular culture in general that followed. Here Bloom's sardonic, titillating style showed itself in full bloom. He imagines a teenage boy doing his homework while wearing headphones or watching MTV, and what does Bloom see in this, his own fantasy? He sees this boy as the inheritor of the progress bequeathed by philosophy and heroism and science: "A pubescent child whose body throbs with orgasmic rhythms; whose feelings are made articulate in hymns to the joys of onanism or the killing of parents; whose ambition is to win fame and wealth in imitating the dragqueen who makes the music. In short, life is made into a nonstop, commercially prepackaged masturbational fantasy."[11] In this sort of language, as one of Bloom's critics on the Right, Harry V. Jaffa, pointed out, there is "a great deal of prurient denunciation of immorality."[12] And no doubt at least part of the book's success can be thus accounted for.

But the flamboyance and prurience of the book's opening sections, with their emphasis on culture, served, perhaps purposely, to obscure the denser argument concerning philosophy and politics later on in the book and, in particular, its theoretical, as opposed to polemical, claims regarding nihilism.

A number of persons are mentioned only once in Bloom's book, including Buddha, Margaret Dumont (who played Groucho's matronly amour in Marx Brothers movies), Michael Jackson, and Pericles. Carl Schmitt is another. Bloom quotes Schmitt, who is unidentified except for his name, as proclaiming, "Today Hegel died in Germany" on the day of Hitler's assumption of power. Bloom wants his readers to think that this denotes the death of the German university, since "Hegel was arguably the greatest university man there ever was," but Schmitt was no Hegelian and in fact joined the Nazi Party three months later, an event and an association Bloom manages not to mention.[13]

But, as many reviewers observed at the time, the most notable notable among the single-referenced is Leo Strauss. When Bloom decries the superficiality of contemporary American nihilism, he calls it "nihilism with a happy ending" or "nihilism without the abyss," to distinguish it from its Old World version.[14] The light-hearted language of "value judgments," he claims, can be attributed primarily to the books of Max Weber and Sigmund Freud taught by the university professors of the postwar period who were themselves either German or had studied in Germany or with the émigré German professors. These professors repressed the "darker side" of Weber and Freud, namely the debt each owed to Nietzsche. The irony here, of course, is that Bloom's professor was the German émigré Leo Strauss, who did not repress the dark side.

Whereas Kristol gladly mentions Strauss as a teacher and inspiration, Bloom's ironic omission is characteristic of a certain obfuscation that one frequently encounters in accounts of Strauss's German period (i.e., before his emigration from Germany in 1931, first to Paris and London, then to the United States), including his own. An example of this obfuscation is Fukuyama's assertion that

> Leo Strauss was a German Jewish political theorist who studied under Ernst Cassirer and who, fleeing the Nazis, emigrated to the United States in the 1930s and taught mostly at the University of Chicago until shortly before his death in 1973. Much of his work can be seen as a response to Nietzsche and Heidegger, who had undermined the rationalist tradition of Western philosophy from within and left modernity without a deep philosophical grounding for its own beliefs and institutions.[15]

It is true that Strauss did his doctoral work in philosophy under Cassirer's direction, but he was so little influenced by him that, in an autobiographical account he gave in 1970, Strauss did not even mention him. Instead, Strauss emphasized the impact of Heidegger, whose lectures he attended in the mid-1920s. As a result of what he heard in Heidegger's lectures, Strauss says he remarked at the time that, "compared to Heidegger, Max Weber, till then regarded by me as the incarnation of the spirit of science and scholarship, was an orphan child."[16] Fukuyama's undoubtedly intentional distorted representation is meant to obscure Strauss's deep-seated anti-Enlightenment sentiments. Although it is certainly true that Strauss was in some sense "responding" to Nietzsche and Heidegger, the nature of that response is very much in question.

Strauss wrote his own book, published in 1952 but originating in lectures he delivered in 1949, ostensibly dealing with American values. In the introduction to *Natural Right and History*, he begins by quoting the passage from the Declaration of Independence enumerating the "self-evident" truths, which include the rights of "life, liberty and the pursuit of happiness." Do Americans still believe in these self-evident truths? he asks. The question is rhetorical because Strauss makes no attempt to answer it. Instead, he quotes the German theologian Ernst Troeltsch to the effect that, whereas Americans still believed so fundamentally in the idea of natural rights that they simply assumed their existence, German thought, under the influence of the "historical sense," had become so relativistic that Germans had to have the American presuppositions spelled out to them. Strauss writes that Troeltsch's remark was made "about a generation ago" and quotes it from an essay published in English translation in 1934. Strauss then states, "Whatever might be true of the thought of the American people," American social science, Catholic social science excepted, had by this time adopted the German attitude. "It would not be the first time," Strauss concludes, "that a nation, defeated on the battlefield and, as it were, annihilated as a political being, has deprived its conquerors of the most sublime fruit of victory by imposing on them the yoke of its own thought."[17]

Obscured in Strauss's opening salvo is his subtle manipulation of the timing and circumstances of Troeltsch's essay. By citing its English publication Strauss reinforces his generational time frame and sets the essay after Hitler's assumption of power. The implication ties the notion of German historicism to Nazism, the defeated nation. Historicism then becomes the yoke imposed on the somewhat naive conquerors. But Troeltsch died in 1923, and his criticisms of historicism were framed in the aftermath of Germany's defeat in the Great War. Having been a defender of historical criticism in theology before the war, afterward he wrote of the "crisis of historicism" and described the intellectual climate in Germany as itself a battle between various combatants:

> culture and progress, skepticism and aesthetics against Christianity, and above all against the long-standing association of culture and Protestantism; realists, modernists, Völkists, expressionists against antiquity, venera-

tors of Christianity with one another and against modern culture, the Dionysian and Apollonian renewers of antiquity against Christianity and modernity together.[18]

Troeltsch attempted to salvage the situation not through a dogmatic rejection of historicism but, rather, through a reconciliation of history and philosophy. However, in the period between Troeltsch's death and the Nazi regime, it was historicism that was predominantly under attack from both right and left. Strauss himself had been a participant in that assault on historical method, Enlightenment rationality, and political liberalism from the political Right until his emigration to the United States.[19]

Strauss elides his own intellectual past by effectively postdating Troeltsch's comment and ignores the actual philosophical and political debates of Weimar Germany by reducing German thought to historicism. There is purpose to this elision. This curious denial of his own identity allows Strauss to pose as a defender of perhaps forgotten American principles against the very tradition that he will deploy in his text to undermine those principles. The key to unraveling Strauss's book is the same key that unlocks his student Bloom's, namely, a particular reading of Nietzsche's writings in relation to those of Max Weber and Martin Heidegger. In both scenarios, Weber plays the fall guy.

Until the neoconservative counter-countercultural revolution, the question of nihilism had not been a particularly American obsession. It was, however, a central question first for German, and then later European, social and political philosophy. Nietzsche was the first to make it the core question as he investigated the aftermath of the French Revolution and its attendant intellectual trends. Strauss follows Nietzsche in his condemnation of what Strauss calls historicism. The so-called historical school, Strauss notes, emerged in reaction to the French Revolution "and to the natural right doctrines that had prepared that cataclysm."[20] Strauss makes a fundamental distinction between these "doctrines," which he calls modern natural right doctrines, and "pre-modern" or "classical" natural right doctrines, a distinction that will be crucial to understanding the implicit criticism of the American version. The latter, he notes, "did not sanction reckless appeal from the established order, or from what was actual here and now, to the natural or rational order."[21] But the historical school "seemed to have realized somehow" that the appeal to universal principles has an unsettling effect "as far as thought is concerned" with reference to the established order. "The recognition of universal principles thus tends to prevent men from wholeheartedly identifying themselves with, or accepting, the social order that fate has allotted to them. It tends to alienate them from their place on the earth. It tends to make them strangers, and even strangers on the earth."[22] Strauss thus notes that although premodern natural right might produce an unsettling effect in thought, it also contains some content that prevents "reckless" abandonment of the established order, unlike modern natural right's universalism. The real question then becomes one of properly distinguishing between the two doctrines of natural right.

The historical school, influenced by Edmund Burke, sought to avoid the revolutionary implications of modern natural right's appeal to universal rights by substituting instead the notion of historical rights. However, this effort produced even more drastically radical consequences than the universalist doctrine it opposed, since it sought to find objective standards in the historically contingent. The historical school proved incapable of establishing the basis for any universal principle that would compel individuals to accept the particular historical situation in which they found themselves. Thus, individuals were in principle free to choose their own standards. "No objective criterion henceforth allowed the distinction between good and bad choices," Strauss observes. "Historicism culminated in nihilism. The attempt to make man absolutely at home in this world ended in man's becoming absolutely homeless."[23]

Strauss "suspects" that historicism is the dogmatism of our times.[24] Historicism undermines itself by denying all transhistorical truths except the truth that all truth is historical. However, Strauss also quietly introduces a variant of historicism that he terms "radical historicism." The basis for radical historicism was laid by Nietzsche. In Strauss's reading, Nietzsche declared that a theoretical position acknowledging the relativity of all comprehensive worldviews "would make human life impossible, for it would destroy the protecting atmosphere within which life or culture or action is alone possible. . . . The theoretical analysis of life is noncommittal and fatal to commitment, but life means commitment." Strauss continues:

> To avert the danger to life, Nietzsche could choose one of two ways: he could insist on the strictly esoteric character of the theoretical analysis of life—that is, restore the Platonic notion of the noble delusion—or else he could deny the possibility of theory proper and so conceive of thought as essentially subservient to, or dependent on, life or fate. If not Nietzsche himself, at any rate his successors adopted the second alternative.[25]

In the paragraph that follows, Strauss outlines the basic principles of radical historicism: all knowledge presupposes a frame of reference or horizon; reason cannot disclose that horizon, since it is its presupposition; consequently there are a variety of comprehensive views and we must simply choose one; however, our choice is constricted by fate, by the horizon of our own historical situation; hence, "we are free either to choose in anguish the world view and the standards imposed on us by fate or else to lose ourselves in illusory security or in despair." Strauss then summarizes the essence of the radical historicist position: "The radical historicist asserts, then, that only to thought that is itself committed or 'historical' does other committed or 'historical' thought disclose itself, and, above all, that only to thought that is itself committed or 'historical' does the true meaning of the 'historicity' of all genuine thought disclose itself."[26] The radical historicist thesis is thus that it is given to fate for a particular historical period to discover the essential historicity of all thought, thus avoiding the problem of relativism that characterized nineteenth-century historicism. Though Strauss never mentions his name in *Natural Right and History,* it is clear to anyone familiar with the relevant texts that the principal "successor" to Nietzsche in question is Martin Heidegger.[27]

The importance of all this becomes clearer if we see that Strauss never attempts to repudiate the radical historicist position. He notes that although Hegel may be read as having postulated the achievement of an absolute historical moment in which the "fundamental riddles" have been solved, "according to historicism . . . the absolute moment must be the moment in which the insoluble character of the fundamental riddles has become fully manifest or in which the fundamental delusion of the human mind has been dispelled."[28] He notes that the implication of this position is that if philosophy is understood as the effort to "replace opinions about the whole by knowledge of the whole," and this is the way Strauss consistently defines philosophy, then philosophy is absurd, since philosophy itself rests on opinion. And then Strauss blinks. "We cannot even attempt to discuss these theses," he writes.

We must leave them with the following observation: radical historicism compels us to realize the bearing of the fact that the very idea of natural right presupposes the possibility of philosophy in the full and original meaning of the term. It compels us at the same time to realize the need for unbiased reconsideration of the most elementary premises whose validity is presupposed by philosophy. The question of the validity of these premises cannot be disposed of by adopting or clinging to a more or less persistent tradition of philosophy, for it is of the essence of traditions that they cover or conceal their humble foundations by erecting impressive edifices on them.[29]

The notion that a reconsideration of the possibility of philosophy rests on an "unbiased" return to its origins Strauss owes precisely to Nietzsche and Heidegger. By following the first of the two paths open to Nietzsche, toward Plato and the "noble delusion," normally termed the "noble lie," Strauss leaves the second path intact.

But before embarking on his path to Plato, Strauss assaults what he considers a lesser foe than Heidegger, namely, Max Weber. According to Strauss, contemporary social science is unable and unwilling to assert that we can have any basis for our "ultimate principles" other than personal preference. Natural right he takes to be a standard against which the ideals of any society, including our own, can be judged. So he draws the conclusion that "[t]he contemporary rejection of natural right leads to nihilism —nay, it is identical with nihilism."[30] Since Max Weber "is the greatest social scientist" of the twentieth century, Strauss makes him the focus of his critique.[31] But Strauss acknowledges that Weber did not reject "timeless values," which "distinguishes Weber's position most significantly from historicism."[32] But the timeless values Weber accepts are not those of standards but, rather, those of science. And since Strauss claimed the impossibility of genuine knowledge of "Ought," he maintains that "Weber's thesis necessarily leads to nihilism or to the view that every preference, however evil, base, or insane, has to be judged before the tribunal of reason to be as legitimate as any other preference."[33] And then Strauss once again misdirects his readers. He undertakes to explain how it was that Weber concealed the nihilistic consequences of his position from himself, and in tracing out the trajectory of Weber's thought, "we shall inevitably reach a point beyond which the scene is darkened by the shadow of Hitler." He adds, "Unfortunately, it does not go without saying that in our examination we must avoid the fallacy that in the last decades has frequently been used as a substitute for the *reductio ad absurdum*: the *reductio ad Hitlerum*. A view is not refuted by the fact that it happens to have been shared by Hitler."[34] How is it that Weber, who died in 1920, is connected to Hitler? What idea did they share? Strauss does not say; the allusion to Hitler is left to do its discrediting work. Nietzsche, whom the Nazis claimed as their own, and Heidegger, who actually joined the National Socialist Party in 1933, are displaced by Weber. Is the criticism of the *reductio ad Hitlerum* meant to spare the social scientist Weber, or the two philosophers whom Strauss took as his critical touchstones?

The assault on relativism as nihilism sets up Strauss's description of classical natural right and his critique of modern natural right. The elementary point about classical natural right is that it is a doctrine discovered by reason that accords with nature. Socrates, Strauss writes, is "said" to have been the first political philosopher, and "to the extent to which this is true," he originated "natural rights teachings."[35] Socrates began his investigations into "the natures of things" from the opinions of his fellow citizens, ascending from opinion to true knowledge. True knowledge is therefore the consistent view, as opposed to the inconsistent views represented in opinions. Strauss emphasizes that this inquiry uncovers a natural hierarchic ordering of the human soul to which corresponds a "natural law" consisting of rules that circumscribe the good life and constitute the correct ordering of life. "The life according to nature," Strauss concludes, "is the life of human excellence or virtue, the life of a 'high-class person,' and not the life of pleasure as pleasure."[36] Based on this premise, Strauss makes a number of assertions regarding classical natural right that are particularly important. "Since the classics viewed moral and political matters in the light of man's perfection, they were not egalitarian," he notes. "Not all men are equally equipped by nature for progress toward perfection, or not all 'natures' are 'good natures.'" And Strauss draws the necessary conclusion: "Since men are then unequal in regard to human perfection, i.e., in the decisive respect, equal rights for all appeared to the classics as most unjust. They contended that some men are by nature superior to others and therefore, according to natural right, the rulers of others."[37]

It is in the context of unequal rule that Strauss introduces the concept of "regime." It is his translation for the Greek *politeia*. Strauss emphasizes that *politeia* is not synonymous with "law" or "constitution." Instead, "the politeia is more fundamental than any laws; it is the source of all laws. The *politeia* is rather the factual distribution of power within the community than what constitutional law stipulates in regard to political power."[38] "Regime" then stands for something like a way of life of a society determined by, but not equivalent to, its form of government. And since classical natural right doctrine stipulates that what is right is what is in accordance with nature, this doctrine "is identical with the doctrine of the best regime. For the question as to what is by nature right or as to what is justice finds its complete answer only through the construction, in speech, of the best regime. The essentially political character of the classic natural right doctrine appears most clearly in Plato's *Republic*."[39]

Why the caveat "in speech"? The answer goes to the heart of Strauss's political theory. Classical natural right, he claims, establishes the notion of human excellence, and the best regime would be one that realizes that excellence in accordance with nature. It would be a regime in which "the best men," those who combine wisdom with virtue, ruled the polity absolutely in a perfect natural order. However, "virtue exists in most cases, if not in all cases, as an object of aspiration and not as fulfillment. Therefore, it exists in speech rather than in deed."[40] The rule of the best men is impractical. The best practical regime is one in which the wise act as legislators, establishing the rule of law according to wisdom and then entrusting the administration of the law to a type of man who can be trusted to apply it in situations unforeseen by the wise. "The classics felt that this type of man is the gentleman."[41] The gentleman is "experienced in things noble and beautiful," and this sets them apart from the wise, who have knowledge of the noble and beautiful, on the one hand, and the vulgar, who have neither such knowledge nor experience, on the other.

This schema of best and second-best regimes has as its common characteristic natural inequality.

Classical natural right in Strauss's construction, then, is an orientation toward nature conceived as hierarchically structured with virtue at the top. The polity built in accordance with it will be similarly structured. This contrasts radically, in his reading, with modern natural right. In contrast to the inegalitarian notion of right in the classical formulation, the modern one is built on individualist and egalitarian grounds. Machiavelli's admonition to cease talking about how men ought to live in favor of how they actually do live, what Machiavelli called the "effectual truth" of things, is highlighted by Strauss as a key turning point. It dictated, Strauss thinks, the move from an attitude toward natural law that was purely rational to one that would seek a grounding in the passions in order to be fully effective. It was Hobbes who accomplished this by basing the notion of natural right in the most powerful of passions, the desire for self-preservation and the fear of violent death. This shifts the focus from the duties required by virtue to the rights demanded by self-preservation.[42] This is a shift from natural law as the foundation from which duties follow to the view that natural rights are fundamental and that laws of nature follow from them. This was Hobbes's position, and, in a controversial move, Strauss argues that it was essentially also Locke's.[43]

Given the presumption that the "self-evident truths" articulated in the Declaration of Independence are grounded in a Lockean understanding of natural right, Strauss's interpretation of Locke discloses the rhetorical game of musical chairs that he plays in his text. The critique of "value-free" nihilism, ostensibly in the name of universal truth, will end with the modern doctrine of natural right left without any support. In his reading of Locke, Strauss sees the effects of the modern natural right doctrine leading to a political society without purpose other than self-preservation and public happiness. But he also shows that the accumulation of property is essential to that purpose. So Locke had to argue, against the traditional moral argument, that the unlimited accumulation of wealth is morally just. In a much-quoted passage, Strauss has this to say about Locke's deployment of the virtue of acquisition:

> the burden of his chapter on property [in the *Second Treatise of Government*] is that covetousness and concupiscence, far from being essentially evil or foolish, are, if properly channeled, eminently beneficial and reasonable, much more so than "exemplary charity." By building civil society on "the low but solid ground" of selfishness or of certain "private vices," one will achieve much greater "public benefits" than by futilely appealing to virtue, which is by nature "unendowed." One must take one's bearings not by how men should live but by how they do live.[44]

Strauss's quotation marks do not refer to Locke but are rather meant to enforce Strauss's view that Locke is a central figure in a more or less seamless modernity stretching from Machiavelli and Spinoza to Hobbes to Bernard de Mandeville's *The Fable of the Bees: Or Private Vices, Publick Benefits* (1714) to Adam Smith and beyond. "Locke's doctrine of property," Strauss notes, "is directly intelligible today if it is taken as the classic doctrine of 'the spirit of capitalism' or as a doctrine regarding the chief objective of public policy."[45] And that spirit Strauss characterizes as a contradictory hedonism, one that demands the deferment of pleasure in constant labor. "Hobbes identified the rational life with the life dominated by the fear of fear, by the fear which relieves us from fear," namely, the fear of sovereign power that dispels the fear of the state of nature. "Moved by the same spirit, Locke identifies the rational life with the life dominated by the pain which relieves pain." For Locke, as for Hobbes, "The way toward happiness is a movement away from the state of nature, a movement away from nature: the negation of nature is the way toward happiness. And if the movement toward happiness is the actuality of freedom, freedom is negativity. Just like the primary pain itself, the pain which relieves pain 'ceaseth only in death.'" So Strauss concludes, "The painful relief of pain culminates not so much in the greatest pleasures as 'in the having those things which produce the greatest pleasures.' Life is the joyless quest for joy."[46] The coincidence of this phrase with Weber's "iron cage" signals that Strauss has come full circle from the critique of the alleged nihilism of value neutrality to the gilded nihilism of liberal-capitalist society and its endless, and unfulfilling, acquisitiveness.

Recall that Strauss claimed that Nietzsche laid open two possible paths to follow in responding to the nihilistic threat posed by historicism. He followed the path back to the "strictly esoteric character of the theoretical analysis of life—that is, restore the Platonic notion of the noble delusion." This refers to the fact that what is right by nature can only be discerned by reason and, thus, knowable only to a few. These few, in turn, must devise means by which to gain the consent of the many, who live according to opinion and convention. "Natural right would act as dynamite for civil society" if not mediated through the noble guile of the rulers.[47] Strauss's guile has produced a rhetorical claim on behalf of what are said to be foundational American principles while he has laid the dynamite carefully between the lines.

In an essay largely devoted to insulating Strauss from the use some Straussians and others have made of him, Mark Lilla emphasizes the long-term impact of *Natural Right and History*. The crucial date in assessing that impact is 1968. The upheavals within American universities that began in earnest in that year had a traumatic effect on many of Strauss's current and former students, Lilla writes. Thanks to *Natural Right and History*, they were "prepared to see the threat of 'nihilism' lurking in the interstices of modern life, waiting to be released, turning America into Weimar."[48] This premise, Lilla notes, underlay Bloom's *Closing of the American Mind*. Illustrating Lilla's point, Bloom there uses Louis Armstrong's popularization of the Brecht-Weill song "Mack the Knife" as a sign of the "astonishing Americanization of the German pathos." Bloom links the song's concept to Nietzsche's *Thus Spake Zarathustra* and to the "supra-moral attitude of expectancy" that "appealed to Weimar and its American admirers." Its American version becomes "less dangerous, although not less corrupt."

"Our stars," he continues, "are singing a song they do not understand, translated from a German original and having a huge popular success with unknown but wide-ranging consequences, as something of the original message touches something in American souls. But behind it all, the master lyricists are Nietzsche and Heidegger."[49]

Bloom's one mention of Strauss comes at the end of a section of several pages in which he largely reiterates his teacher's teaching about Locke. Hobbes, Bloom says, invented the notion of rights, and Locke gave it respectability. Rights, to an American, "are our common sense. Right is not the opposite of wrong, but of duty. It is a part of, or the essence of, freedom. It begins from man's cherished passion to live, and to live as painlessly as possible." Rights represent "a new kind of morality solidly grounded in self-interest."[50] The irony with which Bloom articulates these points was likely lost on many readers. However, against the background of Strauss's *Natural Right and History,* Bloom's paragraph that begins with "Americans are Lockeans" and ends with the sentence, "As Leo Strauss put it, the moderns 'built on low but solid ground,'" displays its fully ironic sense.[51] But aside from the Straussians among them, the neoconservatives largely ignored the irony, and figures such as William Bennett generated and exploited Bloom's commercial success, mindlessly jumbling Plato and Locke, Socrates and Jefferson together while failing to see the worst of Nietzsche threading his way through Bloom's glib and unreasoned pronouncements. It made for attention-grabbing headlines and initiated a largely vacuous but politically astute "debate" on cultural values that proceeded on terms set by the neocons.

It was one of Bloom's students who managed to synthesize various elements of the Straussian liturgy into a useful neoconservative sermon on history and politics. Francis Fukuyama's principal contribution to neoconservative political theory is his much-discussed 1992 book, *The End of History and the Last Man.* In it, Fukuyama beats the Weberian horse one more time. "While Max Weber," he writes, "took a despairing and pessimistic view of the increasing rationalism and secularism of mankind's historical 'progress,' postwar modernization theory gave his ideas a decidedly optimistic and, one is tempted to say, typically American cast."[52] But Fukuyama's text represents a skillful sublimation of the European and American, despairing and optimistic motifs. Whereas Strauss dwelt on what he saw as the disastrous effects of modern science and technology, Fukuyama emphasizes two social aspects of their development: technology allows for advances in military strength and in economic capacity. Thus, science provides the means for people "to gratify their desire for security, and for the limitless acquisition of material goods."[53] Security and the accumulation of wealth are the foundations of the modern notion of right examined and ultimately rejected by Strauss. Fukuyama highlights the limitations of this notion of right, but with a more strategic view toward its needed supplement in the present historical period.

Fukuyama discusses Hobbes and Locke under the rubric of "the first man," focusing on their conceptions of the so-called state of nature.[54] His purpose is to contrast the safety-seeking, acquisitive, rights-bearing liberal individual of Locke with the individual who seeks recognition above all else. Fukuyama derives this "first man" from Hegel's depiction of the struggle for recognition in the *Phenomenology of Spirit*, a struggle that results in the establishment of masters and slaves. The master-type is able to overcome the natural fear of death and risk everything in the struggle, while the slave-type ultimately clings to life. Thus, Locke's individual is the type of the slave, who puts the desire for self-preservation first. And Fukuyama notes, "Thomas Jefferson's 'self-evident' truths about the rights of men to life, liberty, and the pursuit of happiness were not essentially different from Locke's natural rights to life and property." The problem for politics was seen by Locke, Jefferson, and others like them, Fukuyama says, "as being in some sense the effort to persuade the would-be masters to accept the life of the slave in a kind of classless society of slaves."[55]

The "first man" of the liberal imagination is at the same time the "last man" of Fukuyama's title. Although Fukuyama emphasizes his reading of Hegel, as mediated by the Russo-French philosopher Alexander Kojève, his larger conception of recognition is indebted to Bloom's idiosyncratic interpretation and translation of Plato's *Republic*.[56] The crucial notion here is that there is a part of the soul that is characterized by "spiritedness" (*thymos*) that drives individuals to seek recognition. It is a passion and is distinct from desire. The Lockean individual elevates desire for self-preservation and material comfort over this passion. Figuratively, Fukuyama characterizes this elevation, insofar as it is successful, as the victory of the bourgeois over the aristocrat.[57] Nietzsche called the victor the "last man" in *Thus Spake Zarathustra* and described him as an unselfreflective, small man who "makes everything small" while proclaiming himself the inventor of "happiness."[58] The success of science, technology, and liberal democracy, a society of "slaves," poses the problem of the last man for Fukuyama.

Liberal democracy is understood by Fukuyama to be the only long-term political option in the world after the collapse of the Soviet empire. In the short term, forms of authoritarian rule may prevail, but liberal democracy is the only system that provides the possibility of the universal recognition that will increasingly be demanded as education levels increase in accordance with technological (including military and economic) advances. These latter advances are inevitable, given the processes of globalization. But despite this assertion, Fukuyama's analysis is plagued by the specter of the last man. "Liberal principles," he writes, "can be destructive of the highest forms of patriotism which are necessary for the very survival of the community. For it is a widely recognized defect of Anglo-Saxon liberal theory that men would never die for a country based merely on the principle of rational self-preservation."[59] Liberal democracy requires irrational passions to sustain it. The "noble" features of Strauss's critique of modernity return.

In an influential article published in 1996 in *Foreign Affairs,* William Kristol and Robert Kagan drew the consequences of the preceding trajectory of thought from Strauss to Fukuyama. They claimed that American military officers worried that "while they serve as a kind of foreign legion, doing the hard work of American-style 'empire management,' American civilians at home, preoccupied with the distribution of tax breaks and government benefits, will not come to their support when the going gets tough."[60] So they called for greater "moral clarity" in American foreign policy by promoting the "American principles" of "democracy, free markets, respect for liberty."[61] Then they drew the connection: "The remoralization of America at home ultimately requires the remoralization of American foreign policy."[62] The Straussian element in the neoconservative agenda thus contributed to a political project that aimed at exploiting America's unrivaled global military power in order to reverse its cultural decline. The regime it sought to change was the American regime. September 11 presented the opportunity to enact this noble delusion. The result of the assault on nihilism has been its victory.

NOTES

1. Irving Kristol, "The Neoconservative Persuasion," *Weekly Standard* 8, no. 47 (August 25, 2003), available online at http://www.weeklystandard.com/utilities/

printer_preview.asp?idArticle=3000&R=785F27881. All additional quotations from Kristol in following paragraphs are from this article.

2. Alain Frachon and Daniel Vernet, *L'Amerique messianique: Les guerres des néo-conservateurs* (Paris: Éditions du Seuil, 2005), 49.

3. Ibid., 54.

4. Gertrude Himmelfarb, "Democratic Remedies for Democratic Disorders," *Public Interest* (spring 1998), available online at http://www.findarticles.com/p/articles/mi_m0377/is_n131/ai_20632390.

5. Francis Fukuyama, *America at the Crossroads: Democracy, Power, and the Neoconservative Legacy* (New Haven, CT: Yale University Press, 2006), 13. But Fukuyama is perhaps transparent where Kristol is opaque, since Fukuyama precedes this assertion by noting that some (unidentified) neoconservatives have charged their (unidentified) critics with a veiled anti-Semitism in the very use of the term "neoconservative."

6. Ibid., 21.

7. Ibid., 34. The one figure who represents the fusion of Strauss and Wohlstetter is Fukuyama's former classmate and colleague Paul Wolfowitz. Already identified in journalistic accounts of the Straussians within the administration of George W. Bush, the former Assistant Secretary of Defense and current head of the International Monetary Fund was thinly disguised as the character Peter Gorman in Saul Bellow's roman à clef, *Ravelstein*. There, Gorman/Wolfowitz was presented as a dutiful student of Allan Bloom, the real man behind the eponymous Abe Ravelstein, himself the dutiful student of Leo Strauss in the guise of Professor Felix Davarr. In fact, Wolfowitz was a student of Bloom's at Cornell and did attend two classes of Strauss's at the University of Chicago shortly before Strauss retired from the university in 1967. The full extent of his actual Straussianism is not easy to discern, and Wolfowitz himself is clear that, in his mind, the greater influence on him was Wohlstetter, also at the time teaching at Chicago. It is certain that Wolfowitz's career in government was due to his studies with Wohlstetter.

8. Ibid., ix–x.

9. See James Mann, *Rise of the Vulcans: The History of Bush's War Cabinet* (New York: Viking, 2004), 160–63.

10. Allan Bloom, *The Closing of the American Mind: How Higher Education Has Failed Democracy and Impoverished the Souls of Today's Students* (New York: Simon and Schuster, 1987).

11. Ibid., 75.

12. Harry V. Jaffa, "Humanizing Certitudes and Impoverishing Doubts: A Critique of *The Closing of the American Mind*," in *Essays on The Closing of the American Mind*, ed. Robert L. Stone (Chicago: Chicago Review Press, 1989), 129.

13. Bloom, *Closing*, 259.

14. Ibid., 147, 155.

15. Fukuyama, *America at the Crossroads*, 21–22.

16. Leo Strauss, "A Giving of Accounts," in Strauss, *Jewish Philosophy and the Crisis of Modernity: Essays and Lectures in Modern Jewish Thought,* ed. Kenneth Hart Green (Albany: State University of New York Press, 1997), 461.

17. Leo Strauss, *Natural Right and History* (Chicago: University of Chicago Press, 1965), 1–2. Strauss declines to specify any examples. Predictably, Bloom repeats his master's sentiment, but without Strauss's characteristic reticence: "The great influence of a nation with a powerful intellectual life over less well-endowed nations, even if the armies of the latter are very powerful, is not rare in human experience. The most obvious cases are the influence of Greece over Rome and of France on Germany and Russia." Bloom, *Closing,* 152.

18. Quoted in David N. Myers, *Resisting History: Historicism and Its Discontents in German-Jewish Thought* (Princeton, NJ: Princeton University Press, 2003), 108.

19. Myers, *Resisting History,* chap. 4: "Anti-Historicism and the Theological-Political Predicament in Weimar Germany: The Case of Leo Strauss."

20. Strauss, *Natural Right and History,* 13.

21. Ibid.

22. Ibid., 13–14.

23. Ibid., 14.

24. Ibid., 22

25. Ibid., 26.

26. Ibid., 26–27.

27. See Martin Heidegger, *Being and Time,* trans. Joan Stambaugh (Albany: State University of New York Press, 1996), Division Two, V and passim.

28. Ibid., 29. It is clear from the context that Strauss is here referring to what he has categorized as radical historicism.

29. Ibid., 31.

30. Ibid., 5.

31. Ibid., 36.

32. Ibid., 39.

33. Ibid., 42.

34. Ibid., 42–43.

35. Ibid., 120. The use of passive constructions is typical of Strauss. This technique, related to his notion of esoteric writing, allows him at once to articulate conventional views while distancing himself from them. He may or may not be endorsing the view in question.

36. Ibid., 127.

37. Ibid., 134–35.

38. Ibid., 136.

39. Ibid., 144.

40. Ibid., 146. This distinguishes the classical natural right doctrine of the Greek tradition from that of "biblical faith," since, for the latter, the best regime is identical with the City of God and therefore "coeval with Creation and hence

always actual; and the cessation of evil, or Redemption, is brought about by God's supernatural action. The question of the best regime thus loses its crucial significance." Ibid., 144.

41. Ibid., 142.

42. Ibid., 180–81. The opposition between virtue and individuality is what Strauss sees as the central issue in the so-called quarrel between ancients and moderns to which he and his school have repeatedly referred.

43. Ibid., 202–51.

44. Ibid., 247.

45. Ibid., 246.

46. Ibid., 250–51.

47. Ibid., 153.

48. Mark Lilla, "The Closing of the Straussian Mind," *New York Review of Books* 51, no. 17 (November 4, 2004), available online at http://www.nybooks.com/articles/17523.

49. Bloom, *Closing,* 152.

50. Ibid., 166.

51. Ibid., 167.

52. Francis Fukuyama, *The End of History and the Last Man* (New York: HarperCollins, 2002), 68–69.

53. Ibid., 80.

54. Fukuyama's discussion of Hobbes and Locke is derived in its entirety from Strauss's interpretation in *Natural Right and History* and several identifiably Straussian scholars.

55. Ibid., 159.

56. For a cogent interpretation of Fukuyama's book and its inspirations, see Perry Anderson, *A Zone of Engagement* (London: Verso, 1992), 331–57.

57. Fukuyama, *End of History,* 185–87.

58. Friedrich Nietzsche, *Thus Spake Zarathustra,* trans. Walter Kaufmann (New York: Penguin, 1978), 16–19.

59. Fukuyama, *End of History,* 324–25.

60. William Kristol and Robert Kagan, "Toward a Neo-Reaganite Foreign Policy," *Foreign Affairs* 75, no. 4 (July-August 1996): 26.

61. Ibid., 27.

62. Ibid., 31.

Chapter 11

One-Dimensional Men
Neoconservatives, Their Allies and Models

Lawrence Davidson

As we progress into the twenty-first century, there is a sense among many Americans that the policies of the George W. Bush administration are a drastic deviation from what the United States has always stood for: justice, fairness, and a certain civilized moderation in policy. These Americans now hear of the practice of torture, indefinite detentions, the disregard of international law, preemptive war, and they believe that the nation has been led astray. They do not understand how things could have changed so much so quickly. In truth, this assessment is the result of the manipulation and distortion of history. It is the product of a selective presentation of U.S. history that has all but erased the expansionist and exploitive aspects of our national behavior in favor of a long-standing myth of America the benevolent. It is this mythic America that seems to be slipping away.

Ironically, those who now supposedly threaten this vision are very much in the American tradition. They are a contemporary expression of long-standing aggressive and expansionist aspects of the American character. As we will see, they work from an equally deep-rooted philosophy that divides the world into two absolute and opposing camps of good and evil, as well as an ancient conviction that the world is a jungle and aggressiveness is a key to survival. In truth it is their United States, self-righteous, hypocritical, and often violent, that is much more familiar to the rest of the world than the benevolent Sunday-school America that the critics of the Bush administration now mourn.

Who are these people who now, from the very seats of power, appear to be at odds with mythic America? They are known as neoconservatives, and they have a host of allies who help them formulate, support, and rationalize policies that they erroneously claim are innovative. They assert that their new path is an improvement on (and not a betrayal of) the national tradition because it is more attuned to the reality of our times. It should be emphasized that the neocons also believe in the myth of America the benevolent. But for them, benevolence is seen as having degenerated into softness and the inability to do what is necessary to defend America and extend her sway. They demand that the United States, now the world's sole superpower, adopt an attitude of "tough love" toward the world as a whole. For the sake of the good, they now pursue the policies of power and domination.

One-Dimensional Men

At the beginning of the 1970s, neoconservatives in the United States were a loose group of intellectuals lodged in think tanks such as the American Enterprise Institute and journals such as *Commentary* and the *Public Interest*. They were held together by an overriding anticommunism and a philosophical devotion to the power-politics-oriented thinking of such political theorists as Leo Strauss and Irving Kristol.[1] As thinkers and critics of foreign policy, the neocons were known to those in the U.S. government, but they had no direct input into the nation's foreign policy. That would soon change. The last twenty years of the twentieth century would unexpectedly open up opportunities for them, and they would prove ready, for they were a determined and assertive clique. It was a posture that befit their ancient and macabre vision of the world.[2]

That vision was one-dimensional and starkly negative. The neoconservative universe was then, and remains now, a melding of the Hobbesian and the Manichaean conceptions of reality. The reality pictured by Thomas Hobbes placed mankind in a permanent and hostile state of nature where there is "continual fear and danger of violent death."[3] This perspective was recently explained for the citizens of the United States by neoconservative spokesman and author Michael Ledeen, who admonished, "Americans believe that peace is normal, but that is not true. . . . Peace is abnormal."[4]

And what can be said for normality? For the neoconservatives, what is normal is a never-ending war between good and evil that is best characterized by the preaching of the third-century AD religious philosopher Manichaeus.[5] Ledeen spoke for all his associates when he told the BBC, "I know the struggle against evil is going to go on forever."[6] For the neoconservatives, good and evil appear to be absolute in themselves: good is always clear and beyond reproach, and evil is complete. Each side is one-dimensional in its essence, and there is no room for nuance and subtlety.

Of course, Mr. Ledeen and his fellows saw themselves as the ones representing good. And they would do so aggressively. Although most of them were "Yankee intellectuals" from the urban centers of the Northeast, they espoused a cowboy posture that required us all to sleep with our boots on and guns loaded.[7] After all, evil is always out there.

The operative emotions that drove the neoconservatives were fear and loathing. They feared the revival of Nazi politics and anti-Semitism. They feared the USSR and communism. They feared détente. They feared isolationism. They loathed compromise, which they equated with weakness and appeasement. They loathed a liberal approach to foreign policy and its reliance on diplomacy. They loathed the "old Europe." They claimed that they had been "mugged by reality,"[8] and once burnt, twice wise.

Why have they, as a group, been led to see the world this way? Some of them have attributed their worldview of fear and loathing to the experiences of relatives who suffered in the Holocaust. According to neoconservative Richard Perle, the Holocaust was the "defining moment of our history."[9] Here the evil was easy to identify, and one did not need to spend time examining the source of the problem. The appropriate response, at least in hindsight, was clearly active and aggressive resistance rather than appeasement or diplomacy. The message taken away from the experience of the Holocaust was that evil must always be resisted with force. The neocons carried this message over in their reaction to the Soviet Union. They indeed saw the Soviet Union as an "evil empire," and many of them were paranoid enough to always be seeing "reds under their beds." For these neocons the Soviet Union represented the most dangerous empire to have ever existed.[10] It could only be dealt with through the tactics of active resistance and not through diplomacy and negotiation. Hesitation in this regard smacked of appeasement and weakness. And finally, there were others attracted to the neoconservative line who may have just been the type of personalities who are always looking for a fight (John Bolton comes to mind). The neoconservative camp provided them with plenty of opportunities to pick fights.

In any case, this neoconservative world can be interpreted as dangerously oversimplistic. History itself seemed to be all but dismissed by Defense Secretary Donald Rumsfeld with his dubious insight that "stuff happens."[11] As Thomas Wright has put it, what the neoconservatives do is "construct an historical narrative that exclusively associates hawkish positions with success and dovish ones with failure."[12] It should come as no great surprise that such a black-and-white approach has produced very problematic results. As Wright concludes, "advocating one position as an ideology to inform action across all cases—on the basis that it alone holds the key to success—is a recipe for disaster."[13]

Foreign policy was and is the passion of the neoconservatives. Having postulated a fear-filled world and dismissed all counter worldviews as naive and dangerous, the type of foreign policy they advocate flows naturally from their assumptions. The United States required a strong defense because what it really faced was a world where struggle was in the nature of things. The lessons of centuries of experience and effort devoted to the maturation of diplomacy and international law were to be dismissed out of hand in favor of instances where caution and negotiation proved disastrous. Diplomacy was only useful as a form of delay and deceit.

Toward the end of the Cold War neoconservatives found their ideological home in the administration of Ronald Reagan. They joined this president in celebrating America as a land blessed by God—a land that both Reagan and the neoconservatives saw as a political model for all future societies because it embodied democracy and as an economic model because it embodied free enterprise. This being so, the hegemony that America was destined to establish around the globe must be a "benevolent" one. Elliott Abrams, a neoconservative who would get his hands on a bit of power during the Reagan–Bush Sr. era assured all that the United States is "the greatest force for good among the nations of the Earth."[14]

After the Reagan era, the neocons suffered reverses. They were shunned by the Clinton crowd and, at the end of the first Gulf War, their advice to immediately bring down Saddam Hussein was not taken by the elder Bush. However, with George W. Bush's election in 2000, new opportunities presented themselves. They found in Bush Jr. and his entourage truly kindred spirits. The neoconservatives were recruited into the government in droves and quickly made alliances with machpolitik advocates such as Defense Secretary Donald Rumsfeld and Vice President Dick Cheney.

The unexpected demise of the Soviet Union gave some of the neoconservatives a period of intellectual anxiety, but they quickly recovered.[15] They soon realized that the absence of the Soviet Union presented an assumed golden opportunity for the establishment of American hegemony. This would have to be done with dispatch, however, because there now existed a power vacuum, which, if not rapidly filled by an assertive United States, would allow for the emergence of new challengers, such as China or perhaps even Iran. Knowing this to be so, the neocons solemnly warned that it was time to increase, not decrease, military spending.

This continuing aggressive posture was advocated by the neoconservative Charles Krauthammer, a psychiatrist turned editorial writer on foreign affairs. For Krauthammer, the post–Cold War world remained a very dangerous place because advances in technology make peripheral powers and anti-American movements potentially dangerous even to a great power like the United States. Just as during the Cold War, when the Soviet Union was the incarnation of evil, Krauthammer warned of new "embodiments of evil" just on the horizon. After the 9/11 attacks, his message was considered a prophecy come true.[16]

To forestall new challenges and make the world safe for America, Krauthammer and his allies, such as Elliott Abrams, espoused the need for the United States to "act alone" if necessary to disarm countries and movements that were seen as "upsetting world stability."[17] It would also be necessary to alter the "rules of national sovereignty" to allow preventative measures to be taken where needed.[18] This translated into Bush's policy of "preemptive strike" and also of "regime change." Thus, the aggressive use of military power is a required element of neoconservative thinking. Given that their world is one part Hobbesian and one part Manichaean, it could not be otherwise.

One might, therefore, cynically assert that all the talk about promoting democracy that emanates from the Bush White House is only a political cover for the application of "shock and awe."[19] This is almost certainly the case when it comes to Vice President Richard Cheney, Defense Secretary Donald Rumsfeld, United Nations Ambassador John Bolton, National Intelligence Director John D. Negroponte, and others of the machpolitik persuasion. Readers can decide if it is also the case with the Pearls, Wolfowitzes, Abramses, Krauthammers, and President Bush himself. Do they believe that the mayhem, death, and destruction that these men are willing to unleash on the world is going to turn us all into happy, democratically minded entrepreneurs? George W. Bush, ignoring the American-induced chaos in Iraq, likes to remark, "I am confident history will prove the decision we made to be the right decision."[20] We need not wait until some distant future time to know if he is likely right or wrong. There are plenty of historical precedents we can look at.

Past Precedents and Current Models: American Historical Precedents (the "One-Man Majorities")

Many of these precedents are found in American history. As Albert K. Weinberg has shown in an old but elegantly written and very complete work, all of them involve militaristic behavior rationalized by the distortion of information and appeals to security, democracy, and economic necessity.[21] Here are but a few of the notable ones: there was Andrew Jackson (1829–1837), who, believing himself the bravest of men, once proclaimed that "one man with courage makes a majority." While serving his country, he put this adage into practice and indeed acted as if he were a one-man majority. As a general in the U.S. Army, he ignored his orders and illegally invaded Spanish Florida. Later, as president, he consciously ignored the rulings of the U.S. Supreme Court and illegally expelled the Cherokee nation from its homeland.[22] Through a combination of misinformation spread about by yellow journalism, he was able to transform his view of reality into a national view. This set a precedent for those of like character who followed. President James Polk (1845–1849) asserted that "the world has nothing to fear from military ambition in our government"[23] and went on to contrive excuses for starting a war with Mexico (1846–1848).[24] He then concluded that "our beloved country presents a sublime moral spectacle to the world."[25] President William McKinley (1897–1901) reported that he stayed up all night and prayed to God, who then delivered to him a theological justification for seizing the Philippine islands.[26] President Theodore Roosevelt (1901–1909) asserted that "the Monroe Doctrine would go far" if American foreign policy "carried a big stick."[27] He had already helped turn this theory into practice by participating in the Spanish-American War, which he seemed to quite enjoy. Answering a journalist's questions about his experiences in the war's Cuban theater, he replied, "I have had a bully time and a bully fight."[28]

More famous still is President Woodrow Wilson (1913–1921), who, in April 1917, led the United States into World War I because "the world must be made safe for democracy," and democracy in turn was embodied in America's values.[29] This example may be one to which neoconservatives look with particular favor, for they too claim to champion the spread of democracy. However, it should be kept in mind that Wilson's plan proved to be a failure, with negative long-term consequences. After World War I, self-determination was reserved for Central Europeans alone, and even there most of the newly formed postwar countries fell to dictatorship. His "tough love" approach to the Weimar Republic helped pave the way for Adolf Hitler. The Middle East was divided up between the British and French Empires under the guise of mandates—a horrid little deception that fooled no one in the region but made the populations of imperialist Europe feel better. And, last but not least, the Wilsonian effort to spread democracy and self-determination was a cover for the introduction of the Zionist state into Palestine.[30]

As important, throughout the entire nineteenth and twentieth centuries, there was constant intervention in Central America, as if such action was justified by the "international police power" of the United States.[31] More often than not, these interventions were made on the behalf of brutal dictatorships that were cooperating with American corporations. Or they were made to overthrow popular regimes that refused such cooperation. It is interesting to note that, upon realizing themselves to be at the head of the world's sole superpower, our contemporary leaders began treating the rest of the world as the United States has traditionally treated Central America.

Many of the American leaders who were quite willing to launch into foreign wars to expand, dominate, and/or remake the world in America's image are now celebrated in American history as heroes. The fact that they might have quite often lied and even broken the law is largely forgotten, and, instead of staring at us from mug shots, their faces now adorn official portraits and twenty-dollar bills. They appear to have succeeded as men with courage who made their own majorities. Perhaps George W. Bush, who reportedly likes to read presidential biographies, has learned from their examples. However, their reputations as put forth in histories written by American Indians, Mexicans, Cubans, Filipinos, or the excellent but rare iconoclastic histories by writers like Howard Zinn[32] are certainly less heroic. Of course, most Americans—including, no doubt, Mr. Bush—do not read these.

These precedents from the country's history suggest that the neoconservatives are really "yesterday's men" recycling aggressive policies that have come into play over and again. But are these policies really to be judged failures? The answer is yes only if the major goal of U.S. foreign policy was and is to secure the nation by aiming at a relatively peaceful, just, and cooperative world. This goal fits the myth of American benevolence. However, it might be worth considering the possibility that this was not the goal of the presidents listed earlier, nor the goal of the present administration. Perhaps the real goals always were expansion, colonization, economic domination, and the direct or indirect control of the leaders and policies of foreign governments. These ends contradict the goals of a just and peaceful world, and of a democratic one too. However, historians who honor the American myth have either ignored their negative consequences or reinterpreted them as anomalies. Yet, in truth, under these circumstances goals such as democracy and justice degenerate into elements of a cover story that is used to maintain popular sentiment for the real, yet very much more brutal, ends.

Today's neocons add a new layer of cynicism to this historical falsification by proffering a self-fulfilling prophecy that clears their consciences. For if the ends of expansion and domination are expressions of an a priori Hobbesian nature—both of the world we live in and human nature too—their pursuit is both inevitable and indeed "normal." Why then design policies for what is "abnormal"—like peace? The result is "enduring" military bases in Iraq and elsewhere and emergency laws like the Orwellian-named "patriotic" act that never expire because they are tied to an endless war against a tactic (terrorism) that has always been with us and always will be. In many ways this becomes a self-fulfilling prophecy: the neoconservatives and their machpolitik allies interpret the world as Hobbesian and Manichaean. They project onto the world Hobbesian policies. The relationship between states becomes more Hobbesian in nature. The neocons feel vindicated and demand that we must all support them because their interpretation is obviously the correct one.

The Prussian Model (Neoconservatives as Neo-Prussians)

A non-American precedent for the neoconservative approach to foreign policy can be found in the history of Prussian/German "diplomacy" following Kaiser Wilhelm II's dismissal of Otto von Bismarck as Chancellor of Germany in 1890. Bismarck was a political genius, but he was difficult to work with, argumentative, and very set in his ways. Most of all, he was bent on maintaining the balance of power in Europe following the Franco-Prussian War, which ended in 1871. The Franco-Prussian War had paved the way for the final unification of Germany, which then immediately became the dominant industrial and military power on the European continent. However, Bismarck (stubborn but not a one-dimensional thinker) understood that to sustain Germany's position he needed to maintain peace. A provocative and threatening Germany would only engender coalitions against it and eventually upset the balance of power to Germany's detriment.

Neither Wilhelm II, who ascended the throne in 1888, nor his military advisers could understand Bismarck's passivity. For them, it was Germany's destiny to play a dominant political and military role on a world scale—to practice a policy of weltpolitik and thereby achieve glory. War was an essential element of this policy, for only those nations willing to risk war could achieve greatness. This required, as Wilhelm put it, that Germany embark on a "new course" that would allow it to exercise its military might and build an empire as great as that of Great Britain.[33] To proceed along this "new course" the Kaiser replaced Bismarck with General Georg Leo von Caprivi, who immediately started dismantling the alliance system that Bismarck had built to maintain Europe's balance of power.

Over the next decade German diplomacy was transformed into "gunboat diplomacy" as Germany proceeded to claim her "place in the sun." This was pursued through blackmail (the second Morocco crisis of 1911), arms races (Germany's 1898 decision to build a navy that could challenge Great Britain on the high seas), and bravado (the Kaiser telling his troops bound for China that they should give no pardon, take no prisoners, and generally behave "just as the Huns").[34] Wilhelm meant to pursue his "new course" with "an inflexible will which will proceed in the face of all resistance to the goal felt to be right."[35] That narrow-mindedness led straight to World War I, during which over ten million people died.

Wilhelm II has much in common with George W. Bush. Both have "brashly self-assertive" personalities that led them to adopt a personal style of rule that gave reign to their impulsiveness. Both felt that they had a constitutionally granted prerogative over military and foreign policy and were impatient with any attempt to curb their actions in these areas.[36] Wilhelm II (like Bush and the neoconservatives in regard to the United States) believed that Germany was the natural leader and protector of a new Europe but that the old Europe seemed not to understand or appreciate this. He (like his twenty-first-century American counterparts) was utterly convinced of his own correctness and surrounded himself with people who reinforced this view.[37] He felt (as does Mr. Bush and his advisers with regard to the United States) that Germany's military might rendered it invincible. And there is little evidence that, even in defeat, he (or they) ever questioned his decisions or motives. The likenesses are sufficient to suggest that, in their approach to foreign policy and the use of military force, Bush and the neocons behave like neo-Prussians.[38]

There are, of course, some differences. Neither Wilhelm II nor his post-Bismarckian advisers considered themselves intellectuals. But Mr. Bush's neoconservative advisers do think of themselves as such.[39] It is worth noting, though, that as neoconservative practice proves their theoretical assumptions and predictions to be false, they too become just another set of machpolitik politicians—or, to use their critics' term, "thugs in suits."

History has very little good to say about Wilhelm II. After all, Germany did not win World War I. Therefore, it was the British, French, and Americans who shaped the popular images of the last Kaiser. Yet, even taking this bias into consideration, it is hard to deny that destroying the balance of power, substituting gunboats for diplomats, and behaving like a bully in a schoolyard did the Germans (who survived) little good. As we have seen, Mr. Bush has faith that history will vindicate him. But this is likely only if he, unlike the Kaiser or, say, Lyndon Johnson, comes through the slaughter as a "winner." It is questionable whether he and his neoconservative allies are in fact winners. To date they, like the last Kaiser before them, have only managed to turn weltpolitik into weltschmerz.

Israel as a Contemporary Model for Neoconservative Foreign Policy

For the neoconservatives themselves, the most compelling precedent is a contemporary one. If the neocons assert that the United States is a political and economic model for the rest of the world, it is Israel that is a military model for the neocons. In 1967 the United States was losing in Vietnam, and the country was alive with protests and demands for withdrawal. There would be no "staying the course" because increasing numbers of Americans did not believe the course was worth the staying. That same year, the Israelis launched a preemptive attack against Egypt that, seven days later, resulted in a "glorious" victory that allegedly gave the country "safe" borders. It was, indeed, a terrific example of what the bold use of "shock and awe" could accomplish. Subsequently, the Israelis have clung to the Occupied Territories, either absorbing or controlling them, in a thirty-nine-year effort at "staying the course." No end to their steadfastness is in sight.

Men and women who would soon label themselves neoconservatives watched the 1967 Israeli performance with fascination and envy. As one American historian, Melani McAlister, has perceptively put it, in the wake of Vietnam, "Israel and its military played a key symbolic role for those who advocated the remilitarization of U.S. policy. As questions raged both about the morality of the U.S. war in Vietnam and about the role of the U.S. military more generally, Israel came to provide a political model for thinking about military power and a practical example of effectiveness in the use of that power."[40]

Subsequently, Israel's response to Palestinian resistance (which in its extreme modes took on terrorist forms) also became a model for neoconservatives and America's machpolitik leaders. As the "Vietnam syndrome" gripped the United States, the Zionist state seemed to be going about bashing the Palestinians daily. The Israelis were supposedly standing up for themselves, exacting retribution for every attack against them, and behaving like the great and morally righteous power the neoconservatives wanted the United States to be. This image of Israel as the model to be celebrated and emulated was played out in American books and movies throughout the 1960s, 1970s, and 1980s.[41] In these accounts, the Israelis represented the West and therefore goodness and civilization. This picture helped solidify an identification between the United States and Israeli to the point that it was soon assumed that the two nations had "shared values."

So Israel became an exemplar not only of proud military capacity and action but also of moral courage to reject what the neocons considered appeasement (for instance, a two-state solution as part of a compromise peace) and of "stay the course" toughness in the face of terrorist threats to its national security. Indeed, as McAlister points out, "it was the harnessing of moral discourse to military power" that made the Israeli model so potent for many Americans.[42] Therefore, it is unreasonable to expect Mr. Bush and his advisers to chastise or otherwise punish Israel for things that they themselves find exemplary 99 percent of the time. And it should come as no surprise that, subsequently, the neoconservatives created a virtual alliance with a major violent and aggressive Israeli right-wing party, the Likud. Some of the neocons served as advisers to that party's elected prime ministers.[43] Indeed, as Russell Kirk, "one of the founders of the post World War II conservative intellectual movement" has observed, "not seldom it has seemed as if some eminent neoconservatives mistook Tel Aviv for the capital of the United States."[44]

This assertion that Israel set the norm for American foreign and military policy and practice necessitated the systematic distortion of media coverage of both Israel and Palestine.[45] American mainstream media only reinforced the fictional image of Israel displayed in books and movies. It presented Israel as the "only democracy in the Middle East" (completely ignoring Lebanon), while the fact that it treated its Arab citizens much as the United States had treated its minorities prior to civil-rights legislation was never mentioned. Wars of offense were turned into wars of defense; brutal occupation and illegal colonization were explained away or ignored. And, in this case, the media really did end up "blaming the victim" in that the Palestinians were methodically turned into terrorists, their leaders demonized, and the nonviolent aspect of their resistance never mentioned. The Palestinians were the first Arabs to be pictured "hating our values." The neoconservatives were too emotionally enamored of Israeli belligerence (most were Zionists as well) to object to any of this. As Max Boot, the neocon former editor of the *Wall Street Journal* noted, "an attachment to Israel was a key tenet of neoconservatism."[46]

The Evolving Alliance with the Christian Right ("God Is Pro-War")

This identification with Israel was assisted by another powerful factor: the political emergence of fundamentalist Christians in the halls of power. They too were Zionists, but they were led to be so by their own peculiar theological reasoning. This necessitated a successful imperialist Israeli state as a prelude to the second coming of Christ. The second coming in turn presaged Armageddon and the end of the world—once more we are confronted with goals that contradict the search for a peaceful and cooperative world.

Christian fundamentalist concern was not just with Israel's alleged prophetic destiny to conquer all of the Holy Land. It also concerned itself with achieving an aligned American domination of the Middle East and the world in general. Support for American supremacy had a lot to do with the classical battle of good against evil. The United States, being the heartland of evangelical Protestantism, could be no other than a leader of good. Here the Christian fundamentalists shared a somewhat similar attitude as the Manichaean neoconservatives. Indeed, in their advocacy of both a strong Israel and a dominant America, the language used by both groups started to sound like religious or secular variations on the same themes.

It was the neoconservative Richard Perle who once asserted that "the

President of the United States [George W. Bush] on issue after issue, has reflected the thinking of neoconservatives."[47] For the Christian fundamentalist leader Pat Robertson that would tie the neocons to God through the Oval Office, for, according to Robertson, George W. Bush struggles with the "blessing of heaven upon him."[48] If the neocon Michael Ledeen felt that "violent change is the essence of human history,"[49] then the Christian fundamentalist leader Jerry Falwell agreed when he asserted that "America continues to face the realities of a fallen world," adding that "God is prowar."[50] Falwell's answer to terrorism was that "President Bush should blow them away in the name of the Lord."[51] This sounded like a judgment made after taking to heart John Bolton's opinion that "it is a big mistake to grant any validity to international law."[52]

This connection between neoconservatives and extremist Christian fundamentalists smacked of something more than a marriage of convenience. This was an alliance of groups that had a firm conviction that the world was a Hobbesian jungle and that only power saved the day. All of them believed they represented good struggling to survive in a viper's nest. They differed, in practice, mainly in their rationalizations. One might believe that the world had to be made safe for a wrathful Baptist God using both Israel and the United States as his special instruments. The other might believe that the world had to be made safe for Israel and the United States because they embodied modernity and Western civilization itself—and we do not talk about any mystical force that might be casting characters backstage. If there was to ever be a falling out between them, it would have to wait for the end of the world.

In the wake of the Arab-Israeli war of 1973, John R. Walvoord, who was then president of the Dallas Theological Seminary, argued that "Americans would soon have to face a difficult choice: the United States would give in to the Arab world in order to keep access to oil and the friendship of the industrialized nations, or it would support Israel and face the consequences."[53] However, these did not turn out to be the only choices. There would be no "oil blackmail" because neither the ascending Christian fundamentalists nor the ascending neoconservative and machpolitik politicians would allow it. You cannot blackmail God, the world's sole superpower, or its ally who exemplified militant self-righteousness. Those representing good would simply have everything their way: they would support Israel uncritically, suborn most of the dictators of the region, and, where they felt necessary, take the oil by force.

The Fate of Iraq Is the Fate of the Neoconservatives

The one-dimensional outlook that characterized the view of the neocon-servatives and their allies with regard to foreign policy carried over into their way of thinking about the citizens of the United States. Their premise was and is that they, the neocon elite, know better than the electorate. Therefore, to achieve "higher" goals, you can go ahead and lie to and manipulate the voters. As Congressman Ron Paul put it in a speech taking the neoconservatives to task, "They accept the notion that the ends justify the means—that hard-ball politics is a moral necessity. . . . They believe lying is necessary for the state to survive. . . . They believe pertinent facts about how a society should be run should be held by the elite."[54] One can see evidence of this Machiavellian approach in the lies (what Michael Ledeen would call "strategic deception") that surrounded Iraq's supposed weapons of mass destruction, as well as in the suspected manipulation of votes in Florida and Ohio.

It also stands to reason that if you have people in power who take a cavalier attitude toward international law (making John Bolton ambassador to the United Nations is like putting the fox in charge of the hen house), they will sooner or later adopt the same attitude toward domestic laws. This seems to be borne out with President Bush's illegal authorization of large-scale spying on American citizens, the invention of the category of "enemy combatant" that supposedly allows for the suspension of the Geneva Conventions, and the torturing of these same "enemy combatants." Given that the overlapping ideologies of the neocons, the machpolitik politicians, and the Christian fundamentalists postulate a world in constant crisis and beset with never-ending evil, it appears to them to be reasonable and legitimate that they make up the rules (or unmake them) as the situation demands—in other words, that they be allowed to act above the law.

The attacks on September 11, 2001, let loose the, up until then, muted proclivities of the neoconservatives and their allies. It is probably fair to say that the vast majority of those who voted for George W. Bush and Richard Cheney (at least the first time around) had no idea of what they were capable in terms of deception, aggression, and outright criminality. By 2004 they should have had some inkling if they were paying attention to more than the issues of gay rights and abortion. But many were not. Therefore, Bush and his accomplices got their full eight years to try out what Michael Ledeen calls "Machiavelli on modern leadership."[55]

The first seminal neoconservative test case was Iraq. Iraq was most likely targeted by the Bush administration because of its oil reserves and the bellicose nature of its anti-Israel posture. Despite the president's misinformation, there is no evidence that the Iraqi regime, as nasty as it certainly was, had anything to do with the 9/11 attacks. In any case, Iraq was presented to the American people as the epitome of evil, and yet it was supposed to be a cake walk for the representatives of good. Iraq would become a U.S. satellite enjoying manipulated democratic elections and all the benefits of American control of its oil reserves. The Iraqis would be happy with this state of affairs, scattering flowers at the feet of occupying American troops. The oil would flow red, white, and blue, and the Washington-based guardian angels supervising all of this, along with their corporate collaborators, would make a ton of money. So much faith was there in the power of overbearing American force that President Bush reportedly confided to Pat Robertson that he expected there would be no U.S. casualties upon occupation.[56] That Mr. Bush and his neoconservative collaborators could have actually believed that this was the way it would all work out is evidence of their one-dimensional, unreal view of the world. That they have been able to rationalize away their own mistakes and blame all problems on shadowy and elusive terrorist organizations is evidence that most of them are incapable of honestly examining their ideological fantasies.

Apparently the neoconservative game plan did not stop with Iraq. Theirs was a regional focus that placed Iran and Syria on the list of countries to be subjected to preemptive war and regime change. Once more the supposed incontestable nature of U.S. power was to assure easy victory, and the Middle East in general was to be pacified—made safe for both economic exploitation by America and Israeli expansion. As we now know, all these assumptions proved wrong. Instead of opening up a new era of allegedly benevolent American imperial hegemony, what the neocons opened up was a hellish Pandora's box.

The neoconservatives have sped up the transformation of the entire Middle East into a prime breeding ground for anti-American sentiment and, at the extreme, the production of terrorists. It must be admitted, however, that they did not initiate this process. Over the past sixty years, a series of U.S. foreign-policy mistakes have been made due to ignorance, corruption, and short-sightedness that bordered on criminal stupidity. Among these mistakes were the uncritical support of Israel and allowing the pro-Israeli lobby to literally dictate policy when it came to Palestine. This has made the United States complicit in the destruction of

Palestinian society, a process that borders on cultural genocide. Then there was American support of one bloody dictatorship after another, both secular (the Shah's Iran, Mubarak's Egypt, Hussein's Jordan, etc.) and fundamentalist Muslim (the Saudi monarchy and Pakistan). There was the almost glib arming and training of the Mujahadin in Afghanistan as part of a plan to turn that country into the Soviet Union's Vietnam.[57] And finally, there was the draconian application of economic sanctions that killed millions of innocent Iraqis—a house-of-horrors policy that was somehow "worth it" according to former Secretary of State Madeline Albright.[58] It was these policies, among others, that bred the hatred that led to the 9/11 attacks. The deep ignorance among the American people of their country's foreign policies and their consequences made it impossible for them to realize that their leaders had led them to disaster. So, after the Twin Towers came crashing down, instead of doing a thorough policy review and breaking the backs of the Zionist and other interest groups that had substituted their own particular interests for the "national interest," the American electorate followed the neocons over the cliff and into catastrophe. A repeat of 9/11 is likely only a matter of time.

Conclusion

It is impossible to read the works of Albert Weinberg, Howard Zinn, and Melani McAlister without understanding that today's neoconservatives are but the latest manifestation of a long-standing aggressive and self-righteous aspect in the American character. The context in which this character now operates is contemporary, of course, and battered about by such occurrences as the Cold War, the Arab-Israeli conflict, and the concept of nuclear holocaust. The neocon response to all of this has not been unique. These latest representatives of the dark side of the American collective psyche tell us that the world has always been a jungle. The struggle, whether seen in religious or secular psychological terms, is a primordial one wherein good battles evil. And so their policies must fit this worldview. Shock and awe turns out to be a technological update of a rather old tactic fit for an unchanging reality.

Of all the contemporary happenings that have tweaked this reality, the most fortuitous for the neoconservatives was the collapse of the Soviet Union. For nearly eighty years America's struggle with her communist rival reinforced the classic Hobbesian and Manichaean images that make up the neoconservative world. As Ronald Reagan told us, the Soviet Union was the "Evil Empire." America had grappled with that "evil" in a Cold War dance marathon called the "balance of terror." In truth, each side held the other in check. The dance appeared to be all but eternal, and little thought was given to what would happen if one side became exhausted and suddenly dropped out. No one really understood that such an event had the potential to release the pent-up self-righteousness and megalomania of the survivor and expose the world to the torrent of its now unrestrained aggression.

For a moment, following the coming of "glasnost" and then "perestroika," it looked like the future might be different. Some Americans talked of "peace dividends" and the rollback of military-related spending. It might have continued on that happy and truly original path if the opportunity had been taken in the United States to do a thorough policy review with the object of peacefully and rationally addressing all those subsidiary problems (particularly in the Middle East) that now came to the fore. But it was not to be.

The geographic arenas that housed the subsidiary problems were dear to too many American special interests. The Zionists, the Christian Zionists, the oil and large construction corporations, the arms manufactures, and other similar groups all had their influence with Congress and the political parties. Their interests thrived best in the tense world of discord. Therefore, the partisan and short-sighted regional policies that such interests had shaped all along (centering around the arming of friendly dictatorships, the support of Israeli aggression, the indirect and sometimes direct control of foreign resources) were to continue. The negative reactions that these policies had been producing abroad had often been overshadowed by the demands of the Cold War and the myth that American foreign policy was simply the exportation of democracy, development, and modernity (as befitted America the benevolent). Now, however, the "blowback" from these flawed lines of action took center stage. It turned out that an increasing number of people within the non-Western world were repulsed by what the United States had to offer them and were drifting into the orbit of those who were ready to use any means at hand to repel American political, cultural, and certainly military hegemony on their soil. Their actions were ready fodder for the creation of new anti-American evil enemies that would meld themselves into the neoconservative analysis. The clash of civilizations became an ideological basis for a new (and not so cold) war scenario.

Despite the fact that there is an aggressive and exploitative aspect to American history, and indeed to the history of most other nation-states, it is too simplistic and easy to say, as the neoconservatives do, that "realistic foreign policies" must reflect these negative attributes. If the juvenile delinquent appearing before a judge on charges of assault and theft told him that the world in which he grew up was a violent one and that therefore he was only adjusting his behavior to suit the reality around him, it would not be seen as a viable defense. If, in turn, he asserted that it was only human nature, or perhaps original sin, that made him a violent little thief, he might be told to consider a plea of temporary insanity. Just so, the Hobbesian laments of the neoconservatives are no excuse for the mess we have, in truth, created for ourselves. Rather than the Hobbesian jungle or flawed human nature, our problems stem in good part from popular ignorance of the importance of foreign policy and its possible repercussions on the domestic sphere of life.[59] It is such ignorance, deepened by systematic misinformation, that has helped lead Americans to allow myopic and corrupt leaders to make decisions that affect us all. These men and women are myopic and corrupt because they, more often than not, respond only to the particular demands of dominant interest groups. It turns out that in America, when it comes to the formulation of foreign policy, there is no real sense of "national interest."

There is nothing necessary about our present situation and policies. Even the tragedy of September 11, 2001, opened more than one option for the American nation. But if we are to create new policies, we must stop listening to the discredited neoconservatives and machpolitik politicians. We must remove the Christian fundamentalists and Zionists from the halls of power and send them back, for good, to their tabernacles. We must once more take the notion of checks and balances seriously and make "the big lie" a big crime. Most of all we must develop a sense of national interest that builds on the maturation of diplomacy and international law—a national interest that secures the nation by seeking to create a just, cooperative, and peaceful world.

Ignorantia neminem excusat: ignorance no longer excuses any of us.

NOTES

1. See Anne Norton, *Leo Strauss and the Politics of American Empire* (New Haven, CT: Yale University Press, 2004), and Irving Kristol, *Neoconservatism: The Autobiography of an Idea* (New York: Free Press, 1995).

2. For a detailed account of the origins of the neoconservatives, see John Ehrman, *The Rise of Neoconservatism: Intellectuals and Foreign Affairs, 1945–1994* (New Haven, CT: Yale University Press, 1995).

3. The quotation is from Hobbes, *Leviathan,* chap. 13, e-text version: etext .library.adelaide.edu.au/h/hobbes/thomas/h681/chapter13.html.

4. Ledeen's quotation is in Dick Polman's article, "Neoconservatives Push for New World Order," *San Jose Mercury News,* May 4, 2003. Ledeen is the author of such texts as *The War against the Terror Masters* (New York: St. Martin's, 2002), *Machiavelli on Modern Leadership* (New York: St. Martin's, 1999), and *Freedom Betrayed: How America Led a Global Democratic Revolution, Won the Cold War, and Walked Away* (Washington, DC: AEI Press, 1996).

5. Manichaeus taught that the world was dominated by two warring principles: lightness or good and darkness or evil. Mankind had to choose between them.

6. BBC interview, May 18, 2003.

7. If we are to use Carl Oglesby's terms, coined in his famous essay *Yankee and the Cowboy War* (New York: Berkley, 1977), the "Yankees" have deserted to the "cowboys."

8. The saying is attributed to Irving Kristol, the "godfather" of neoconservatism.

9. Jim Lobe, "What Is a Neoconservative Anyway?" *Asia Times,* August 13, 2003.

10. See Ehrman, *Rise of Neoconservatism,* 104–109.

11. CNN, "Rumsfeld on Looting in Iraq: Stuff Happens," by Sean Loughlin, April 12, 2003.

12. Thomas Wright, "American Neoconservatives—All Muscle, No History," *Globalist,* September 15, 2004.

13. Ibid.

14. Lobe, "What Is a Neoconservative Anyway?"

15. Ehrman, *Rise of Neoconservatism,* 104–109.

16. Ibid., 190.

17. Ibid., 182–183

18. Ibid., 183. Elsewhere, Richard Perle stated that "[w]e are going to have to take the war [against the terrorists] often to other people's territory, and all the norms of international order make it difficult to do that. So the president has to reshape fundamental attitudes toward those norms, or we are going to have our hands tied by an antiquated institution [the prevailing system of international law and diplomacy]." Quoted on the Web page of the *Christian Science Monitor,* http://www.csmonitor.com/specials/neocon/neoconQuotes.html.

19. Making the world safe for America and also safe for democracy can, in fact, turn out to be contradictory. Democracy, at least in the Middle Eastern and Muslim worlds, is now most likely to produce anti-American Islamic governments. But in the world of the neoconservatives all such complications are made

to disappear. After all, if President Bill Clinton can arbitrarily redefine what "sexual relations" means, President George W. Bush and his neoconservative advisers can choose how the world should define "democracy." In their world, democracy must produce pro-American governments; otherwise it is not democracy.

20. Press conference, July 30, 2003.

21. For a rundown of most of them, see Albert K. Weinberg, *Manifest Destiny* (Chicago: Quadrangle, 1963).

22. Howard Zinn, *A People's History of the United States, 1492–Present* (New York: HarperPerennial, 1995), 131–146. When the Supreme Court ruled against Jackson and forbade the removal of the Cherokees, Jackson reportedly said, "Well, John Marshall [the Chief Justice] has made his decision, now let him enforce it."

23. Quotation can be found at James K. Polk Quotes, www.home.att.net/~jrhsc/polk.html.

24. Polk asserted that the Mexican army "has passed the boundary of the United States, has invaded our territory and shed American blood upon the American soil." At the time, he was aware that the assertion that the Rio Grande was the southern border of Texas was an arbitrary claim and that the traditional border between Texas and Mexico was the Nueces River some 150 miles north of all the alleged Mexican aggressions. See Zinn, *People's History,* 147–148, 150.

25. James K. Polk Quotes.

26. Zinn, *People's History,* 305.

27. Theodore Roosevelt, in a speech at the Minnesota State Fair, September 2, 1901.

28. Quoted on the Spanish American War Centennial Website, www.spanamwar.com/tr2.htm.

29. Wilson's Declaration of War address to Congress, April 2, 1917.

30. For a history of this tragedy, see Lawrence Davidson, *America's Palestine: Popular and Official Perceptions from Balfour to Israeli Statehood* (Gainesville: University Press of Florida, 2001).

31. See Weinberg, *Manifest Destiny,* chap. 14. Between 1848 and 1996, the United States intervened in Central America twenty-seven times overtly using American troops and forty-five times in a covert manner. See www.zompist.com/latam.html.

32. See Zinn, *People's History.*

33. See R. R. Palmer and J. Colton, *A History of the Modern World* (New York: Knopf, 1984), 582.

34. See Michael Sidney Tyler-Whittle, *The Last Kaiser* (New York: Times Books, 1977), chap. 10.

35. Ibid., 185.

36. See David Frum's assessment of George W. Bush in Walter Shapiro, "Hype and Glory," *USA Today,* January 7, 2003, available online at www.usatoday.com/news/opinion/columnist/shapiro/2003-01-07-hype_x.htm.

37. Wilhelm II allowed his opinion on military strategy to be overruled but

once, and, ironically, this proved fatal. He sought to restrict the opening fighting in World War I to the eastern front, but von Moltke, his Chief of the General Staff, told him that the Von Schlieffen Plan for conducting the war made this impossible. Therefore, with all the trouble coming from the east, Germany struck west at France. Emil Ludwig, *Wilhelm Hohenzollern: The Last of the Kaisers* (New York: Putnam's Sons, 1927), 453.

38. Andrew Bacevich, a professor of international relations at Boston University, wrote in an article entitled "Bush's Grand Strategy" (*American Conservative,* November 4, 2002, p. 1) that the administration's national-security strategy read like an "unlikely collaboration between Woodrow Wilson and the elder Field Marshal von Moltke."

39. This is perhaps a warning to us all that those who come from academia and the world of think tanks can create political and foreign-policy disasters as readily as anyone else. One can add the neocons to a list of intellectuals that includes the likes of Woodrow Wilson and Henry Kissinger.

40. Melani McAlister, *Epic Encounters* (Berkeley: University of California Press, 2001), 157.

41. The most famous was the novel *Exodus* by Leon Uris, which was soon followed by the film.

42. McAlister, *Epic Encounters,* 187.

43. A group of American neoconservatives led by Richard Perle served as consultants for Israel's Likud Party. In 1996 they produced a document entitled "A Clean Break: A Strategy for Securing the Realm." It suggested, among other things, that Israel abandon its alleged strategy of negotiating "land for peace" and instead take "preemptive action" to secure the territory supposedly necessary for Israeli security.

44. Ehrman, *Rise of Neoconservatism,* 186. After the September 11, 2001, terrorist attacks, forty neoconservatives petitioned President Bush in an open letter to immediately attack Hezbollah in Lebanon as well as Syria and Iran if they did not cease supporting Hezbollah. Hezbollah, of course, had nothing to do with the 9/11 attacks. It was, however, a central player in the Likud Party's "empire of Terror." See Patrick Buchanan, "Whose War?" in *American Conservative,* March 24, 2003.

45. Edward Abboud, *Invisible Enemy: Israel, Politics, Media, and American Culture* (Reston, VA: Vox, 2003). This distortion was not unlike that practiced on America history in creating and sustaining the myth of benevolence.

46. See Buchanan, "Whose War?"

47. Quoted on the *Christian Science Monitor* Web site, www.csmonitor.com, "In Their Own Words," September 3, 2003.

48. CNN report, October 21, 2004.

49. *Christian Science Monitor* Web site, "In Their Own Words," September 3, 2003.

50. "God Is Pro War," WorldNetDaily, January 31, 2004.

51. See Greg Warner, "Call to Kill Terrorists in the Name of God," *Baptist Standard,* November 5, 2004, available online at www.baptiststandard.com.

52. Tom Barry, "John Bolton's Baggage," *Counterpunch,* March 14, 2005.

53. McAlister, *Epic Encounters,* 173.

54. Speech before the House of Representatives, July 10, 2003.

55. This is the name of a book Ledeen published in 1999 and subsequently distributed free of charge to the Republican members of Congress.

56. See David Kirkpatrick, "Robertson Says Bush Predicted No Iraq Toll," *New York Times,* October 21, 2004.

57. Jimmy Carter's National Security Adviser, Zbigniew Brzezinski, wrote a memo to the president the day after the December 25, 1979, Soviet invasion of Afghanistan suggesting that "we now have the opportunity to give the Soviet Union its Vietnam." See Zbigniew Brzezinski, Wikipedia, subsections on Afghanistan and quotations.

58. *60 Minutes* interview, May 12, 1996.

59. It is Thomas Jefferson who told us what we have either forgotten or ignored, "if a nation expects to be ignorant and free, in a state of civilization, it expects what never was and never will be." As quoted in Saul Padover, *Thomas Jefferson: Passionate Pilgrim* (Lanham, MD: Madison Books, 1939), 89.

Chapter 12

Resisting the Right
Challenging the Neoconservative Agenda

Stephen Eric Bronner

The ideal of American manhood and culture isn't a lot of
cranks sitting around chewing the rag about their Rights
and their Wrongs, but a God-fearing, hustling, successful, two-fisted Regular Guy, who belongs to some church
with pep and piety to it, who belongs to . . . any one of
a score of organizations of good, jolly, kidding, laugh-
ing, sweating, upstanding, lend-a-handing Royal Good
Fellows, who plays hard and works hard, and whose answer to his critics is a square-toed boot that'll teach the
grouches and smart alecks to respect the He-man and
get out and root for Uncle Samuel, USA!
>   —Sinclair Lewis, *Babbitt* (1922)

Let me count this day, Lord, as the beginning of a new
and more vigorous life, as the beginning of a crusade for
complete morality and the domination of the Christian
church through all the land. Dear Lord, thy work is but
begun! We shall yet make these United States a moral
nation!
>   —Sinclair Lewis, *Elmer Gantry* (1927)

Politics is generally understood as the art of the possible. Too often, however, the possible is simply equated with the immediate demands of the
moment.[1] For professional politicians constituting the mainstream of the
Democratic Party, especially those in the Democratic Leadership Council,
the moment is all that there is. There is no before and there is no after.

Everything other than what contributes to winning that election they consider impractical and utopian. Incoherence of program is mixed with a profound underestimation of neoconservative ideology and its power. Unwilling to articulate an independent agenda and a worldview, these unpragmatic pragmatists have much to learn from their neoconservative and intensely ideological opponents. Right-wing Republicans were already aware with the defeat of Senator Barry Goldwater (R-AZ) in the presidential election of 1964 that their political future depended on having a program and a message that would unify what had been the two constantly warring factions of their party. Ronald Reagan initially sealed the alliance between those committed to an assault on the "socialist" welfare state in the name of free trade and individualism and those committed to an assault on "liberalism" in the name of a traditional understanding of "community." Thus, the basis was laid for the "victory" of George W. Bush in 2000.[2]

The neoconservative agenda introduced by President Bush touched on foreign affairs, economic policy, national politics, and cultural mores. It went beyond the immediate bread-and-butter demands of the moment. In foreign affairs, according to neoconservative thinking, the United States must exercise its military might. That is because the world is a "dangerous place," bereft of law, in which states are—following Thomas Hobbes[3]—involved in an ongoing "war of each against all."[4] This assumption underpins the neoconservative preoccupation with an "endless war" on terror and the "preemptive strike." It also explains the contempt of neoconservatives for the United Nations, the dictates of international law, and the possibilities of diplomatic rather than military resolution of conflicts. In economic affairs, the neoconservative aims of the Bush administration were evident from the beginning. Not only were its major thinkers bent on castigating the New Left for its critical attitude toward inequality and capitalism,[5] but there is also something symbolically important about the failed attempt by House Republicans to replace FDR with Ronald Reagan on the face of the dime. The Bush administration was, from the first, intent on redistributing wealth upward to the top 0.01% of the population, rolling back programs associated with the New Deal and the War on Poverty and creating new subsidies for large corporations like Bechtel and Halliburton. Then, too, on the political plane neoconservatism has sought to invigorate the type of American nationalism undercut by the "Vietnam trauma." September 11 was manipulated to justify a new nationalism and a new reliance on militarism.[6] Constriction of civil liberties and a preoccupation with national loyalty, combined with a staggering increase in funds for "security" and "defense," helped fuel the imperialist experiments with "regime change" in Afghanistan and Iraq and later—using the same propagandistic mixture of projection, hysteria, and manipulated "facts on the ground" —with the threats directed to Iran and Syria. In cultural terms, not even to mention the neoconservative emphasis on the conflict between Judeo-Christian and Arab societies in what Bernard Lewis and then Samuel Huntington called "clash of civilizations," our new reactionaries have highlighted a concern with "family values" and "intelligent design." The assault on abortion and reproductive rights have become intimately connected in an attempt to transform the culture and constrict the individual choices associated with sexuality.[7] Intellectual traditions, some particularly perverse, have been used to justify the new outlook, including its attempt to blur the lines between church and state. Not only do neoconservatives deny the deism of America's founding fathers and their general lack of concern with intrinsically theological questions[8]—George Washington never once mentioned God in his letters—but they also perversely view the Enlightenment in general as providing a foundation for the "compassionate conservatism" of the Bush administration in its supposed acceptance of religion, respect for tradition, and belief in what Edmund Burke termed a "benevolent imperialism."[9]

Eastern intellectuals and public figures may have articulated the tenets of neoconservatism. Some of them may have originally been influenced by the sectarian anticommunism of the later Trotsky and others perhaps by the philosophy of Leo Strauss. But there is a sense in which the intellectual pretensions of the neoconservatives have been taken far too seriously. From the time when that first election of President Bush was being contested, and photos were printed by the major newspapers depicting virtual mobs threatening the vote counters, liberal intellectuals have been intimidated and too refined in their encounter with the neoconservatives. As Jane Jacobs once remarked at a meeting of some planning commission from which she was removed in 1961: "We had been ladies and gentlemen and only got pushed around." The neoconservative message has never been primarily directed toward other intellectuals but rather to those everyday people thriving in the least cosmopolitan and economically developed parts of the United States. Few writers have exposed the underside of Middle America better than Sinclair Lewis. His most famous character, George Babbitt, evidenced the self-serving ignorance and complacent self-assurance of the provincial booster of small-time capitalism. Lewis also knew that an inner bond connected this everyday reactionary with the religious huckster, and, in the character of Elmer Gantry, America's first Nobel Prize laureate for literature provided the fictional prototype for our more modern Bible-thumpers.

Babbitt and Elmer both liked to bend the law for their own profit, though neither would admit any such thing. Both would undoubtedly have turned a blind eye to the manipulation of public opinion by the Bush administration to justify the Iraq war and the bribing of important reactionary politicians like former House Majority Leader Tom DeLay (R-TX) and scions of the religious Right like Ralph Reed, who founded the Christian Coalition. George Babbitt and Elmer Gantry would surely have agreed that the willingness to serve God and Mammon is "the very glue that holds together the awkward marriage of Christian moralism and high-rolling Republicanism."[10]

The Bush administration has generated a culture of lying and corruption not known since the days of President Warren Harding.[11] By way of contrast with that administration, however, neoconservatives have supplemented blatant corruption with a more surreptitious institutional sort that they justify through particular interpretations of presidential power.[12] Republicans have self-consciously employed their ideology to cover their rear and—in the words of Karl Rove—"mobilize the base." In this respect, they are very different from the Democrats. Pragmatic and "flexible," the mainstream of the Democratic Party has become defined by the agenda of its Republican opponents. Suggestions that the Democrats have had trouble developing a "program" of their own or "sending a message" simply miss the point. They have no program, and they have no message. The "triangulation" strategy employed by Bill Clinton, which involved placing his party just a whiff to the left of Republicans on any major issue, took care of that. It has indeed proved a disaster for his successors.

The House and the Senate have been in the hands of Republicans for more than a decade. In the meantime, the majority of Democrats embraced "welfare reform," supported the invasion of Iraq, compromised on the Patriot Act, and constantly appeared as posturing nationalists with a religious bent. The mainstream of the Democratic Party still looks like it is pandering to those good citizens of Peoria at the expense of its urban base —and it is. Its partisans lack message, conviction, and courage. There was hardly a single Democratic senator in the chamber when Senator Russell Feingold (D-WI) presented his argument for censuring President Bush on the basis of patently illegal wire-tapping. There is also little willingness to present a national strategy in 2006 or put forward a "contract" like the Republicans did in 1994. The only concern of individual Democratic politicians is with winning, and most seem content with helping President George W. Bush slide in the opinion polls by attacking the competence and honesty of his administration and then picking up his more disillusioned supporters with uncontroversial issues like rising gasoline prices.

Winning is, of course, important. Turning away from elections entirely can only lead the radical Left to become defined by what it opposes. Getting out of the electoral trap calls for more than participating in endless discussions over whether to support a right-wing Democrat against a Republican, as if an election were somehow a moral testing ground, or even simply working for left-wing candidates. There is no magic formula about what to do when entering the voting booth. If a genuine progressive like Senator Feingold or Representative John Lewis (D-GA) is running, or if there really is a "lesser of two evils" in a given campaign, then the "choice" is self-evident. Accepting the lesser evil can, of course, backfire. But there is usually a better probability of achieving a "progressive" result by voting for the "lesser evil" than by not voting or voting symbolically for a fringe candidate. The real problems emerge when a progressive is faced with Senator Joseph Lieberman (D-CT) or Senator Benjamin Nelson (D-NE) running against some mainstream Republican opponent. In such instances, the "lesser evil" may not exist: not voting or voting symbolically might then make sense. Making a decision on how to vote, in any event, should depend less on moral considerations than on an empirical comparison of the candidates and their records.

Very different criteria apply when it comes to building the ideological context in which the vote should be cast. If the Left is seriously going to challenge the prevailing neoconservative agenda, its partisans must move beyond the "pragmatism" that failed the Democratic Party so miserably in the last three elections. Issues must take center stage that pertain to the failed Iraqi war, the upward distribution of wealth, the rollback of civil liberties, and the trends working toward the creation of a national-security state. It is incumbent on progressives to pressure the Democratic Party to develop plans for a new foreign policy, the full public financing of elections, single-payer health coverage, and a new version of the War on Poverty. Even while voting for the lesser of the two evils, progressives should begin thinking less about winning elections *at any ideological cost* than about imagining or, better, reimagining the possible in ways that might inspire and mobilize the core constituencies of the Democratic Party: people

274 STEPHEN ERIC BRONNER

of color, union workers, the poor, students, and women. It is the task of progressives to articulate an interconnected set of what Andre Gorz once termed "non-reformist reforms" that—together—offer a genuine alternative to neoconservatism.

Imperialism, hypernationalism, and militarism have never been discrete phenomena. They have been interconnected and parts of the arsenal employed—to put it bluntly—by retrograde capitalist interests in what has become nothing short of class war and an assault on liberal democracy. That is as much the case today as it was in the early twentieth century. Only the lies that veil these tendencies are different. The invasion of Iraq and the geopolitics attendant on the "endless" war on terror orchestrated by the Bush administration have resulted in a precipitous decline of American prestige abroad. That, in turn, has only increased the provincial feelings of a nation under siege while fostering a new form of "imperial presidency" contemptuous of congressional interference in its prerogatives and intent on constricting civil liberties through legislation like the Patriot Act. The heightened militarism required by these imperialist policies, and justified by a resurgent American nationalism, is meanwhile bankrupting the welfare state and undermining the commitment to social justice. It is unnecessary to consult *Das Kapital* to figure out that a war, whose actual cost lies somewhere between the $450 billion allocated in the budget and the $2.2 trillion estimated by the Nobel Prize–winning economist Joseph Stiglitz, tends to justify radical reductions in social programs crucial to the existence of working people and the poor. The Republicans have already pushed through legislation that will cut $50 billion from close to 150 programs next year, and they are developing a budget with more than $600 billion in reductions over the next five years.

Imperialism, militarism, hypernationalism, and class war: ignoring the "totality," refusing to connect the dots, undermines the possibility of offering a coherent response to neoconservatism and what more than one Nobel Prize winner has called the most reactionary administration in American history. Understanding the totalizing character of this neoconservative reaction in its drastic impact on social welfare, political democracy, and foreign policy is a matter of utmost importance. Many people who are dissatisfied are content to believe that, sooner or later, the pendulum will swing back the other way, without recognizing that it would take a virtual policy revolution—something tantamount to the legislation of the 1930s and the 1960s—to bring the country back to where it was in 1968. In fact, however, this is an enormous undertaking. Its difficulty is perhaps what has produced such timidity by adherents of the mainstream in the Democratic Party. Or so they say.

But perhaps there is another reason. It might just be that the leaders of the Democratic Party, along with its coterie of advisers and experts, are fearful of the core constituencies within their own organization. The Democratic Party is a party of reform, but it is a party that still recognizes the imperatives of capitalism, and its advisers have increasingly been drawn from the corporate sector. Perhaps why the Democratic Party is unwilling to set an alternative agenda with a new ideological justification is because a genuinely radical program—a program that connects the dots —would also threaten its own elites. Simply emphasizing a raise in the minimum wage, a rollback of the existing prescription-drug law, a probe of the misuse of intelligence during the Iraqi war, a commitment to implement homeland-security measures, and a reinstatement of lapsed budget-deficit controls may provide a safe way of letting the Republicans lose the election.[13] But this package of issues does nothing to contest the neoconservative agenda. That is where "the Left" must enter the scene. What the Democratic Party appears incapable of doing is precisely what intellectuals and activists outside its confines must begin to do. But this calls for dealing with three interlocking constraints: the *translation* problem, the *coordination* problem, and the *communication* problem. These are not problems that can be solved in a short essay such as this one, but they can at least be described, with some indication given for their solution.

With respect to the *translation* problem, it is defined by a seeming inability of the Democratic Party and other attendant organizations of the political establishment to turn progressive public sentiment on given issues into either progressive legislation or elements of an articulated progressive agenda. The translation problem became particularly evident when hardly a single major figure within the mainstream of the Democratic Party even acknowledged the hundreds of thousands of Americans and millions of people throughout the world who marched against the Iraqi war. It appeared again in the inability of the mainstream to either generate a serious critique or a serious opposition to the Patriot Act and to the stacking of the courts by the Bush administration. It has been manifest in the inability of the Democrats to even foster a debate over a single-payer health-insurance program, let alone a serious program for dealing with dental matters. There are also environmental issues ranging from global warming to the subsidies offered for SUVs to the rape of Alaska and the Amazon that are being decided less by reference to the public good than by particular interests with particular ambitions. The translation problem becomes manifest in the general opposition to the intrusion of right-wing religious fanaticism into public life by a bulk of the American citizenry. It is easy to build the list of issues that genuinely concern the public but that are increasingly decided against its interests.

Coming to terms with the translation problem, in the first instance, means remembering that the great moments of progressive reform occurred when there were people in the streets, when mass demonstrations took place, and when the system was threatened with disruption. Looking back to the abolitionists, the 1890s, the aftermath of World War I, the 1930s, and the 1960s makes it clear how the threat to withhold cooperation from the system generated pressure on the more progressive elites within the Democratic Party and their elite advisers.[14] Or, to put it a different way, radical reform was embraced when mainstream liberals got scared. Unfortunately, they are not scared now. People are currently not in the streets but instead are a progressive mass constituency "out there." The (stolen?) election of 2004 was not a mandate for George W. Bush. The vote instead reflected a deep division within the country that, especially given the incompetence and corruption of the neoconservative cabal within the Bush administration, has created new opportunities for the Democratic Party. Whether this party of the "Left" has taken advantage of them is the question.

Republicans might just lose their majority less because of anything that the Democrats do than because of their own actions. Most Americans are against cutting welfare programs in the name of tax cuts.[15] A growing unease exists over the constriction of civil liberties by a new imperial presidency; environmental degradation increasingly influences everyday life; and invading Iraq is now seen as a mistake by a majority of Americans. Noteworthy is the way in which the mainstream of the Democratic Party has refused to take the lead—or begin a national debate—on any of these concerns. The base of the Democratic Party is dissatisfied, but it remains a matter of translating such dissatisfaction into an agenda. That this has not come to pass can only be explained by the alienation of the Democratic Party from its base. Articulating the dissatisfaction of the base, after all, would force elites within the Democratic Party to confront their own complicity in the disastrous policies of the Bush administration. Better for the "pragmatists" to worry over the way in which a more radical politics upset and alienate "swing voters." In fact, however, the loss of "swing voters" can be offset by increased mobilization of African Americans, public-sector employees, union workers, students, and women.[16] It therefore becomes incumbent on genuine progressives to stress militant tactics, ideological values in determining the quality of "advisers," the failures of the liberal mainstream, and the concerns of the party base.

As far as the *coordination* problem is concerned, ironically, the issue is less important when people are in the street than when the need exists under quieter circumstances for placing pressure on the Democratic Party. This requires a unity of purpose and ideological outlook—ultimately perhaps an organization something like the Poor People's Movement—even while the Left is today composed of ever more and increasingly autonomous interest groups. The sheer number of these groups produces a replication of tasks, a division of loyalties, and constant labyrinthine and internecine battles over the priorities of progressive politics. There is little doubt that it was ultimately necessary, both practically and existentially, for the spate of particular and identity movements to have emerged as the 1960s drew to a close.[17] Initially these movements and groups were founded on transclass categories like race, gender, or sexual preference. But the concern with identity took on its own dynamic. For example, the concern with women soon enough generated a concern with black women, black-gay women, Hispanic women, Hispanic gay women, and the like. There is little doubt that this development built the cultural confidence of new constituencies and made possible the *political* representation of new interests. By the same token, however, this led to fierce internecine competition for resources and the emergence of interest-group bureaucracies whose interest lies in maintaining autonomy and whose leaders challenge one another over the priorities of progressive politics. For all the *cultural* benefits achieved by these new social movements, in *political* terms, the result is a situation in which the Left—not merely the Democratic Party[18]—constantly finds itself with a hundred different issues and a willingness to fight for ninety-nine of them at the same time.

That is why the whole of the Left appears far weaker than the sum of its parts. Dealing with this situation requires both practical and ideological work. Careerists in different Left organizations have a stake in suppressing calls for intragroup solidarity in favor of autonomy so that they can maintain their own positions of authority. Given their populist roots, moreover, many on the American Left have an exaggerated fear of hierarchy and bureaucracy. By the same token, however, the Left should not succumb to its own brand of provincialism by dismissing the cultural gains made during the 1960s. Looking at the problems created by partisans of the counterculture and identity politics is not to dismiss their importance. Viewing "cultural" concerns like abortion as bereft of "politics," as secondary to purely economic issues, or as open to compromise in the quest for that elusive "swing voter" is an enormous mistake. Cultural issues have mobilized people, and they speak to the exercise of freedom. The point is to begin developing practices and criteria to further a sense of radical solidarity. Activists within different groups and organizations need to be brought together more regularly and in a more organized fashion in order to develop the appropriate themes of a movement. It is essential to begin conceiving of a "class ideal" that can help in shaping the type of program that speaks to the interests of working people in all groups but privileges none in particular.[19] Success in pressuring the more conservative elements and aiding the more progressive forces within the Democratic Party depends—especially when action in the street is *not* taking place—on the degree of coordination between the existing interests groups, community organizations, and unions that, loosely speaking, constitute the Left.

Finally, there is the *communication* problem. Ultimately the distortion of democracy rests in the way that big money influences legislative programs and decisions of public organizations. Republicans have traditionally been the recipients of greater private financial support than Democrats. Rather than push the elephant of private money out of the room by passing a bill that would provide public financing of elections, the House has now approved campaign-finance legislation that would bar 527 nonprofit committees, which mostly supported the Democratic Party, even while lifting the limits of party spending in support of their candidates. Money is not the whole story,[20] of course, but it is a big part of the communication problem. Given the way in which the major newspapers and other media outlets have ever more surely become parts of huge corporate conglomerates, it only makes sense that everyday Americans should increasingly be questioning their credibility. Everyone knows that newspapers are not publishing everything that is fit to print, that skewed coverage is more the norm than the exception on television, and that the range of political debate is narrowing in public forums. The way in which newspapers like the *New York Times,* fearful of being condemned for its "liberal" prejudices, echoed the lies justifying the invasion of Iraq constitutes a scandal whose implications have still not been fully appreciated.[21] A serious reckoning of what the Iraqi people and the surrounding nations affected by this catastrophe have suffered over the past few years still remains to be calculated. Seeing Left public intellectuals with enormous popular appeal like Noam Chomsky cited for their political scholarship in the academic mainstream,[22] let alone in the mainstream media, still remains the rare exception rather than the rule.

Neoconservatives in alliance with the Christian conservatives have, from the first, sought to narrow the accepted range of discourse and eradicate the freedoms associated with what Norman Podhoretz termed the "adversary culture" of the 1960s. Irving Kristol has weighed in on the need for censorship, and constricting the academic discourse is the prime purpose of David Horowitz, who became the driving force behind the Academic Bill of Rights and organizations like Campus Watch.[23] Pat Robertson, a former Republican presidential candidate and host of the *700 Club*, stated in his television program of March 21, 2006, that about thirty or forty thousand "termites" or left-wing professors "have worked into the woodwork of our academic society."

If only the academy were as institutionally left wing as its right-wing critics believe it is. In the humanities and social sciences, it is an open secret that the most innovative and radical research does not take place in the most highly touted professional journals. There is also little concern with bridging the gap between academics and a new general reading public. Overcoming the chasm, or at least mitigating its enormity, is an essential part of any new communicative politics by progressives. Improving the current situation would require little more than that progressive academics, in spite of the pressures associated with tenure and promotion, devote even just a bit of their time to writing for online magazines and journals. The Internet has changed the face of the public discourse and political organizing. It has altered the nature of fund-raising, raised the stakes for lying, and expanded the possibilities for participating in the public sphere.[24] The Left has a stake in insisting on more perspectives from more news outlets in public debate and in the classroom. The politically curious can now get information, cheaply and quickly, from a score of international sources and rely less on the established media. Truthout and MoveOn have profoundly influenced the American political landscape and the character of electoral campaigning. They have shown that informing the public and mobilizing it are flip sides of the same coin.

There is a way of shifting responsibility in dealing with the translation, coordination, and communication problems. Too often the source of the problem is simply projected outward, and too rarely does the Left look in the mirror. It is perhaps time for progressives—activists as well as intellectuals—to admit that they have become too satisfied with the electoral path, too unctuous to march with the masses, and too "responsible" to insist on the need for disruption to shake things up. It is also perhaps time for progressives to project beyond the immediate demands of this or that interest group, beyond the immediate demands of the moment, and beyond the formula race + gender + class. Perhaps it is time, once again, to begin conceptualizing what Andre Gorz called "non-reformist reforms" and—in the demands made no less than in the actions undertaken—what Carl Boggs termed the "prefiguration" of the new society we would like to see.

The translation of discontent is impossible without coordination, and coordination requires a communicable set of radical aims. Articulating them calls for imagination. More important than the overt attempts to constrain discourse is the kind of self-censorship born less of fear from being on some "list" compiled by an intelligence agency than the fear of being labeled "utopian," thereby subverting the quest for academic reputation and the desire to be taken seriously by the "mainstream." The Left must keep one foot inside and the other outside the Democratic Party. Legislative acts and electoral victories obviously have an impact on the concrete lives of individuals. Building a Left requires more than discrete legislative acts and electoral victories. It also calls for challenging existing political priorities and the reactionary values of civil society that set them. Even should the White House and the Congress change hands, even should a new "consensus" come to pass, the Left will remain on the defensive. That is why its primary concern must involve establishing the public presence of a rational radicalism capable of highlighting the palpable yet unacknowledged problems of social and political life. There is a sense in which that is also its tradition. Thus, once again, the Left must begin to think of itself less as a party of career politicians than a party of protest, justice, and qualitative change.

NOTES

1. For a more extensive discussion, see Stephen Eric Bronner, *Imagining the Possible: Radical Politics for Conservative Times* (New York: Routledge, 2002), pp. 1ff.

2. Kurt Jacobsen, "Tin Foil Hats, the MSM, and Election Mischief," in *Logos: A Journal of Modern Society and Culture* (winter 2005), available online at www.logosjournal.com.

3.

Europe is turning away from power, or to put it a little differently, it is moving beyond power into a self-contained world of laws and rules and transnational negotiation and cooperation. It is entering a post-historical paradise of peace and relative prosperity, the realization of Immanuel Kant's "perpetual peace." Meanwhile, the United States remains mired in history, exercising power in an anarchic Hobbesian world where international laws and rules are unreliable, and where true security and the defense and promotion of a liberal order still depend on the possession and use of military might. That is why on major strategic and international questions today, Americans are from Mars and Europeans are from Venus.

Robert Kagan, *Of Paradise and Power: America and Europe in the New World Order* (New York: Knopf, 2003), p. 1.

4. Even the most superficial reading of Hobbes, ironically, leaves the impression that militarily deposing the sovereign will plunge a nation back into the lawless "state of nature." Those who planned the invasion of Iraq apparently did not heed the advice offered by the author of *Leviathan.*

5. John Ehrenberg, *Servants of Wealth: The Right's Assault on Equality* (Lanham, MD: Rowman and Littlefield, 2006).

6.

The United States and its allies spent roughly 73% of total global military allocations in 2003. Pentagon outlays are conservatively expect to reach $500 billion for 2008 and close to $550 billion for 2010, according to the Pentagon's own estimates—a figure that would account for easily half the world's total. These amounts do not include money for intelligence agencies (nearly $70 billion in 2003), for homeland security (another $38 billion), or for the occupation and reconstruction of Iraq (untold billions)—numbers that could easily skyrocket beyond expected levels with just one more devastating terrorist attack. Such resource allocations, without parallel in history, are becoming the mark of something akin to a full fledged garrison state.

Carl Boggs, *Imperial Delusions: American Militarism and Endless War* (Lanham, MD: Rowman and Littlefield, 2005), p. 26.

7. Russell Shorto, "Contra-Contraception: Is This the Beginning of the Next Culture War?" *New York Times Magazine,* May 7, 2006.

8. David L. Holmes, *The Faiths of the Founding Fathers* (New York: Oxford University Press, 2006).

9. Gertrude Himmelfarb, *The Roads to Modernity: The British, French, and American Enlightenments* (New York: Knopf, 2004). For a critical review, see Stephen Eric Bronner, "Neocons and Philosophes," *Washington Post,* September 12, 2004.

10. Bob Moser, "The Devil Inside: Ralph Reed Hits the Evangelical Movement in the Gut," *Nation,* April 17, 2006, p. 15.

11. See Matthew Continetti, *The K Street Gang: The Rise and Fall of the Republican Machine* (New York: Doubleday, 2006).

12. Charlie Savage, "Bush Challenges Hundreds of Laws," *Boston Globe*, April 30, 2006.

13. Jonathan Weisman, "Confident Democrats Lay Out Agenda: Party Plans Probes of Administration If It Wins the House," *Washington Post*, May 7, 2006.

14. Frances Fox Piven, *Challenging Authority: How Ordinary People Changed America* (Lanham, MD: Rowman and Littlefield, 2006).

15.

Public opinion was clearly and consistently hostile to the top-heavy skew of the Bush tax cuts. . . . Lest doubt remain on this point, consider some of the poll findings from 2000 and 2001. Versus Social Security, tax cuts lost by a 74 to 21 percent margin. Versus Medicare, the margin is 65 to 25 percent. Even when Social Security is taken out of consideration, 69 percent of respondents preferred using extra monies on "education, the environment, health care, crime-fighting, and military defense" rather than a tax cut, which garnered just 22 percent support.

Jacob S. Hacker and Paul Pierson, *Off Center: The Republican Revolution and the Erosion of American Democracy* (New Haven, CT: Yale University Press, 2005), pp. 50–51.

16.

Predictably, the strategy of pandering to the right was an abject failure: Reagan was elected, the ERA lost. If an ambivalent public hears only one side of a question, the conservative side, passionately argued—if people's impulses to the contrary are never reinforced, and they perceive that the putative spokespeople for feminism and liberalism are actually uncomfortable about advancing their views—the passionate arguers will carry the day. . . . The left did not learn the obvious lesson—that to back away from fighting for your beliefs on the grounds that you have no hope of persuading people to share them is to perpetrate a self-fulfilling prophecy. On the contrary, the appeasers could see in their defeats a confirmation of their pessimism. This scenario has been repeated countless times as the country has moved steadily to the right, yet it appears to have inspired no second thoughts.

Ellen Willis, "What's the Matter with Tom Frank (and the Lefties Who Love Him)?" *Situations* 1, no. 2 (2006): pp. 5ff.

17. For a more extensive discussion, see Stephen Eric Bronner, *Moments of Decision: Political History and the Crises of Radicalism* (New York: Routledge, 1992), pp. 101ff, 121ff.

18. Cf. Molly Ivins, "Enough of the D.C. Dems," *Progressive* (March 2006), available online at http://progressive.org/mag_ivins0306.

19. For a more complete discussion, see Stephen Eric Bronner, *Socialism Unbound,* 2nd ed. (Boulder, CO: Westview, 2000), pp. 158–167.

20. Thomas Ferguson, *Golden Rule: The Investment Theory of Party Competition and the Logic of Money-Driven Political Systems* (Chicago: University of Chicago Press, 1995).

21. Michael Massing, "The Press: The Enemy Within," *New York Review of Books,* December 1, 2005.

22. Note the interesting article by Lawrence T. Woods, "Where's Noam? On the Absence of References to Noam Chomsky in Introductory International Studies Textbooks," *New Political Science* 22, no. 1 (March 2006): pp. 65ff.

23. Eighteen states have already passed legislation, and in ten there are bills pending, to strengthen the conservative presence in the university and thereby foster "diversity." Note the map provided in *On Campus,* the magazine of the American Federation of Teachers, vol. 25, no. 6 (March-April 2006), available online at www.aft.org.

24. Jerome Armstrong and Markos Moulitsas Zuniga, *Crashing the Gate: Netroots, Grassroots, and the Rise of People-Powered Politics* (New York: Chelsea Green, 2006).

Contributors

Stanley Aronowitz is Distinguished Professor of Sociology at the Graduate Center, CUNY. He is the author or editor of twenty-three books, including *False Promises* (1973), *Education under Siege* (with Henry Giroux; 1985); *Science as Power* (1988); *Postmodern Education* (with Henry Giroux; 1991), *Roll Over Beethoven* (1993), *The Jobless Future* (with William DiFazio; 1994), *From the Ashes of the Old* (1998), *The Knowledge Factory* (2000), *Paradigm Lost* (edited with Peter Bratsis; 2002); *Implicating Empire* (edited with Heather Guatney; 2003), *How Class Works* (2003), and *Just Around the Corner: The Paradox of the Jobless Recovery* (2005).

Chip Berlet is senior analyst at Political Research Associates near Boston and has studied the political Right for over twenty-five years. Berlet is coauthor (with Matthew N. Lyons) of *Right-Wing Populism in America: Too Close for Comfort* (2000) and editor of *Eyes Right! Challenging the Right Wing Backlash* (1995), both of which received a Gustavus Myers Center Award for outstanding scholarship on the subject of human rights and bigotry in North America. A journalist by trade, Berlet's byline has appeared in publications ranging from the *New York Times* and *Boston Globe* to the *Progressive* and *Amnesty Now*. Berlet has also written chapters in academic books and articles in scholarly journals and is on the editorial advisory board of the journal *Totalitarian Movements and Political Religions*.

Stephen Eric Bronner is Distinguished Professor of Political Science and a member of the Graduate Faculties of Comparative Literature and German Studies at Rutgers University. He received his B.A. from the City College of New York and his Ph.D. from the University of California–Berkeley. The Senior Editor of *Logos: A Journal of Modern Society and Culture,* his many works include *Socialism Unbound* (2000); *Imagining the Possible: Radical Politics for Conservative Times* (2002); *A Rumor about the Jews: Anti-Semitism, Conspiracy, and the "Protocols of Zion"* (2003); *Reclaiming the Enlightenment: Toward a Politics of Radical Engagement* (2004), and most recently, *Blood in the Sand: Imperial Fantasies, Right-Wing Ambitions, and the Erosion of American Democracy* (2005).

Lawrence Davidson is Professor of History at West Chester University in West Chester, Pennsylvania. His specialization is in the history of American relations with the Middle East. He is also a contributing editor to *Logos.* He is the author of two recent books: *America's Palestine: Popular and Official Perceptions from Balfour to Israeli Statehood* (2001) and *Islamic Fundamentalism* (2003). He has also written numerous articles on U.S. perceptions of and policies toward the Middle East. He has traveled extensively in the region. Over the past twenty years Professor Davidson has taken on the role of public intellectual and has sought to heighten public awareness of the nature and consequences of U.S. policies in the Middle East.

Greg Grandin teaches Latin American history at New York University. He has written for *Harper's* and the *Nation* and is the author of a number of books, including *The Last Colonial Massacre: Latin America in the Cold War* (2004) and *Empire's Workshop: Latin America, the United States, and the Rise of the New Imperialism* (2006).

Philip Green is Visiting Professor of Political Science in the Graduate Faculty of the New School for Social Research. He is the author, most recently, of *Cracks in the Pedestal: Ideology and Gender in Hollywood* (1998); *Equality and Democracy* (2000); and *Primetime Politics: The Truth about Conservative Lies, Corporate Control, and Television Culture* (2005). He is also a member of the editorial board of the *Nation.*

Diana M. Judd is Assistant Professor of Political Science at William Paterson University. She received her B.A. from Columbia University and her Ph.D. in political science from Rutgers University. She is the author of *Questioning Authority: Sir Francis Bacon, Political Resistance, and the Birth of the Scientific Method* (forthcoming). Her current research interests include issues of separation of church and state in the United States, as well as the relationship between religion and politics more generally.

Thomas M. Keck is Assistant Professor of Political Science in the Maxwell School of Citizenship and Public Affairs at Syracuse University. He is the author of *The Most Activist Supreme Court in History: The Road to Modern Judicial Conservatism* (2004) and is currently working on a book examining the conservative legal assault on affirmative action from 1978 to 2006.

Charles Noble is professor and chair of the Department of Political Science and director of the International Studies Program at California State University, Long Beach. Specializing in American politics, public policy, and comparative political economy, he has written several books and numerous articles on subjects ranging from labor-union politics to government regulation of the environment. He is most recently the author of *The Collapse of Liberalism: Why America Needs a New Left* (2004).

R. Claire Snyder is Associate Professor of Government and Politics in Political Theory at George Mason University. She is also a Faculty Fellow at the Women and Politics Institute at American University and an active member of New Political Science. Snyder's undergraduate and graduate teaching interests include the history of political thought, normative political theory, feminist theory, and women and politics. She is the author of *Citizen-Soldiers and Manly Warriors: Military Service and Gender in the Civic Republican Tradition* (1999) and *Gay Marriage and Democracy: Equality for All* (2006), as well as numerous articles and essays on topics related to democratic theory and citizenship. Her current research agenda includes projects on Third Wave feminism, intersections between democratic and feminist theory, the Christian Right, civic republicanism, and the welfare state. Snyder holds a Ph.D. from Rutgers University and a B.A. cum laude from Smith College.

Michael J. Thompson is Assistant Professor of Political Science at William Paterson University and the founding editor of *Logos: A Journal of Modern Society and Culture*. His next book, *The Politics of Inequality: A Political History of the Idea of Economic Inequality in America*, is forthcoming from Columbia University Press.

Nicholas Xenos is Professor of Political Science at the University of Massachusetts, Amherst. He has been a Visiting Professor of Rhetoric at the

University of California, Berkeley, and is an Alumnus Fellow of the Society of Fellows in the Humanities at Columbia University. The author of *Scarcity and Modernity* (1989) and of essays and reviews in the *Nation, Grand Street,* the *London Review of Books, Logos,* and other periodicals, he is currently completing a book on Leo Strauss and his influence on neoconservative foreign policy.

Index